Walk in the Light Series

Pagan Holidays

Examining the Ancient Origins
and Propriety of Various
Religious Holy Days

Todd D. Bennett

Shema Yisrael Publications

Pagan Holidays
Examining the Ancient Origins and Propriety
of Various Religious Holy Days

First printing 2012
Copyright © 2012 by Shema Yisrael Publications. All rights reserved. No part of this book may be used or reproduced in any manner whatsoever without written permission of the publisher, except in the case of brief quotations in articles and reviews.

For information write: Shema Yisrael Publications, 123 Court Street, Herkimer, New York 13350.

ISBN-10: 0985000414
ISBN-13: 978-0-9850004-1-7
Library of Congress Number: 2012907735

Printed in the United States of America.

Please visit our website for other titles:
www.shemayisrael.net

Pagan Holidays

Examining the Ancient Origins and Propriety of Various Religious Holy Days

*"² Do not learn the way of the heathens . . .
³ For the customs of the peoples are futile . . ."*
Jeremiah 10:2-3.

Table of Contents

Acknowledgements
Introduction   i
Chapter 1   In the Beginning   1
Chapter 2   Paradise   20
Chapter 3   Out of Paradise   27
Chapter 4   Judgment and Restoration   36
Chapter 5   Babylon   55
Chapter 6   Out of Babylon   69
Chapter 7   Egypt   88
Chapter 8   Out of Egypt   100
Chapter 9   Yisrael   121
Chapter 10   Out of Yisrael   140
Chapter 11   Daniel   151
Chapter 12   Hellenism   175
Chapter 13   The Messiah   194
Chapter 14   Division   203
Chapter 15   Pagan Christianity   221
Chapter 16   Pagan Society   239
Chapter 17   In the End   255
Endnotes   282

Appendix A   Tanak Hebrew Names
Appendix B   Hebrew Language Study Chart
Appendix C   The Walk in the Light Series
Appendix D   The Shema
Appendix E   Shema Yisrael

Acknowledgments

I must first and foremost acknowledge my Creator, Redeemer and Savior who opened my eyes and showed me the Light. He never gave up on me even when, at times, it seemed that I gave up on Him. He is ever patient and truly awesome. His blessings, mercies and love endure forever and my gratitude and thanksgiving cannot be fully expressed in words.

Were it not for the patience, prayers, love and support of my beautiful wife Janet, and my extraordinary children Morgan and Shemuel, I would never have been able to accomplish this work. They gave me the freedom to pursue the vision and dreams that my Heavenly Father placed within me, and for that I am so very grateful. I love them all more than they will ever know.

Loving thanks to my father for his faithfulness along with his helpful comments and editing. He tirelessly watched and held things together at the office while I was away traveling, researching, speaking and writing.

Special thanks to my friend and brother Eliyahu David ben Yissachar for all of his assistance relative to editing and, in particular, calendar and dating issues. Because of his efforts this work was made better, and most importantly, more accurate.

Introduction

This book is part of a larger body of educational work called the "Walk in the Light" series. In fact, it is a compilation of various content found throughout the rest of the series, which was written as a result of my search for the truth. Having grown up in a major protestant denomination since I was a small child, I had been steeped in doctrine which often times seemed to contradict the very words contained within the Scriptures. I always considered myself to be a Christian although I never took the time to research the origins of Christianity or to understand exactly what the term Christian meant. I simply grew up believing that Christianity was right and every other religion was wrong or deficient.

Now my beliefs were founded on more than simply blind faith. I had experienced a "living God," my life had been transformed by a loving Redeemer and I had been filled with a powerful Spirit. I knew that I was on the right track, regrettably I always felt something was lacking. I was certain that there was something more to this religion called Christianity; not in terms of a different God, but what composed this belief system that I subscribed to, and this label which I wore like a badge.

Throughout my Christian walk I experienced many highs and some lows, but along the way I never felt like I fully understood what my faith was all about. Sure, I knew that "Jesus died on the cross for my sins" and that I needed to believe in my heart and confess with my mouth in order

to "be saved." I "asked Jesus into my heart" when I was a child and sincerely believed in what I had done, but something always felt like it was missing. As I grew older, I found myself progressing through different denominations, each time learning and growing, always adding some pieces to the puzzle, but never seeing the entire picture.

College ministry brought me into contact with the baptism of the Holy Spirit and more charismatic assemblies yet, while these people seemed to practice a more complete faith than those in my previous denominations, many of my original questions remained unanswered and even more questions arose. It seemed that at each new step in my faith I added a new adjective to the already ambiguous label "Christian". I went from being a mere Christian to a Full Gospel, New Testament, Charismatic, Spirit Filled, Born Again Christian; although I could never get away from the lingering uneasiness that something was still missing.

For instance, when I read Matthew 7:21-23 I always felt uncomfortable. In that Scripture most English Bibles indicate that Jesus says: *"Not everyone who says to Me, Lord, Lord, will enter the kingdom of heaven, but he who does the will of My Father Who is in heaven. Many will say to Me on that day, Lord, Lord, have we not prophesied in Your name and driven out demons in Your name and done many mighty works in Your name? And then I will say to them openly (publicly), I never knew you; depart from Me, you who act wickedly [disregarding My commands]."* The Amplified Bible.

This passage of Scripture always bothered me because it sounded an awful lot like the modern day Christian Church, in particular, the charismatic churches which I had been attending where the gifts of the Spirit

were operating. According to the Scripture passage it was not the people who *believed* in the spiritual manifestations that were being rejected, it was those who were *actually doing* them. I would think that this would give every Christian pause for concern.

First of all "in that day" there are *many* people who will be calling Him "Lord." They will also be performing incredible spiritual acts in His Name. Ultimately though, the Messiah will openly and publicly tell them to depart from Him. He will tell them that He never knew them and specifically He defines them by their actions, which is the reason for their rejection; they acted wickedly or lawlessly. In short, they disobeyed His commandments. Also, it seems very possible that while they thought they were doing these things in His Name, they were not, because they may have never known His Name. In essence, they did not know Him and He did not know them.

I think that many Christians are haunted by this Scripture because they do not understand who it applies to or what it means and if they were truly honest they must admit that there is no other group on the face of the planet that it can refer to except for the "Christian Church." This series provides the answer to that question and should provide resolution for any who have suffered anxiety over this verse.

Ultimately, my search for answers brought me right back to the starting point of my faith. I was left with the question: "What is the origin and substance of this religion called Christianity?" I was forced to examine the very foundations of my faith and to examine many of the beliefs which I subscribed to and test them against the truth of the Scriptures.

What I found out was nothing short of earth

shattering. I experienced a parapettio, which is a moment in Greek tragedies where the hero realizes that everything he knew was wrong. I discovered that many of the foundations of my faith were not rocks of truth, but rather the sands of lies, deception, corruption and paganism. I saw the Scripture in Jeremiah come true right before my eyes. In many translations, this passage reads: *"O LORD, my strength and my fortress, My refuge in the day of affliction, The Gentiles shall come to You from the ends of the earth and say, "Surely our fathers have inherited lies, worthlessness and unprofitable things. Will a man make gods for himself, which are not gods?"* Jeremiah 16:19-20 NKJV

I discovered that I had inherited lies and false doctrines from the fathers of my faith. I discovered that the faith which I had been steeped in had made gods which were not gods and I saw very clearly how many could say "Lord, Lord" and not really know the Messiah. I discovered that these lies were not just minor discrepancies but critical errors which could possibly have the effect of keeping me out of the New Jerusalem if I continued to practice them. (Revelation 21:27; 22:15).

While part of the problem stemmed from false doctrines which have crept into the Christian religion, it also had to do with anti-Semitism imbedded throughout the centuries and even translation errors in the very Scriptures that I was basing may beliefs upon. A good example is the next verse from the Prophet Jeremiah (Yirmeyahu) where most translations provide: *"Therefore behold, I will this once cause them to know, I will cause them to know My hand and My might; and they shall know that My Name is the LORD."* Yirmeyahu 16:21 NKJV.

Could our Heavenly Father really be telling us that His Name is "The LORD"? This is a title, not a name and

by the way, won't many people be crying out "Lord, Lord" and be told that He never knew them? It is obvious that you should know someone's name in order to have a relationship with them. How could you possibly say that you know someone if you do not even know their name. So then we must ask: "What is the Name of our Heavenly Father?" The answer to this seeming mystery lies just beneath the surface of the translated text. In fact, if most people took the time to read the translators notes in the front of their "Bible" they would easily discover the problem.

You see the Name of our Creator is found in the Scriptures almost 7,000 times. Long ago a false doctrine was perpetrated regarding speaking the Name. It was determined that the Name either could not, or should not, be pronounced and therefore it was replaced. Thus, over the centuries the Name of the Creator which was given to us so that we could know Him and be, not only His children, but also His friends, was suppressed and altered. You will now find people using descriptions, titles and variations to replace the Name such as: God, Lord, Adonai, Jehovah and Ha Shem ("The Name") in place of the actual Name which was given in Scriptures. What a tragedy and what a mistake!

One of the Ten Commandments, also known as the Ten Words, specifically instructs us not to take the Name of the Creator "in vain" and *"He will not hold him guiltless who takes His Name in vain."* (Exodus 20:7). Most Christians have been taught that this simply warns of using the Name lightly or in the context of swearing or in some other disrespectful manner. This certainly is one aspect of the commandment, but if we look further into the Hebrew word for vain - שוא (pronounced shav) we find that it has a

deeper meaning in the sense of "desolating, uselessness or naught."

Therefore, we have been warned not only to avoid using the Name lightly or disrespectfully, but also not to bring it to naught, which is exactly what has been done over the centuries. The Name of our Creator which we have the privilege of calling on and praising has been suppressed to the point where most Believers do not even know the Name, let alone use it.

This sounds like a conspiracy of cosmic proportions and it is. Anyone who believes in the Scriptures must understand that there is a battle between good and evil. There is an enemy, Ha Shatan, who understands very well the battle which has been raging since the beginning. He will do anything to distract or destroy those searching for the truth and he is very good at what he does. As you read this book I hope that you will see how people have been deceived regarding the Scriptural Appointed Times and certain holy days with pagan origins.

My hope is that every reader has an eye opening experience and is forever changed. I sincerely believe that the truths which are contained in this book and the "Walk in the Light Series" are essential to avoid the great deception which is being perpetrated upon those who profess to believe in, and follow the Holy One of Yisrael.

This book, and the entire series, is intended to be read by anyone who is searching for the truth. Depending upon your particular religion, customs and traditions, you may find some of the information offensive, difficult to believe or contrary to the doctrines and teachings which you have read or heard throughout your life. This is to be expected and is perfectly understandable, but please realize that none of the information is meant to criticize anyone or

any faith, but merely to reveal truth.

The information contained in this book had better stir up some things or else there would be no reason to write it in the first place. The ultimate question is whether the contents align with the Scriptures and the will of the Creator. My goal is to strip away the layers of tradition which many of us have inherited and get to the core of the faith which is described in the Scriptures.

This book should challenge your thinking and your beliefs and hopefully aid you on your search for truth. May you be blessed in your journey of faith as you endeavor to Walk in the Light.

I

In the Beginning

The Scriptures describe the process of creation when the physical universe came into existence. That description of creation begins with the well known phrase, "In the beginning God created . . ." The use of the word God, while popular, is not accurate. The term "God" is a very general descriptor, and could be used by any religion to describe very different entities than the Creator of the Universe described within the Hebrew Scriptures. The Scriptures were originally written in the Hebrew language, and the title used to refer to the Creator in those texts is Elohim (), not God.[1]

This is a very simple example of an inherited tradition which, throughout time, has misled untold numbers of people. Understanding that Elohim created, rather than "God," identifies and connects the Creator with the Hebrew language. "God" is a general English term used to identify countless "deities." It is appropriate to use the term "Elohim," as Hebrew is the language through which the Creator chose to reveal Himself.[2]

Much of this book will be examining traditions. Now not all tradition is bad, but when a tradition clouds truth, it must be identified and discarded. It is essential when searching for truth that we attempt, in every way possible, to go back to the origins of the text in order to discern the original meaning. Part of this process will involve an analysis of the language.

It is important to understand that the so-called "Modern Hebrew" language does not represent the original Hebrew language. Modern Hebrew was brought back from Babylon after the exile of the House of Yahudah.³ It was not the language spoken by the very ancient patriarchs, so throughout our investigation for truth, we will be examining the Ancient Script, which actually tells a story through pictographs.⁴

If we look at the first five English words, "In the beginning Elohim created," we see only three Hebrew words – "Beresheet bara Elohim." Now if this were written in Ancient Hebrew it would read from right to left as follows:⁵

ᴍㄣᄽㄱᄇ ᄇ⑨◻ ✕ㄣw ᄇ⑨◻.

There are many mysteries contained in the Hebrew script, which cannot be readily discerned from simply reading a translation. In fact, if we look at the first word, we see a great mystery.

✕ㄣw ᄇ⑨◻

The first Hebrew word in the Scriptures, translated as "in the beginning," is "beresheet." As seen above, it begins with the letter "bet" (◻) which means: "house." The character actually represents the floor plan for a tent or a house. This particular bet (◻) is quite unique, because it is the second letter in the Hebrew alphabet, and the first letter in the Scriptures. Many question why the Scriptures did not begin with the aleph (ᄇ), which is the first letter in the Hebrew alphabet. This is a mystery only understood in the timing of the creation of the spiritual universe before the physical

universe.⁶

The bet is also unique because it is larger than the other letters. While some might think that this is simply a decorative touch, or illuminated letter, added by a scribe, they would be missing a tremendous truth. You see, throughout the Hebrew text there are instances of these "jots and tittles" which are intended to emphasize a point or send a message.⁷

So we can see right from the beginning of the Scriptures that there is an emphasis on "the House." As it turns out, all of creation is intended as a House, and through the process of time, Elohim is building a "family" to fill that House. Indeed, from this "first" word we can discern many things. For instance, if we remove the House, the bet (⌂), we are left with "resheet" (X⌐w ⋎ ⍟). Resheet means: "first – choicest." It is sometimes translated as "firstfruits." So then the House is for the firstfruits of Elohim.

We also see the word "brit" (X⌐⍟⌂) surrounding the word "aish" (w ⋎). Brit means: "cutting or covenant" and aish means: fire. So we should be looking for a covenant involving fire as a means of gathering the Firstfruits into the House. We also see the Aleph Taw (X⋎) surrounding the mysterious word "shi" (⌐w), which means: "gift or present."⁸ So we see the gift or offering couched within the Aleph Taw (X⋎) – the Messiah.

Analyzing the pictograms of the Paleo-Hebrew text is one way of studying the Scriptures. Another way is through Gematria, which involves studying the numerical values of words. It is important to understand that each Hebrew character has a numerical value. There is no separate set of numbers in the Hebrew language, so every word has multiple dimensions of meaning as well as a numerical value. The values for each character can

be seen in the Hebrew Language Study Chart in the Appendix.[9]

Throughout this text we will, at times, examine the numerical values of the words which can expand our understanding, and reinforce certain ideas. For instance, the numerical value of "beresheet" is 913. The word for house is "beit" (X⌐◻), and it has a numerical value of 412. The word for head is "rosh" (W⅄⍥), and it has a numerical value of 501. When combined, their values equal 913 – the same as beresheet.[10]

Now each of these words, "beit" and "rosh," actually have individual Hebrew characters associated with them. As we already discussed the Hebrew character bet (◻), means "house." The Hebrew character "resh" (⍥) means: "head." When we combine "bet" and "resh" we have "bar" (⍥◻), which is not only the first two letters of "beresheet," but also the word for "son." The possibilities and avenues of discovery are endless, and they reveal the beauty and spirituality of the Language of the Creator. Indeed, it is the very language of Creation.

Aside from the first word, which is a study in and of itself, the rest of the first sentence has more profound information about how this house will be filled, and even provides a framework for time. Here is the entire sentence.

```
+⍥⅄Ψ X⅄? ᴍ⌐ᴍWΨ X⅄ ᴍ⌐Ψ1⅄ ⅄⍥◻ X⌐W⅄⍥◻
 7    6    5    4    3    2      1 ←
```

Now remember that Hebrew reads from right to left. That is why you see the first word Beresheet, all the way to the right. Phonetically the sentence reads as follows:

Beresheet bara Elohim et ha'shamayim v'et ha'eretz

→ 1   2   3   4   5   6   7

If you read it out loud, you just spoke Hebrew. There are seven words, although only six are translated into English. In a basic English translation you will read "In beginning Elohim created the heavens and the earth." There is something critical that never gets translated out of the Hebrew. It is essential to understanding how the Covenant House would be built.

This verse actually contains two instances of the mysterious Aleph Taw (ᵡᵾ). While it is spoken in Hebrew, pronounced "et," it goes unnoticed in the English. The aleph (ᵾ) is the first letter in the Hebrew alphabet. It symbolizes a "bull or ox" and means: "strength." The taw (ᵡ) is the last letter in the Hebrew alphabet. It represents a "mark or covenant." So this "strength of the covenant" is present 2 times in the first seven Hebrew words of the Scriptures.

In the first instance we see the Aleph Taw (ᵡᵾ) stand alone in position 4, untranslated but spoken. In the second instance it is in position 6, attached to a vav (ו), which represents a "peg" or a "nail." Again, in the second instance the Aleph Taw (ᵡᵾ) is untranslated but spoken.

Some interpret this untranslated but spoken Aleph Taw (ᵡᵾ) as representing the Messiah, revealed as the Word, sometimes referred to as the Memra.[11] The reason is because the Aleph Taw (ᵡᵾ) contains within it all the characters of the Hebrew language. Therefore, it is believed that the Messiah is the manifestation of Elohim within creation, all of which was accomplished through the language – the spoken word.[12]

In the second occurance of the Aleph Taw (ᵡᵾ), the Aleph Taw (ᵡᵾ) is attached to a "nail" or a "stake,"

represented by the letter vav (𐤅). Therefore, it literally stands between the heavens (ᵚᵞᵚᵂᵞ) and the earth (✝𐤒𐤏ᵞ), connecting them. That fits in perfectly with the notion that Creation is all about a House for the first son, the Messiah, Who will be the head of the House filled with the firstfruits of His harvest. This will become clearer as we continue this discussion.

It is commonly believed that this verse begins a pattern of sevens that will be repeated throughout the Scriptures, providing seven millennium as the framework for time. As we continue to examine the text, we read about how Elohim actually created everything in six days and rested on the seventh. So these seven words reveal the pattern of sevens. The phrase "in the beginning" is essentially describing the beginning of the physical existence that we know and observe. It also describes the very beginning of time. We know that time is a physical dimension and as with other matters in this physical creation, it can be measured.[13]

Indeed, during the creation process we read about the sun and the moon as the actual "hands on the clock." "[14] *Then Elohim said, "Let there be lights in the firmament of the heavens to divide the day from the night; and let them be for signs and seasons (moadim), and for days and years;* [15] *and let them be for lights in the firmament of the heavens to give light on the earth" and it was so.* [16] *Then Elohim made two great lights: the greater light to rule the day, and the lesser light to rule the night. He made the stars also."* Genesis (Beresheet) 1:14-16.

The sun, known as "shemesh" (ᵂᵚᵂ) in Hebrew is referred to as the greater light and the moon, known as "yerach" (🄷𐤒ᵞ) is referred to as the lesser light. Now it is important to recognize that these "lights" were created on the fourth day of the Creation week, but light had already been separated from darkness in the physical

realm on Day 1. This begs the question: What was the difference in these lights. To answer this question let us return to the Creation account describing the First Day.

> "³ And Elohim said, Let there be light: and there was light. ⁴ And Elohim saw ×ᘔ-the light, that it was good: and Elohim divided the light from the darkness. ⁵ And Elohim called the light Day, and the darkness He called Night. And the evening and the morning were the first day." Beresheet 1:3-5.

Now it is important to understand that this light was not the light emitted from the sun. The sun was not created until the fourth day. (see Beresheet 1:14). So this light was not the light we typically associate with photons emitted from the sun. In Hebrew it is called "owr" (ᛋᛁᛒ).

Other Scripture passages actually provide hints regarding this mysterious light. In fact the Proverbs describe the Torah (ᛎᛋᛁ×) as light (ᛋᛁᛒ). (Proverbs 6:23). This would make sense since the Torah is the instruction of Elohim which provides distinctions and often separates right from wrong, righteousness from evil, the way of light from the way of darkness. The Torah reveals the way of the Creator and establishes the rules of His Kingdom reflected through creation.[14]

Therefore, this light was spoken into the very fabric of creation. It is interesting to examine these words in the original Hebrew describing the bringing forth of light. Essentially, we read that the Creator said "Let it be" and "it was." In each case the word describing the existence of light is yihey (ᛦᛎᛦ). The word includes two yuds (ᛦ), which symbolize arms as can plainly be seen in the Ancient Hebrew Script.

The two arms surround a hey (𐤄) which often is understood to represent spirit, breath or wind, but in the Ancient Hebrew Script is more representative of a man. There is something very interesting about this light, and in the passage there are two representations of this "spirit man." This word is closely linked with the description and Name of the Creator revealed as 𐤄𐤅𐤄𐤉, often depicted as YHWH in English. (See Shemot 3:14-15).[15]

So, if we look at this text in Hebrew we will see some important details and connections that are not properly conveyed in translated "Bibles."[16] Translations do not always effectively convey the complete meaning of the text, and it is very helpful to review and amplify the text using the original language.[17]

If we read further, we start to learn more about this light. Here is what we see in the Hebrew text:

𐤀𐤋𐤄𐤉𐤌-𐤕𐤀 𐤌𐤉𐤄𐤋𐤀 𐤀𐤓𐤉𐤅

Literally this reads: "and saw Elohim et-the light." The "et" is the Aleph Taw (𐤀𐤕) which is actually connected with the light. Again, we already mentioned the Messianic significance of the Aleph Taw (𐤀𐤕), and in the text we see the Aleph Taw (𐤀𐤕) actually connected to the light. It is specifically described as "good." This essentially reveals that the Messiah was that Light. This makes perfect sense when we understand that all of Creation was made to be a House for the Head Son - the First Son - the Messiah.

There then came a time when Elohim spoke light into existence, and light was then divided from the darkness to help delineate time. The light was called day, which is "yom" (𐤉𐤅𐤌) in Hebrew. The darkness was called night, which is "lilah" (𐤋𐤉𐤋𐤄) in Hebrew. What comes next is critical to our understanding of time. A

common translation reads:

> "And the evening and the morning the first day."
> (Beresheet 1:5).

We can see here that the concept of a day began in the evening. This is consistent with the pattern of Creation as Creation started in darkness, and then there was light added to Creation.

Interestingly, many translations miss what really went on here. During this event we see a separation and then a unification, which resulted in the creation of a day. Elohim actually took darkness and light and united them together as a day. We know this from the very Hebrew text which literally states: *"And the evening and the morning the unified (echad) day."* The text includes the word "echad" (ד ח א) which can mean: "one or unified."

Through this unification Elohim actually created a day which would progress in a cycle from evening to night to morning to day. The two divided and separate concepts of night and day, darkness and light, were essentially stitched together at evening and morning to form a cycle.

As the creation account unfolds we are presented with another important cycle and pattern - the cycle of seven repeating days that constitute a week. It is within this period of time that the pattern for all of Creation is contained, and it is within the first 6 days that everything was created.

So then we have an account of creation occurring within 144 hours followed by a period of 24 hours rest.[18] Interestingly, while each of the first six days ends with the phrase *"and there was evening and there was morning"*, it is absent on the seventh day.

"*² By the seventh day Elohim had finished the work He had been doing; so on the seventh day He rested from all His work. ³ And Elohim blessed the seventh day and made it set apart, because on it He rested from all the work of creating that He had done.*" Beresheet 2:2-3.

The absence of the phrase "*and there was evening and there was morning*" on the seventh day prophetically signifies that the seventh millennium will be different. It is believed that before the flood, a vapor canopy with fiber optic qualities enveloped the earth. At evening it was still light as the sun's light was optically conducted to the dark side of the earth.

When the earth is restored to paradise in the Millennial Kingdom, it is likely that this firmament, called "raqiya" (◯⤳𖤐𖦹) in Beresheet 1:6-8, will be restored. The prophet Isaiah (Yeshayahu) may have actually spoken directly to that fact. "*Moreover the light of the moon will be as the light of the sun, and the light of the sun will be sevenfold, as the light of seven days. In the day that YHWH binds up the bruise of His people and heals the stroke of their wound.*" Isaiah (Yeshayahu) 30:26.

At the time YHWH heals His people, they will already be "in the House." This is the scene that John (Yahanan) saw in the Book of Revelation. "*¹ After these things I heard a loud voice of a great multitude in heaven, saying, Halleluyah! Salvation and glory and honor and power belong to YHWH our Elohim! ² For true and righteous are His judgments, because He has judged the great harlot who corrupted the earth with her fornication; and He has avenged on her the blood of His servants shed by her. ³ Again they said, Halleluyah! Her smoke rises up throughout the age and to eternity! ⁴ And the twenty-four elders and the four living creatures fell down and worshiped Elohim who sat on the* throne, saying, Amen! Halleluyah! ⁵ Then a voice came from the throne, saying, Praise our Elohim, all you His servants and those who fear Him, both small and great! ⁶ And I heard, as it were, the voice of a great multitude, as the sound of many waters and as the sound of mighty thunderings, saying, Halleluyah! For YHWH Elohim Omnipotent reigns! ⁷ Let us be glad and rejoice and give Him esteem, for the marriage of the Lamb has come, and His wife has made herself ready. ⁸ And to her it was granted to be arrayed in fine linen, clean and bright, for the fine linen is the righteous acts of the set apart ones. ⁹ Then he said to me, Write: Blessed are those who are called to the marriage supper of the Lamb! And he said to me, These are the true sayings of Elohim." Revelation 19:1-9.

Notice that prior to this great wedding feast and restoration there will be judgment. Take special note of the "great harlot" also known as the "great whore." This will be the prevailing subject of this book, which is a warning to help people avoid falling under the judgment associated with this "harlot." The idea is to be in the House and be part of the "bride." The bride must be pure and undefiled, unlike a harlot.

So there is great prophetic significance associated with the seventh day of creation, which was blessed and set apart from the other days. It was clearly different from the others, and it was even given a name – Shabbat. So the seventh day Shabbat completes the pattern of seven, although the seventh day was mysteriously left open ended. It is an important day to be observed by the bride – a day which the harlot defiles.

The cycle of seven days that was established when Elohim divided light from darkness on Day 1 continues to this day. This cycle is a simple seven day count, and relies upon nothing other than the elapse of seven yom cycles.

From this Creation account we can see there were

things that went on before time was created. There is a back story to all of this which is not provided at this point, although there are hints throughout the Scriptures. There was a creation and existence of the spiritual realm before the creation of this physical.

As a result, there were things that occurred in the spiritual realm, outside of the time of our present physical existence. Therefore, everything that occurred after Beresheet 1:3, when Elohim separated light from darkness on Day 1, occurred in the physical universe, within our present understanding of time. Time, in the physical universe, was created on day one. It is finite. In other words, it has a beginning and an end. The Creator provides us with a reckoning of days divided into four general units, evening, night, morning and day.

Within the framework of the first six days of Creation, Elohim also established a mechanism for reckoning other durations of time greater than a week. He established units of time that are known as months and years which are determined by the sun and the moon.

In the midst of the seven day cycle we are told about the Creation of the sun and the moon and the stars on day four.

> "*14* And Elohim said, 'Let there be lights in the expanse of the sky to separate the day from the night, and <u>let them serve for signs and for seasons (moadim) and days and years,</u> *15* and let them be lights in the expanse of the sky to give light on the earth.' And it was so. *16* Elohim made two great lights - the greater light to govern the day and the lesser light to govern the night. He also made the stars. *17* Elohim set them in the expanse of the sky to give light on

the earth, [18] to govern the day and the night, and to separate light from darkness. And Elohim saw that it was good. [19] And there was evening, and there was morning - the fourth day." Beresheet 1:14-19

Again, it is important to note that the day count existed before the sun and the moon were created on day four. The sun and the moon were later created to separate between the newly created periods of time called the day and the night. The sun was the greater light and the moon was the lesser light.

So we have the cycle of days, determined by the passage of evening and morning – two parts. The sun and the moon were created on the fourth day to mark the passage of days on this particular planet. The way we calculate time is unique to our environment. We then have the cycle of weeks, which consists of seven days ending with a special day named Shabbat, also known as the Sabbath. The sun and the moon were also created to mark cycles of months and years.

It is important to note, the weekly count is distinctive and independent of the month and the year. This is very important to understand as we continue to study time. There are cycles within cycles. So here we have these two related, but separate reckonings of time occurring simultaneously.

Some attempt to construe that the stars are involved in telling time. The text is quite clear that the greater light and the lesser light separate the day from the night, and are for determining time. The sun and the moon "rule" over the day and the night. They are the hands on the clock for our planet. It just so happens that all of the celestial bodies, including the stars, were also made on the fourth day. That is why they are mentioned,

but not in the context of reckoning time.

This is not to diminish the role of the stars in any way. Indeed, when one views pictures from deep space there are not sufficient words to describe the vastness and grandeur of the cosmos. They are extraordinary creations set far outside of our solar system. They are one way that the Creator provides a witness, and signs, in the sky.[19] That one simple sentence, "He also made the stars," involved a lot of creating.

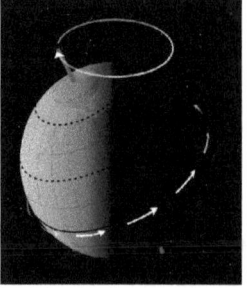

Due to the procession of the equinoxes, the constellations are continually "moving." In other words, they are not in regular, fixed positions that provide a constant and continuous cycle which would allow us to mark days, months and years - that is left to the greater light and the lesser light. The stars are for signs, but the greater light and the lesser light are made for telling time in months and years. This is confirmed through the Psalms (Tehillim): "He appointed the moon for seasons (moadim): the sun knoweth his going down." Tehillim 104:19.

You may have noticed the word "moadim" in parenthesis in the passage quoted above as well as with Beresheet 1:14. That is the actual Hebrew word found in the text, and it does not mean "seasons." While it is true, to a certain extent, that the sun and the moon traverse "righteous cycles" (Psalm 23:3) which can be divided into four discernable seasons, that is not the focus of the text.

The Hebrew word "tequfah" means "turn or circuit" and there are four tequfot each year described as equinoxes and solstices. Each solar cycle of 365.242 days is divided into four tequfahs, or rather "turns" and they are intimately tied with the four seasons. Now the Scriptures really only describe two seasons – summer

and winter. As a result, some argue that there are only two tequfahs known as the vernal (spring) equinox and the autumnal (fall) equinox. Each equinox is a point, or turn, when the day and night are equal. Therefore, it could be argued that the autumnal equinox marks the end of summer and the beginning of winter while the vernal equinox marks the end of winter and the beginning of summer.

There are two other distinct points in this grand yearly cycle. Not only were the sun and the moon created to mark time, but the earth is obviously integral to the process of reckoning time. It is constantly revolving on a tilted access, and both of these factors are critical for life to exist on the planet, and for providing markers for the year. The tilting results in a constant change in the amount of sunlight that strikes various points on the planet. It is this tilting that results in the four general demarcation points, or turns, in the cycle.

While the equinoxes mark the two points when day and night are equal, there are two remaining tequfot called the solstices. The summer solstice is the turn when the day is longest and the night is shortest. The final tequfah is the winter solstice, when the day is the shortest and the night is the longest. The winter 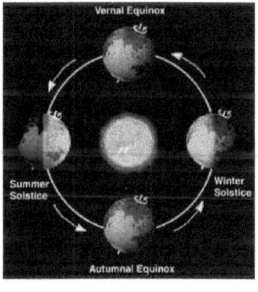 solstice is likely the most well recognized and celebrated due to the fact that it used to fall on December 25.

That date is infamous as the source of many pagan traditions revolving around sun god worship. Since the days start to get longer, the pagans who worshipped the sun saw it as a "rebirth" of the sun as the days grew longer.[20] As we shall see, the very physical universe has become the object of worship, and the

source of many false religions and traditions.

Due to the procession of the equinoxes, the winter solstice now falls on December 21. Christians continue to revere the past solstice date of December 25, due to the pagan traditions adopted into the religion 2 millennia ago.

The first stated purpose in Beresheet 1:14 for the creation of the sun and the moon was for signs. The signs referred to here are solar and lunar eclipses. Eclipses occur every year, and when a historical record was made that referred to an eclipse, it became an important piece of evidence for the reconstruction of history. The second stated purpose for the sun and the moon was for "seasons" (moadim). The third stated purpose for the sun and the moon was for days, and the fourth purpose was for years. The fact that Elohim states in His word that the sun and moon were created to determine years has obviously not been contemplated by many, but should not be ignored.

Now that is all interesting background information, but it is important to reiterate that the Hebrew text in Beresheet 1:14, regarding the second purpose for the creation of the sun and the moon, does not actually say "seasons." Again, in the Hebrew we read the word "moadim" which is commonly translated as Appointed Times.

The word "moadim" is a very unique and special word. It might have looked something like this ᛖᛥᚒᚖᚎᛖ in the most ancient Hebrew script. It is understood to mean: "Appointed Times," which are precise calendrical dates determined by the moon cycle. Interestingly, the text of Beresheet does not provide any more details concerning these Appointed Times, despite the fact that the sun and the moon have been set in their courses to mark these events. This stands out as a great mystery from the beginning.

In fact, this first mention of the word "moadim," in the plural sense, is the only time the word can be found in the entire text of Beresheet. It is specially located and stands out in many ways to draw our attention to its significance. The only other usage in Beresheet is in the singular sense. Three times the word moad is found involving the birth of Isaac (Beresheet 17:21; 18:14; 21:2).[21]

The word itself is quite mysterious. It begins and ends with mem (ᨇ) which represents "water." At the heart of the word we see ayin-dalet (ᨈᨆ), which literally means: "see the door." Therefore, if we interpret this word using the ancient symbols as a guide we would see the following concept: "as we pass through the waters (ᨇ), held back in their place (ᔑ)

we see the door by the arm (ᔑ) of Elohim. The door, of course is the door to the House of Elohim that was alluded to at the beginning.

When I look at this word in the Ancient Script, I immediately see a picture of the children of Yisrael[22] passing through the waters of the Red Sea, and the Jordan River. Of course, as we shall see, these moadim are for Yisrael – the people in Covenant with YHWH.[23] Just as the Yisraelites once passed through the waters on their way to the Promised Land, the Covenant people "pass through" these Appointed Times as they progress toward the House of YHWH.

We see this concept right at the beginning on the sixth day when Elohim created man. The word for man in Hebrew is Adam (ᨇᨈᨆ). Notice the dalet (ᨈ), which

means: "door." The door is located at the center of this word surrounded by the word am (ᴹᵹ) which means: "assembly or people."

The common definition of moadim is "Appointed Times," and time is a very important aspect of the moadim. If we are going to concern ourselves with the times appointed by the Creator, then we should understand how He reckons time.

The word moadim does not only involve time though. There is another dimension that we must consider – space. The very idea of an appointment involves being at a set place at a set time. It also involves meeting with someone for a purpose.

In the case of the moadim, at the heart of the word is "ad" (ᵾ☉) which is translated: "witness" or "testimony." Remember that in the ancient symbols it would mean "see the door" so we can equate seeing the door with the witness or testimony. We will see this notion of the witness and the testimony take on physicality through the Ark of the Covenant and the Tabernacle, which actually becomes an important focal point of the moadim. As it turns out, time is actually connected with a place at these Appointed Times.

In fact, the singular form of the word is "moad" and it actually means: "place of assembly." So through the moadim we see specific times where we assemble at a specific place. As previously mentioned, each letter in the Hebrew language has a numeric value. Through the study of these numerical values and relationships we can find intriguing connections and enhanced meaning. The numerical value for the word moad (ᵾ☉ᛁᴹ) is 120 (ᴹ = 40, ᛁ = 6, ☉ = 70, ᵾ = 4).[24] This will become more significant as we examine the flow of the moadim through the cycles of time.[25]

So with all of this we know that time is

intimately linked with creation. Indeed the markers of time are built right into creation. Through and within this framework of created time, YHWH is building a house.

2

Paradise

So from the beginning we can see that time plays a very significant role in creation. In fact, there are special times, known as Appointed Times that the sun and the moon were created to mark. We are also shown, from the beginning, that a house is the focus of creation.

After the Creation account we actually learn about this house. It was a special place known as the Garden of Eden. The Scriptures are short on detail considering the importance of this special place. We can glean some very significant information from the text when reading about the creation of man.

It is on the sixth day that we read how Elohim decided to create man. "*²⁶ Then Elohim said, 'Let Us make man in Our image, according to Our likeness; let them have dominion over the fish of the sea, over the birds of the air, and over the cattle, over all the earth and over every creeping thing that creeps on the earth.' ²⁷ So Elohim created man in His own image; in the image of Elohim He created him; male and female He created them.*" Beresheet 1:26-27.

We see that man was special and different from all other created beings. Man was made in the "image" of Elohim, which is "tselem" (ᵐ ᴧ+) in Hebrew. Man was made after the "likeness" of Elohim, which is "demuwt" (ⅩꝒᵐႱ) in Hebrew. In fact, man and woman were in the image of Elohim. It should be noted that the title Elohim is plural. The text does not state: "let Me create," but

rather, "let Us create."

Therefore, by using the plural term "Elohim" instead of the singular form "El," we are given a clue concerning the nature of the Creator. The image of Elohim is not complete until the man and the woman are joined together. This joining completes and unifies the image into one – echad. This joining, through intimate relationship, is something that Elohim has been trying to teach from the beginning.

Now we read something even more special about this relationship. After Elohim created man, He rested. *"¹ Thus the heavens and the earth, and all the host of them, were finished. ² And on the seventh day Elohim ended His work which He had done, and He rested on the seventh day from all His work which He had done. ³ Then Elohim blessed the seventh day and set it apart, because in it He rested from all His work which Elohim had created and made."* Beresheet 2:1-3.

Elohim rested on the Sabbath, the seventh day. So the first full day of mankind's existence was a rest day. Elohim blessed it and set it apart. It is, and remains a special day, different from all others – from the beginning. We already mentioned the existence of Appointed Times that were determined by the sun and the moon. This is the first "Appointed Time" of YHWH. It is a rest day that occurs every seventh revolution of the earth on its axis. It is a day when both YHWH and man rest from their work so that they can commune together.

We will see the importance of this time of communing as we continue the discussion. This also has profound significance as we look forward to the seventh millennium, but for now it is important to recognize that the seventh day was a special day.[26] It was set apart by YHWH as a rest day, for both Himself and for man,

who was made in His image.[27]

Let us now continue with the text. "[4] *This is the history of the heavens and the earth when they were created, in the day that YHWH Elohim made the earth and the heavens, [5] before any plant of the field was in the earth and before any herb of the field had grown. For YHWH Elohim had not caused it to rain on the earth, and there was no man to till the ground; [7] And YHWH Elohim formed man of the dust of the ground, and breathed into his nostrils the breath of life; and man became a living being. [8] YHWH Elohim planted a garden eastward in Eden, and there He put the man whom He had formed. [9] And out of the ground YHWH Elohim made every tree grow that is pleasant to the sight and good for food. The tree of life was also in the midst of the garden, and the tree of the knowledge of good and evil. [10] Now a river went out of Eden to water the garden, and from there it parted and became four riverheads. [11] The name of the first is Pishon; it is the one which skirts the whole land of Havilah, where there is gold. [12] And the gold of that land is good. Bdellium and the onyx stone are there. [13] The name of the second river is Gihon; it is the one which goes around the whole land of Cush. [14] The name of the third river is Hiddekel; it is the one which goes toward the east of Assyria. The fourth river is the Euphrates. [15] Then YHWH Elohim took the man and put him in the garden of Eden to tend and keep it. [16] And YHWH Elohim commanded the man, saying, 'Of every tree of the garden you may freely eat; [17] but of the tree of the knowledge of good and evil you shall not eat, for in the day that you eat of it you shall surely die.'"* Beresheet 2:7-15.

The first thing that should draw your attention is the continued repetition of YHWH Elohim. This is the first time that the Name YHWH is used in the Scriptures, and it is combined with Elohim 7 times. The Name of YHWH is intimately connected with man. This tells us that YHWH desires relationship with Him.

He reveals His Name to man so that man can "know" Him.

YHWH Elohim is used 5 times describing the creative process involving man. YHWH Elohim "formed, planted, made, took and then commanded." So YHWH Elohim first formed man. There is something very interesting in the Hebrew that cannot be seen in the English. The Hebrew mechanically reads: "*And formed YHWH Elohim ×𐤏-the adam.*"

So we can see that the Aleph Taw (×𐤏) is actually attached to the adam – the man. He was taken from "the dust of the ground." The Hebrew word for "dust" is apar (𐤏𐤓𐤏). Interestingly, in this word we see the the symbols for man's primary functions – see, eye (𐤏), speak, mouth (𐤓) and mind, head (𐤏). The dust came from the ground, which is "adamah" (𐤄𐤌𐤃𐤀). Thus the name for man was "adam" (𐤌𐤃𐤀), because he came from the ground.

YHWH breathed into the man. He imparted something into the man called "the breath of life." The breath of life is "neshemah chai" (𐤉𐤇 𐤄𐤌𐤔𐤍). The word for "breathed" is "neyphach" (𐤇𐤐𐤍), and it is where we derive the word for "soul." You can see the symbol for "life" represented by the nun (𐤍). So thousands of years before the development of a microscope, the "seed of life" was depicted by a pictograph, which graphically represents a sperm. This should give us a hint of the special nature of the Ancient Hebrew language.

So this "seed of life" from Elohim was planted by the arm of YHWH represented by the yud (𐤉). It was "spoken" into the man through the mouth (𐤐) of YHWH. The seed of life from YHWH was placed in a container of flesh, represented by the chet (𐤇) which is a "fence or barrier."

Once this process was accomplished, man became

a living "soul" which is "nephesh" (w ?ᔕ) in Hebrew. So this is how man was made in the "image" of Elohim. Man represents a likeness to Elohim, but he is not Elohim. He has the life of Elohim imparted within him, and he is meant to be like Elohim.

YHWH Elohim then "planted" a garden, "made" good and pleasant trees for food. He "took" man and placed him in the garden. YHWH Elohim then "commanded" man. He gave man instructions for living in the home.

So this is what it all comes down to. Are we willing to become molded into the image of YHWH, by doing His will, or do we refuse to conform and walk in disobedience. The reader must understand that this is the continuing theme of the Scriptures from the beginning to the end. YHWH is looking to fill His House with a family, His seed who will become righteous immortal beings. For Messiah said that those who attain to the resurrection of the righteous and the Kingdom Age in the seventh millennium will be as the angels of Elohim in Heaven. (see Luke 20:35-38; Mattityahu 22:30-32).

Those who obtain this immortality are those who walk according to His instructions, keep His commandments, and live according to the "rules" of His House. Man was made to live with YHWH, so let us take a look at this House established by YHWH Elohim from the very beginning.

We are told of a place named Eden. Eden (ᔕ ⋃ ☉) means: "paradise." A literal intereprerpation of the characters is: see (☉) the door (⋃) to life (ᔕ). So man was placed in paradise where there was life. This should give you a pretty good understanding of the Creator and His desire for man. He wants the best for us. We then read about a special garden within Eden, geographically located to the east.

The word for garden in Hebrew is gan (𐤂𐤍). It means: "an enclosed or protected space." This is very important to understand. Man was not simply placed on the earth to wander aimlessly. He was placed in a specific location within paradise and given a specific purpose. Within the garden were many trees that were good for food and was permitted to eat. There was also the Tree of Life and the Tree of Knowledge of Good and Evil.

Man was actually charged with watching over this garden and taking care of it. The Scriptures describe: "*And took YHWH Elohim ✕𐤏-the man and put him in the garden of Eden to tend and keep it.*" Beresheet 2:15. Notice the Aleph Taw (✕𐤏), once again, connecting Elohim with the man. Man was given two distinct tasks while in the garden. The word for "tend" is "abad" in Hebrew. Abad (𐤏𐤁𐤃) means: "to work, to serve, to labor, to till."

So even in Paradise, man's life was only complete when he had a task to fulfill. Man found a purpose to his life in taking care of YHWH's garden. At the same time he could reap the benefits of living in the garden. Through this service, the man would "see the door to the house." In other words, by being a faithful servant, the man was able to see the door to the House of YHWH.

His other task was to "keep" it. The word for "keep" is "shamar" in Hebrew. Shamar (𐤔𐤌𐤓) means: "to keep, to watch, to preserve." So the man was to be a watchman over the garden. This is consistent with the fact that the garden was a protected, fenced in space. So the man was to keep out intruders and guard it from harm.

He was given responsibility and dominion. This was essentially the Kingdom of YHWH, and the garden was the castle. It was the place where YHWH would dwell and commune with man. It was from this place

that man would rule. It was the source of life – the Tree of Life. It was the place from which the waters flowed throughout the rest of the lands, which we will later see are the Covenant lands promised to Abram.

There were, no doubt, many instructions given to man. After all, he was made in the image of YHWH and expected to live and exist like YHWH. Interestingly, we are not given a list of all the commands, although we are told specifically about what man was permitted to eat. First, we read about the food given for every being that has life - "nephesh chayah" (every soul that has life) - "*I have given every green herb for food*" Beresheet 1:30. In the beginning, man ate a vegetarian diet.

We also read a command concerning two specific trees. "*[16] And YHWH Elohim commanded the man, saying, 'Of every tree of the garden you may freely eat; [17] but of the tree of the knowledge of good and evil you shall not eat, for in the day that you eat of it you shall surely die.'*" Beresheet 2:16-17. So man was given charge of the garden. There was great responsibility and trust associated with his assignment. He was given extraordinary freedom, and as far as we can see there was only one thing that he was specifically told not to do. In fact, that one thing had severe consequences – death.

Man was infused with the breath of life from YHWH Elohim, and had direct access to the Tree of Life. As a result, he was supposed to live forever in paradise. His status as a resident of paradise required his obedience to the commandments, which were the rules of the Kingdom. Failure to obey would result in death – expulsion out of the garden.

3

Out of Paradise

Thus far we have talked about the man, called Adam, because he was the one first created and given the commandments. We already saw that Elohim created both man and woman in His image, and the Scriptures give a very interesting account of the creation of the woman.

"*[18] And YHWH Elohim said, 'It is not good that man should be alone; I will make him a helper comparable to him.' [19] Out of the ground YHWH Elohim formed every beast of the field and every bird of the air, and brought them to Adam to see what he would call them. And whatever Adam called each living creature, that was its name. [20] So Adam gave names to all cattle, to the birds of the air, and to every beast of the field. But for Adam there was not found a helper comparable to him. [21] And YHWH Elohim caused a deep sleep to fall on Adam, and he slept; and He took one of his ribs, and closed up the flesh in its place. [22] Then the rib which YHWH Elohim had taken from man He made into a woman, and He brought her to the man. [23] And Adam said: 'This is now bone of my bones and flesh of my flesh; She shall be called Woman, because she was taken out of Man.' [24] Therefore a man shall leave his father and mother and be joined to his wife, and they shall become one flesh. [25] And they were both naked, the man and his wife, and were not ashamed."* Beresheet 2:18-25.

We are told that during this "birthing process"

Adam was placed in a "deep sleep." The Hebrew word used here is "tardemah" (ΨᵐՍ⊕X) - which means more than just deep sleep. In fact, it means: "trance or stunned - like death." So what we see is a picture of Adam dying so that his bride could live. Adam was then "brought back to life," or "resurrected" so that he and his bride could dwell together in paradise. This was a pattern established at the very beginning which would have profound implications in the future.

The word for man is "aish" (wﾉϑ) in Hebrew and the word for woman is "aishah" (Ψwϑ). Aishah means "taken out of man." Notice that there is a Hebrew letter hey (Ψ) added to the word. The hey (Ψ) symbolizes a man standing with arms raised and means: "behold." It is meant to announce something and can also mean: "to reveal."

The hey (Ψ) also represents breath, which is life - the Spirit of Elohim. Interestingly, the passage of Scripture detailing this event includes the untranslated Aleph Taw (Xϑ) in the Hebrew, which is drawing our attention to a deeper meaning hidden in the text involving the Messiah.

This entire birthing process is an important event that we are meant to learn from. YHWH could have easily created a woman directly from the ground as He did with Adam. Instead, He chose to create a new being, similar, but very different from Adam. The woman was taken from a living being. Both the man and the woman were unique in their beings, and in the fashion in which they were created.

Now along with man, the woman was chosen to dwell in a special place, and to perform a specific purpose. The woman is often described as a "help mate" for the man, but she was really much more. The Hebrew Scriptures describe that no "ezer k'negedow" (lՍ⋀ﾑw

𐤀𐤅𐤎) could be found, so woman was created. Adam needed an intelligent, powerful, capable, equal partner and so Elohim created woman.

The word "ezer" is used by the writer of Psalm 121:1-2 to describe the powerful help that comes from YHWH. If the word "k'neged," which means equal, were not there, the woman would have been more powerful than the man. Elohim did not create the woman to serve the man, He created the woman to serve with the man.²⁸ Adam had work to do in the garden and he needed help.

Again, while in the Garden man was commanded *"to tend and keep it."* Beresheet 2:15. The Hebrew word for "tend" is "abad" (𐤏𐤁𐤀) and the Hebrew word for "keep" is "shamar" (𐤓𐤌𐤔). Both of these words are verbs and they involve action. These concepts are very important as we shall see throughout our discussion, and another way of describing Adam's mission is *"to work and to watch"* or *"to do and to guard."*

The Scriptures record an incident when the woman was deceived by a serpent that had entered the Garden. Adam and the woman both transgressed a command – they partook of the fruit of the tree of knowledge of good and evil - better known as the tree of all knowledge.

It has been suggested that "the phrase [tov v'ra] 𐤏𐤓 𐤅𐤈𐤁 translated *good and evil*, is a merism. This is a figure of speech whereby a pair of opposites are used together to create the meaning *all* or *everything*, as in the English phrase, 'they came, great and small', meaning just that they all came. So the *Tree of Knowledge of Good and Evil* they take to mean the *Tree of All Knowledge*. This meaning can be brought out by the alternative translations *Tree of Knowledge of Good and of Evil* (the word *of* not being expressed in the Hebrew) or *Tree of*

Knowledge, both Good and Evil."²⁹

Prior to the incident involving the Tree of All Knowledge, the Scriptures provide that *"they were both naked, the man and his wife, and they were not ashamed."* Beresheet 2:25. When Adam and the woman partook of this forbidden fruit, their eyes were suddenly opened to their "nakedness" which is arom (ᵐ𐤉𐤏𐤏) in Hebrew. They were suddenly afraid and made for themselves coverings of leaves, likely leaves from the very tree from which they partook the fruit.³⁰

Most people who read this account will ask: "What could have possibly happened to cause such a sudden change in their perception, and how could eating a piece of fruit do such a thing?" While the fruit of that particular tree may have had special "powers" there is likely more to the story than meets the eye. This episode was a sensual event and we read in the text the emphasis placed upon the senses of touching, tasting and seeing.

The act of eating, drinking and tasting is at times used in the Scriptures in a metaphorical fashion to describe intimacy. For example in Song of Solomon we read, *"Like an apple tree among the trees of the woods, so is my beloved among the sons. I sat down in his shade with great delight, and his fruit was sweet to my taste."* Song of Solomon 2:3 NKJV. The Proverbs speak about a man drinking water from his own cisterns and not being enraptured by an immoral woman. (Proverb 5:15). We are encouraged to: *"Taste and see that YHWH is good."* Psalm 34:8

The key is that they now "knew" that they were naked. The fact that they were naked had not changed, rather the fact that they "knew," which is "yada" (𐤏𐤃𐤉) in Hebrew. Interestingly, the man and the woman were not the only ones who were naked during this event. The Scriptures record that the serpent was

also "arom" (ᴹ𐤉𐤏𐤎), which was the same word to describe the man and woman as naked. Relative to the serpent, the word "arom" (ᴹ𐤉𐤏𐤎) is usually translated as "cunning."

The word translated "the serpent" is "hanachash" (w𐤇𐤍ψ) in Hebrew. The noun "nachash" (w𐤇𐤍) can mean a "snake, serpent or one who practices divination." The adjective "nachash" (w𐤇𐤍) means: "bright or brazen." So was it actually a snake or was it some bright, angelic being?

No matter how you describe this "serpent," something happened here which should draw our attention to the prohibitions found within Leviticus (Vayiqra) 18-20. Most commentators allude to the fact that something sordid and graphic occurred, but typically shy away from the details.

Something clearly occurred that was offensive to the Creator. The man and the woman, who thought they would be like YHWH, were suddenly ashamed because they had done something wrong. This prompted them to cover themselves and hide. They had not only eaten from the Tree of All Knowledge, they had participated in evil – through their disobedience they had sinned.

When confronted concerning their newly donned apparel, they both participated in the blame game. The man blamed the woman, and the woman blamed the serpent. It did not work, each was held accountable for their actions. Various punishments were meted out and the following was directed to the serpent by YHWH: "*I will put enmity between you and the woman, and between your seed and her Seed. He will crush your head and you shall crush His heel.*" Beresheet 3:15.

This is considered by many to constitute a direct reference to the Messiah. In other words, there would be One that would come from the woman Who would

crush the head of the one that deceived mankind and helped bring sin into the world. Some who take a strictly literal interpretation of the Hebrew text proclaim that there is no such promise, and this verse could simply be translated as a curse without the hope that many read into the text.

The interesting part of the passage is that there are also seed from the serpent that will be in opposition to the Seed from the woman. This begs the question why it was the Seed of the woman, and not the Seed of the man. Since it is the male that has the seed, and not the woman, what could possibly be meant by this statement?

The easy answer is that this verse simply refers to offspring. Another view proposes that the woman represents the Bride of YHWH who will consist of both men and women, thus the existence of seed. The Messianic interpretation hints of a virgin birth. In any case, the timing of the promise is critical to understanding the verse.

An important shift had just occurred in the relationship between Elohim and mankind made in His image. Man and woman had violated His commands, which necessitated punishment. They would be subjected to separation and death, which would be the end of these marvelous creatures unless there was some sort of atonement made on their behalf.

Clearly, by meting out individual punishments to all of the perpetrators, YHWH was revealing that He was not pleased with any of them. He told them that they would die if they disobeyed, but He was also providing hope by revealing the avenue through which He would provide restoration for mankind. How, when, where and by Whom were all questions left unanswered – they would become clearer in the future. For the time being mankind would have to be satisfied with this promise – the promise of a Seed from a woman.

Despite this hope of a future fix, their transgression resulted in immediate punishment followed by atonement, which bought mankind some time. While YHWH told man that he would die if he ate the fruit of the forbidden tree, he did not immediately experience physical death because there was atonement for the man and the woman.

This atonement consisted of blood being shed on their behalf, and they were then each clothed with the skin of the dead animal that was killed. They were literally and symbolically clothed with death because of their transgression. While they chose fig leaves to cover their nakedness, YHWH chose skins. This is a powerful picture provided for us to learn and understand.

It vividly demonstrates the model of atonement through the shedding of blood – which is the essence of the life of the sacrifice. It also demonstrates substitution – one life taken on behalf of another. Both of these concepts are intimately involved in the eventual restoration of mankind through the promised Seed – the Messiah.

Therefore, what occurred in the Garden is not just a story from days gone by. It is filled with images and concepts that we must learn about and understand. It not only shows us the problem created by the sin of the first man and woman, but also the path to a solution.

It was only after the transgression that we are told how Adam named the woman Hawah (ΨIH) which means: "life-giver." Man was originally created to live as a complete being, dwelling in paradise, communing with Elohim for eternity. After the transgression in the Garden, Adam and Hawah were expelled and denied access to the Tree of Life. This resulted in the introduction of death to mankind, which again, was

directly linked to the rest of creation. The impact was immediate although the process of both physical and spiritual death took their own unique courses.

Prior to the fall, Adam was "plugged in to Elohim" spiritually. Adam could commune directly with Elohim in an intimate fashion which no created being was able to do after the fall. Once he was expelled from the Garden and from the presence of Elohim, he experienced spiritual death.

Death began to take hold of his physical body as well as the rest of creation. Those things that were made to last forever began to die. While Adam was originally created in the image of Elohim (Beresheet 5:1), the offspring of Adam were begotten in the image and likeness of Adam, as is said of Seth. (Beresheet 5:3). Adam contained the "breath of Life" which cannot be killed, although he existed in a body, which was once eternal, but now subject to death. As a result, his offspring were born in this same state.

The problem is evident although the solution was not so clear. Adam was expelled from paradise, because he had broken the Covenant. Adam chose not to live according to the rules of the House so he was evicted. As a result, all of his offspring were also excluded from the House, which is the source of eternal life. This is the condition that we, as the descendents of Adam, have inherited. We are all living in exile from the Garden.

To solve this problem, mankind needs to somehow regain entrance to the House and receive life. This is the rest of the story that we read about in the Scriptures. The underlying theme is the restoration of mankind to the Garden.

It would turn out to be a long journey, as we shall see, and mankind ultimately became divided between the few who followed the ways of YHWH and the many

who chose to rebel against their Creator. This is the distinction that we see to this very day. There is a difference between those who follow YHWH in the way that He commands, and those who insist upon doing things their own way. One path leads back to the garden, and the other path leads to death and destruction.

4

Judgment and Restoration

The punishment of Adam and Hawah involved banishment from the House, and ultimately death. Their disobedience impacted all of mankind and creation. We are supposed to learn from their mistake. Amazingly, there are those who currently claim to follow the Creator, yet they continue to disregard and ignore His commandments.

After the man and the woman were expelled, blood was shed, and they were covered with animal skin. This provided a pattern that blood must be shed to cover sin until the issue is ultimately settled, and an end is made of sin at the 70th seven to fulfill the prophecy of Daniel 9:24. That first blood-shedding event did not resolve the disobedience. The man and the woman were still punished, and they still died. The blood of the animal provided a temporary atonement, or rather covering.

We know that things did not go well with Creation after sin was introduced. It spread like a disease. Following the expulsion from paradise, Hawah bore both Cain (Qayin) and Abel (Hebel).[31] They were apparently conceived the same day Adam and Hawah were expelled from the Garden.[32] The Scriptures describe the births of Qayin and Hebel, and a mechanical translation of Beresheet 4:1 reads *"the Man (Adam) had*

known ✗ƴ Hawah his woman and she conceived and she brought forth ✗ƴ Qayin and she said I purchased a man with ✗ƴ YHWH."³³

Notice the three instances of the Aleph Taw (✗ƴ) in this passage and that each Aleph Taw (✗ƴ) is immediately next to a name: Qayin, Hawah and YHWH. They are clearly pointing to something important. Was Qayin intended to be the Seed of woman that would restore mankind, or is this simply showing us a shadow picture of how the Messiah will enter Creation.

There is actually ancient and intriguing speculation concerning the origin of both Qayin and Hebel. We do not have the space to fully investigate that subject, but I will simply point out that the text only records Adam as "knowing" Hawah once, but it describes two births.³⁴ When a person studies the Scriptures, over time it becomes apparent that nothing is by chance - neither omissions, inclusions or repetitions - everthing has a purpose.

Some speculate whether they were twins or whether only one of them was from Adam. No doubt these two brothers both came from the womb of Hawah, and they were unique beings. Not long after the description of their birth, we read a disturbing story telling how Qayin killed his brother Hebel. Tradition holds that this took place when they were both 40 years old.³⁵ We are told of an incident when they both presented offerings to YHWH *"at the conclusion of days"* or *"in the process of time."* Here is an account of what happened.

> "² Now Hebel was a keeper of sheep, but Qayin was a tiller of the ground. ³ And at the conclusion of days (in the process of time) it came to pass that

Qayin brought an offering of the fruit of the ground to YHWH. ⁴ Hebel also brought of the firstborn of his flock and of their fat. And YHWH respected Hebel and his offering, ⁵ but He did not respect Qayin and his offering. And Qayin was very angry, and his countenance fell." Beresheet 4:2-5.

We can safely deduce that this was not just any arbitrary day, but rather a special time called a "moad" (𐤌𐤏𐤃), also known as an Appointed Time. The brothers knew that they were supposed to bring offerings to YHWH at this particular time, and they both presented their offerings at the same place. The offering of Qayin was not looked upon favorably by YHWH. This passage reveals that there was an established time and method of worship which was known from the beginning. There was a right way and a wrong way to come before YHWH with gifts – Hebel did it properly while Qayin did not.

This is particularly significant since Qayin is the firstborn son, which is bakar (𐤁𐤔𐤓) in Hebrew. Adam was the firstborn of all creation, and thus he bore the responsibility as priest for all mankind. It is interesting that Adam was not present in this instance, but as the firstborn son, Qayin would have bourn the responsibility of priest in the absence of his father. As such, he should have known how to properly present offerings before YHWH.

The major clue to our linking this event with an Appointed Time is the phrase, *"in the process of time"* which is "m'qetz yomim" in Hebrew (𐤌𐤉𐤌𐤉 𐤒𐤑𐤌). The word "m'qetz" means: "to chop or cut off." The word "yomim" is literally spelled yom yom, or "day day" and is translated as "days."

The phrase is understood to mean: "end of days"

or a time when the days were ended or cut off. Interestingly, chopping and cutting is intimately connected with harvesting something. So this was not just any day that they chose to present offerings before YHWH, it was likely when the days of harvesting had ended

It is within this context that we must view the sacrifices which were rendered by these two individuals. Not only were they expected to be some place at a particular time, but they were also supposed to bring something and do something. There was a right way and a wrong way, and YHWH's reaction was determined by each individuals actions.

This event reveals a pattern that is repeated in the Scriptures, and shows us behavior that is pleasing, and that which is displeasing to YHWH. This is a lesson in worshipping YHWH, and we all need to pay close attention.

The Scriptures reveal that Qayin brought an offering of the fruit of the ground to YHWH, and Hebel also brought the firstborn of his flock and their fat. It is possible that Hebel brought an offering of the fruit of the ground to YHWH, and also brought the firstborn of his flock. The Hebrew word used for flock is tsone (𐤑𐤀𐤍) which implies a goat or a lamb.

Hebel knew what YHWH required and he complied. He brought the firstborn - the bakar (𐤁𐤊𐤓) of his flock. This was pleasing to YHWH. Qayin must have also known what pleased YHWH. Adam surely was given this information when he received the instructions from YHWH, and he must have transmitted the instructions to his sons. In fact, we are told that YHWH has declared the end from the beginning.[36] So Adam was aware, and as the "High Priest" of mankind, he was obligated to instruct his

descendents regarding how to worship the Creator.

The patterns and the ways of YHWH go back to the beginning, and they are revealed through cycles - one of those cycles being harvests. Throughout the Scriptures we see the terms "in the beginning" (beresheet) referring to the beginning of a harvest or the first of a harvest, and the term "in the end of days" (miqetz yomim) would bring us to the end of that harvest.

Many understand from the passage involving Qayin and Hebel that raising animals was better than tilling the ground, but this is not the relevant point. We see that Hebel offered his firstfruits, while there was no mention of this for Qayin. Also note that the offering of Hebel involved blood, while the offering of Qayin did not. Thus, the offering of Qayin was not acceptable - it did not include blood, and he did not receive atonement. As a result, he was overtaken by sin and he ultimately did shed blood - the blood of his brother. This provides us with a very important pattern.

The event reveals that there was a time and a place, as well as a right way and a wrong way, to meet with YHWH. Those times are marked by the sun and the moon, and are essentially built into the fabric of creation.

We first read a formal listing of these Appointed Times in the Wilderness, detailed to the people in Covenant with YHWH known as Yisrael. They were written by a man named Mosheh[37] and given in the Torah. It is clear that those instructions were known from the beginning. After the death of Hebel, things continued to deteriorate for hundreds of years until YHWH was forced to intervene.

After the passage of ten (10) generations, the Scriptures record the condition of Creation during the life of a man named Noah. "*5 And Elohim saw that the wickedness of man was great in the earth, and that every imagination of the thoughts of his heart was only evil continually . . . ¹¹ The earth also was corrupt before Elohim, and the earth was filled with violence. ¹² And Elohim looked upon the earth, and, behold, it was corrupt; for all flesh had corrupted his way upon the earth." Beresheet 6:5, 11-12.

We read an interesting passage as YHWH looks upon the Earth and actually repented for having made man. "*And YHWH said, My Spirit shall not strive with man throughout the ages (olam), for that he also is flesh: yet his days shall be an hundred and twenty years.*" Beresheet 6:3.

Now on its face, the text appears to indicate that mankind had another 120 years until they would be wiped out. In fact, the Book of Yasher specifically interprets the prophecy in this manner. However, not all flesh was destroyed in the flood, so this passage must therefore have a deeper meaning. In fact, it could also be read to put a limit on time itself. YHWH actually stated that He will not strive with man "forever" which is "olam" (ᴍ ꓶ ◎).

Olam is a very mysterious word, often misunderstood to mean "eternity." It actually can be translated as "until the most remote time." Instead of the abstract notion of "eternity," the word "olam" is meant to express a range between the "remotest time and perpetuity."[38] So "olam" could be interpreted as meaning: "until the end of the age." It is very important to understand the concept of ages when dealing with creation and time. Time has limits and it has been divided into ages, which include cycles. This becomes evident as we further explore the text of Beresheet 6:3.

The word translated as "years" is shanah (ψ⌐w). While "shanah" is commonly translated as "year," it essentially means a revolution or cycle of time. It is commonly understood to mean a year, but it can mean a

whole age.³⁹ Therefore, on another level of understanding, one could interpret the text to describe 120 "cycles."

We already referred to the Jubilee Cycle, which is a 50 year cycle. As a result, YHWH may have been placing a limit on the time that He would strive with mortal man as being 120 Jubilee cycles or 6,000 years. This makes sense when one understands that a thousand years is commonly linked to a day for Elohim. Thus, 6,000 years is like 6 days to YHWH.⁴⁰ This fits perfectly within the 6 day pattern established at creation, followed by a 1 day Sabbath.

So then we must make a distinction between time in general, and time associated with our present physical existence. The Scriptures seem to be indicating that the time that mankind exists in corruptible bodies on the Earth will be a total of 6,000 years, followed by a millennial Sabbath where YHWH will reign for 1,000 years. We therefore understand that the end of 6,000 years will be the end of an age, and the beginning of another age that will last 1,000 years with the redeemed of mankind.

It is within this time frame, up through "the end of this age" (olam), that we see the plan of YHWH develop through His Covenants. He desires to fellowship with mankind intimately in paradise. This is what we saw in the Garden. Eden actually means: "paradise." The Creator wants the best for His Creation, but through the disobedience of man, that ideal was disrupted.

Ever since then, YHWH has sought for those who would be obedient to work out His restoration plan. He found such a man in Noah. The Scriptures proclaim that *"Noah was a just man and perfect in his generations, and Noah walked with Elohim."* Beresheet 6:9. The Hebrew provides more insight into the character of Noah. The

word for "just" is tzedek (ᐈᐊᐁᐂ) and refers to "righteous conduct toward Elohim." The word for "perfect" is tamiym (ᐃᐊᐃᐄ) which means "upright, undefiled, clean." So we have a picture of Noah as one who walked according to the ways of YHWH.

Noah obviously knew the way that YHWH had established for men to live. The commands which were given in the Garden were surely transmitted by Adam through his descendents. As a result, Noah walked with YHWH and was righteous. That meant he followed the instructions of YHWH and was obedient. This provides us with some interesting insight into who YHWH decides to establish His Covenant with. He establishes a relationship with those who obey Him.

The word "covenant" is brit (ᐅᐊᐆᐇ) and it derives from the word "bara" (ᐈᐆᐇ) which means to "select" or "create." Thus the party included in a covenant with YHWH must be selected or "chosen." So in the Scriptural sense, when we talk about a "chosen people" or a "chosen generation" we are talking about those who are in a Covenant relationship with YHWH, and as such, those who walk according to His ways.

Noah was chosen by YHWH to enter into a Covenant relationship. He was told about the Covenant that YHWH would establish with him. "*¹⁷ I am going to bring floodwaters on the earth to destroy all life under the heavens, every creature that has the breath of life in it. Everything on earth will perish. ¹⁸ But <u>I will establish ᐅᐈ My Covenant with you, and you will enter the Ark - you and your sons and your wife and your sons' wives with you.</u> ¹⁹ You are to bring into the Ark two of all living creatures, male and female, to keep them alive with you. ²⁰ Two of every kind of bird, of every kind of animal and of every kind of creature that moves along the ground will come to you to be kept alive. ²¹ You are to take every kind of food that is to be eaten and store it*

away as food for you and for them. [22] *Noah did everything just as Elohim commanded him."* Beresheet 6:17-22.

YHWH informed Noah that He was going to wipe out life on the planet by a global flood. YHWH would establish His Covenant with Noah. The word "establish" derives from the Hebrew word quwm (ᵚᵠ) which means "to stand" or "raise up." The Aleph Taw (×⌶) is an integral element of "establishing" the Covenant which specifically belonged to YHWH. He chose Noah to enter into His Covenant relationship.

As a result, Noah would be saved along with his family and some select creatures. While this was certainly good news for Noah, it was only the beginning of the Covenant process. It was simply a promise that came with conditions and specific instructions. Noah was required to perform his part - he had to build the vessel of his deliverance, which would protect him from the judgment of YHWH. It was also incumbent upon him to store all of the food required for the Ark's passengers. This was a lot of hard work, and it was imperative that he follow the instructions of YHWH precisely.

If Noah did not build the Ark, he would have been killed along with the rest of mankind. Instead, Noah believed the promise, and his actions were consistent with his belief. Thus, through the obedience of Noah we see the continuation of man and animals. Noah was, in essence, like Adam. He was the father of all of mankind, and because of his obedience, men would continue their physical existence.

Because of his walk, Noah found favour in the eyes of YHWH, and he and his family would be spared from the flood. Noah was not an arbitrary choice. He was chosen, because of his walk, to build an Ark - a vessel that would save a portion of creation.

The word "ark" in the modern Hebrew text is tebah (תבה). It is a very curious and unique word, and if you look at most Hebrew dictionaries you will find that the origin of the word is at question. Some actually believe that it is borrowed from Egyptian or Arabic where similar sounding words refer to a "chest" or a "coffin." Essentially the word has been given its meaning from the context of the passage, not necessarily because of the root meaning.

In cases like this it is often helpful to look at the ancient language, and in the case of "tebah" (ЧⅡ×) we see the taw (×), the bet (⊓) and the hey (Ψ). Once again, the taw (×) is a mark which means: "covenant." The bet (⊓) means: "house" and the hey (Ψ) represents a "window." In the most ancient Hebrew pictographic texts the hey (Ψ) appears as a man with his arms upstretched which means: "behold." It shows that something important is being revealed.

This word tebah (ЧⅡ×) seems to be describing much more than a boat, it is pointing us to something important. A literal definition from the ancient script could mean: "behold the covenant house." It is demonstrating that if we follow the instructions of YHWH, and remain in Covenant with Him, we can enter into His House, where there is protection from judgment.

There was a window, so this was not a coffin, as many liken the word. In this protected place man could see and be seen – it was a place of safety meant for the living. It was not a place for the dead, it was a place separated and apart from judgment and death. Death was on the outside, and life was on the inside.

After YHWH gave the promise, there came a time when He commanded Noah to actually build the Ark. According to the Dead Sea Scrolls, Noah was told by a messenger that a flood would occur after a certain number of Shemitah cycles. Most people are unfamiliar with the concept of Shemitah cycles, but it is a most important pattern established on the first week of creation – the pattern of sevens. In the case of the Shemitah cycle, it is a pattern of seven years.

As discussed previously, every seventh year in the count is a Shemitah year or a Sabbath year – a year of rest. These Shemitah years are then counted seven times and after the seventh Shemitah year is a Jubilee year. (Vayiqra 25:8-10). This is how the Creator gauges time, and it is this calculation of time which is imbedded within the Covenant relationship with YHWH.

Therefore, every Jubilee cycle contains seven Shemitah cycles each consisting of seven years. The seven Shemitah cycles, totaling 49 years, are followed by one Jubilee Year. These 50 years form a Jubilee cycle. You might be wondering why this is important when talking about the story of the flood. The reason why it is mentioned again here is because, according to the Dead Sea Scrolls 1 QapGen Col. 6, the flood was to occur in the year that followed a Shemitah cycle.[41]

The point is that YHWH had Noah counting Shemitah cycles. So Noah understood how YHWH reckoned time and he was aware of what time it was. This is critical for anyone in Covenant with YHWH, so they can know and keep the Covenant appointments – the Appointed Times. The importance of the Shemitah count is extremely significant when examining creation, time and the future.[42] This is especially true in light of the fact that through the Jubilee cycles we can discern  that mortal man was given a finite amount of time upon

the earth - namely 6,000 years.

The Scriptures record that: "*Noah did everything just as Elohim commanded him.*" Beresheet 6:22. Notice that he did not do what he felt like doing. He did not follow some tradition or custom that he learned or inherited concerning building boats. No - he did everything exactly as Elohim commanded. There is an element of precision and detail in his obedience that is important to recognize and imitate.

As a result, the Ark was ready to deliver him and his family when the flood waters came. "*¹ YHWH then said to Noah, 'Go into the Ark, you and your whole family, because I have found you righteous in this generation. ² <u>Take with you seven (7) of every kind of clean animal, a male and its mate, and two (2) of every kind of unclean animal</u>, a male and its mate, ³ and also seven (7) of every kind of bird, male and female, to keep their various kinds alive throughout the earth. ⁴ Seven (7) days from now I will send rain on the earth for forty (40) days and forty (40) nights, and I will wipe from the face of the earth every living creature I have made.*" Beresheet 7:1-4.

The Scriptures again specifically emphasize the fact that: "*Noah did all that YHWH commanded him.*" Beresheet 7:5. The point is quite clear, Noah obeyed the instructions of YHWH. Notice that Noah was commanded to take seven (7) pairs of clean animals. Previously we read about two (2) of each animal and now we read about seven (7) clean animals. It is important to understand that there is, and always was, a distinction between clean and unclean, righteousness and sin. We currently find those instructions written in the Torah, but they were ever present before mankind.[43]

Noah knew those distinctions and we already discussed that he was literally described as "righteous" and "clean." The instructions of YHWH were no doubt

handed down by Adam although, by this time, very few were actually following them.

When all preparations were completed, YHWH closed the door of the Ark, sealing Noah and his family, along with the animals inside the "House of the Covenant."

The rains began to fall: "*17 For forty (40) days the flood kept coming on the earth, and as the waters increased they lifted the Ark high above the earth. 18 The waters rose and increased greatly on the earth, and the Ark floated on the surface of the water. 19 They rose greatly on the earth, and all the high mountains under the entire heavens were covered. 20 The waters rose and covered the mountains to a depth of more than 15 cubits. 21 Every living thing that moved on the earth perished - birds, livestock, wild animals, all the creatures that swarm over the earth, and all mankind. 22 Everything on dry land that had the breath of life in its nostrils died. 23 Every living thing on the face of the earth was wiped out; men and animals and the creatures that move along the ground and the birds of the air were wiped from the earth. Only Noah was left, and those with him in the Ark. 24 The waters flooded the earth for a hundred and fifty (150) days. 8:1 But Elohim remembered Noah and all the wild animals and the livestock that were with him in the Ark, and He sent a wind over the earth, and the waters receded. 2 Now the springs of the deep and the floodgates of the heavens had been closed, and the rain had stopped falling from the sky. 3 The water receded steadily from the earth. At the end of the hundred and fifty (150) days the water had gone down, 4 and on the seventeenth day of the seventh month the ark came to rest on the mountains of Ararat. 5 The waters continued to recede until the tenth month, and on the first day of the tenth month the tops of the mountains became visible. 6 After forty (40) days Noah opened the window he had made in the ark 7 and sent out a raven . . .*" Beresheet 7:17-8:7.

One will notice again that Noah knew exactly how to reckon days, months and years from all the specific dates that are given – even when the entire earth was flooded by water. As Noah was a righteous man, he would have had to know how to reckon time. He used the sun and the moon to reckon days, months and years. This is an important point to appreciate when some today are promoting adherence to man-made calendars, or calendars that determine months and years based upon factors that are not prescribed by the Scriptures.

The flood waters receded and Noah, along with the occupants, exited the Ark safely. It is then that we are told of a Covenant established by Elohim. "*⁸ Then Elohim spoke to Noah and to his sons with him, saying: ⁹ 'And as for Me, behold, <u>I establish My Covenant with you and with your descendents after you,</u> ¹⁰ <u>and with every living creature that is with you</u>: the birds, the cattle, and every beast of the earth with you, of all that go out of the ark, every beast of the earth. ¹¹ <u>Thus I establish My Covenant with you: Never again shall all flesh be cut off by the waters of the flood; never again shall there be a flood to destroy the earth.</u>' ¹² And Elohim said: 'This is the sign of the Covenant which I make between Me and you, and every living creature that is with you, for perpetual generations: ¹³ I set My rainbow in the cloud, and it shall be for the sign of the Covenant between Me and the earth. ¹⁴ It shall be, when I bring a cloud over the earth, that the rainbow shall be seen in the cloud; ¹⁵ and <u>I will remember My Covenant which is between Me and you and every living creature of all flesh</u>; the waters shall never again become a flood to destroy all flesh. ¹⁶ The rainbow shall be in the cloud, and I will look on it to remember the everlasting Covenant between Elohim and every living creature of all flesh that is on the earth.' ¹⁷ And Elohim said to Noah, 'This is the sign of the Covenant which I have established between

Me and all flesh that is on the earth.'" Beresheet 9:8-17.

According to the Book of Jubilees 7:1-13, this Covenant was made between YHWH and Noah in the fifth year after the flood, on the first day of the week, on Day 1 of Month 1. The same information appears in the Dead Sea Scrolls in the Tales of the Patriarchs 1 QapGen, Column 12, Lines 13-17. Both accounts appear to confirm Day 1 of Month 1 in the year 2,323 BCE.*

It is important, once again, to note that YHWH repeatedly refers to the Covenant as "My Covenant." In other words, it belongs to Him and none else. This Covenant is an everlasting Covenant – a Covenant throughout the ages. It went beyond the life of Noah, or his immediate descendents for that matter. YHWH promised that He would never again  cut off all flesh by a flood, and never again would He use a flood to destroy the entire earth.

There was no corresponding duty or obligation required from man or the animals. It was a promise accompanied by a sign – the bow. The fact that there was a sign attached to the Covenant is significant. The Hebrew word for sign is owt, spelled (אות) in the Babylonian derived modern Hebrew Script, and (×𐤉𐤏) in ancient Hebrew. It can mean a "mark" or a "token" and is intended to be a visible sign or reminder of the Covenant.

One very important sign for the Covenant people is the Sabbath Day. It is a weekly sign for all who are in a Covenant relationship with the One Who made the seventh day Sabbath.[44] We shall see that YHWH often attaches these marks or signs to His Covenants. In the

case of the Covenant with Noah and creation, we see the bow as the sign of that particular Covenant. It was a sign placed in the sky visible to all creation.

The word for bow in Hebrew is qesheth (☓w𐤏). It is interesting that the bow consists of seven colors which correlate to the seven Spirits described by the Prophet Isaiah (Yeshayahu)[45] in Chapter 11 and verse 2 of the text attributed to him. The sign of the Covenant is also the same bow described as being in the Throne Room of Heaven.[46] There is meaning to every color in the rainbow and I encourage the reader to examine this subject deeper.

In addition, from Elohim's perspective in the heavens, the bow was held backward, an ancient sign by which warriors often indicated that a battle was over.[47] We can still see the bow to this day. It is a reminder of His Covenant, which is essentially a demonstration of His mercy and restraint.

There is a pattern established here. As YHWH makes Covenant with His creation, He uses a man as the mediator. In this instance, Noah represented mankind and creation. Part of this Covenant process also involved the shedding of blood.

A literal rendering of the Scriptures provides that: "[20] *Noah built an altar to YHWH, and took of every clean animal and of every clean bird, and offered burnt offerings on the altar.* [21] *And smelled YHWH* ☓𐤏 *a soothing aroma. Then YHWH said in His heart, 'I will never again curse* ☓𐤏 *the ground for man's sake, although the imagination of man's heart is evil from his youth; nor will I again destroy* ☓𐤏 *every living thing as I have done.'"* Beresheet 8:20-21.

Man could not save himself from judgment, and the only way to life was through obedience. Ultimately, it was YHWH Who provided the salvation. To emphasize this point, there are three instances of the untranslated Aleph Taw (𐤀𐤕) in Beresheet 8:21 when the burnt offerings were being made to YHWH. There are also three instances of the Aleph Taw (𐤀𐤕) when YHWH declares that He will make a Covenant. (Beresheet 9:9-10).[48]

YHWH did not have to enter into this Covenant with man. He could have easily stated, "If you continue to sin I will flood the planet again until you learn your lesson." On the contrary, He unilaterally stated that He would never do such a thing again. This is very telling.

When Adam and Hawah transgressed His commandments, YHWH could have killed them and annihilated all of Creation. Likewise when the planet was corrupted during the age of Noah, He could have destroyed everything. Instead He continued to work with certain men to bring about a restoration.

This is the repeating theme that we shall see throughout the Scriptures - the Covenants are specifically designed to bring about "the restoration of all things." YHWH always preserves a righteous line through which He operates His Covenant promises. Thanks to the mercy of the Almighty and the obedience of Noah, we are alive today to participate in this process.

The phrase "the restoration of all things" is associated with two concepts in Hebraic thought. It is ultimately linked with the restoration of earth to paradise in the seventh millennium. However, it is also linked with the idea of the Jubilee year, which was the year of the restitution of all things in Ancient Yisrael, when the Jubilee was being counted and its specific laws observed. Both concepts are the subject of the prophecy in Acts 3:21, which indicates that the heavens will release the Messiah in a Jubilee Year to bring about the Kingdom of Elohim in the Sabbath millennium.

"*[19]* *Repent therefore and be converted, that your sins*

may be blotted out, so that times of refreshing may come from the presence of YHWH, [20] and that He may send Yahushua Messiah, Who was preached to you before, [21] Whom heaven must receive until the times of restoration of all things, which Elohim has spoken by the mouth of all His set apart prophets since the world began." Acts 3:19-21.

There are some who teach that through this Covenant, YHWH established what are commonly referred to as The 7 Noahic Laws. This is an erroneous doctrine which teaches that Gentiles are only required to obey 7 laws to be deemed righteous, but only Jews are required to obey the Commandments of YHWH outlined in the Torah.

Those who teach and believe this doctrine believe that the world is essentially divided into two categories: 1) Jews, and 2) non-Jews – called Gentiles. This is simply preposterous and is not supported by the Scriptures.[49]

The label "gentile" is actually equivalent in meaning to the word "heathen." It means "the nations" and refers to those who are not in Covenant with YHWH. A fundamental teaching in the Scriptures is that righteousness is determined by the heart, and is demonstrated through a person's conduct – whether they obey the instructions of YHWH.

The Scriptures specifically and repeatedly teach that YHWH Elohim is not a respector of persons.[50] This concept is difficult for people entrapped in religion to grasp, but it is critical to understand. YHWH is only in Covenant with those who believe, and therefore obey Him. YHWH does not make allowances for disobedience toward Him based on race, ethnicity, wealth or religious affiliation. This was a revelation to certain Judeans 2,000 years ago, but has been true since the beginning.

In the New Testament text of John (Yahanan)[51]

we are given a warning against being deceived on this very issue: "⁷ Little children, let no one deceive you. He who practices righteousness is righteous, just as He is righteous. ⁸ He who sins is of the devil, for the devil has sinned from the beginning. For this purpose the Son of Elohim was manifested, that He might destroy the works of the devil. ⁹ Whoever has been born of Elohim does not sin, for His seed remains in him; and he cannot sin, because he has been born of Elohim." I Yahanan 3:7-9.

As we shall see, there is no special provision made for Gentiles. There was no such thing as a Jew or even a Hebrew, when Noah participated in this Covenant. In fact, the first Hebrew would not arrive on the scene for another ten (10) generations through Noah's son Shem. That man was named Abram, and his name was later changed to Abraham after he too was chosen by YHWH and entered into Covenant with YHWH.

Sadly, even after this worldwide deluge and the promise of YHWH, mankind rebelled again. The Scriptures briefly describe an incident at Babylon. We know from history that it was at Babylon where mankind developed a religious system that focused on the creation, rather than the Creator.

5

Babylon

It did not take long after the flood for mankind to, once again, fall away from the ways of YHWH. There is much that we can learn from the incident of Babel which gives insight to many of the problems that we see in the world today. We read a very brief but telling portion of history in the Scriptures when it describes Babylon.

"*¹ Now the whole earth had one language and one speech. ² And it came to pass, as they journeyed from the east, that they found a plain in the land of Shinar, and they dwelt there. ³ Then they said to one another, 'Come, let us make bricks and bake them thoroughly.' They had brick for stone, and they had asphalt for mortar. ⁴ And they said, 'Come, let us build ourselves a city, and a tower whose top is in the heavens; let us make a name for ourselves, lest we be scattered abroad over the face of the whole earth.*" Beresheet 11:1-4 NKJV.

This was not simply about a building project. The inhabitants of the Earth had established their own political and religious system. They were going to build a city *for themselves* and make a name *for themselves.*

Contrast this city with Jerusalem, which ultimately represents the Garden. Jerusalem is a city where YHWH has placed His Name by building His House. It is the city where YHWH meets with His people. It is a city on earth representing YHWH in the temporal realm, while Jerusalem above represents YHWH in the spiritual realm. (Galatians 4:26, Hebrews

12:22, Revelation 3:12, 21:2). Babylon was in direct contrast with the desire of the Creator for His Creation on earth.

Mankind had become haughty and arrogant. They had failed to learn the lesson from the Garden or the flood. They glorified their own intelligence and abilities rather than giving the honor and esteem to YHWH. They refused to worship YHWH, and they disobeyed His Commandments. We see that much of modern civilization shares the same haughty attitude as mankind once had in Babylon as they built a Tower *"to the heavens."* (Beresheet 11:1-9).

Today, we share more with Babylon than mere attitude or architectural accomplishments. In fact, what  many fail to recognize is that it was the counterfeit religious system established by men that was at the heart of the Babel incident. While many popular paintings show a round tower reaching to the heavens, the tower was more likely an ancient ziggurat, which served as the centerpiece to sun god worship established through Nimrod and his mother Semiramis.

It was at Babylon that we see Nimrod being worshipped as a god. Legend has it that Shem, the righteous son of Noah, killed Nimrod for this abomination and scattered his body throughout the earth.[52] Despite his death, a religious system developed wherein Nimrod became deified, and an  entire religious Trinitarian system developed which directed worship away from YHWH toward a false system of worship which is commonly called "sun god worship." It was not limited to the worship of the sun, and included other celestial bodies. Essentially, it involved worshipping the creation rather than the true

Creator.

As we shall see, most of the religious systems in existence today actually derive some of their practices from Babylon. In fact, Babylon represents the attempt of mankind to establish a system of worship which is not condoned by Elohim. Babylon was a religious and political system that was challenging the authority and government of Elohim. Babylon does not worship the Elohim of the Scriptures called YHWH. It always represents a false system of worship, and we have already seen where that leads - judgment.

The Scriptures tell us that Noah's son Ham had a son named Cush who married a woman named Semiramis. Cush and Semiramis then had a son and named him Nimrod. They further report that Nimrod *"began to be a mighty one in the earth. He was a mighty hunter before YHWH: wherefore it is said, even as Nimrod the mighty hunter before YHWH. And the beginning of his kingdom was Babel, and Erech, and Accad, and Calneh, in the land of Shinar."* Beresheet 10:8-10.

Most people do not quite grasp the meaning of this passage. They typically posit that Nimrod was

simply skilled with the bow and arrow. There are many different legends, some claim that "mighty hunter" should actually be interpreted as "giant hunter" because he slew giants and conquered lands. Others claim that his great success in hunting (comp. Gen. x. 9) was due to the fact that he wore the coats of skin which [Elohim] made for Adam and [Hawah] (Gen. iii. 21). These coats were handed down from father to son, and thus came into the possession of Noah, who took them with him into the ark, whence they were stolen by Ham. The latter gave them to his son Cush, who in turn gave them to Nimrod, and when the animals saw the latter clad in them, they crouched before him so that he had no difficulty in catching them. The people, however, thought that these feats were due to his extraordinary strength, so that they made him their king.[53]

The Hebrew word translated as "mighty" is gibor (𐤂𐤁𐤅). It essentially means: "mighty, superior or valiant." Interestingly, this word contains the word "ger" (𐤂𐤅), which means: "stranger." So couched within the word ger (𐤂𐤅) we see the bet (𐤁), which means: "house." If we view the meaning of the word gibor (𐤂𐤁𐤅), looking at the ancient symbols, we see "strange house or foreign house" which stands in contrast to the Covenant House of YHWH. Indeed, Nimrod was creating a "strange house" that was diametrically opposed to the Garden. His was a house of rebellion, disobedience and defiance.

"Until Nimrod, mankind was governed by the patriarchal system where the heads of families heard from [Elohim] and guided their individual tribes. Nimrod, more accurately a "mighty hunter against YHWH," usurped patriarchal rule, and crowned himself the first human king in all of history. Now man ruled instead of Elohim."[54]

As common tradition has it, Nimrod became a god-man to the people. Semiramis, his wife and mother, became the Queen of ancient Babylon. Nimrod was eventually killed by an enemy, some say it was Shem the son of Noah. His body was apparently cut into pieces and sent to various parts of his kingdom to demonstrate that he was a man and he was dead. This was supposed to put an end to his being worshipped as a god but here is where Semiramis steps in. She had all of Nimrod's body parts gathered, except for one part that could not be found - his phallus.

Semiramis claimed that Nimrod could not come back to life without it, and told the people of Babylon that Nimrod had ascended to the sun and was now to be called "Baal," the sun god. She was creating a mystery religion, and claimed to have been immaculately conceived, establishing herself as a goddess. She became known as Ishtar, or Easter, and purportedly descended from the moon in a giant moon egg that fell into the Euphrates River at the time of the first full moon after the spring equinox. This is the origin of moon worship. Ishtar soon became pregnant and claimed that it was the rays of the sun-god Baal that caused her to conceive.

The son that she brought forth was named Tammuz, who was believed to be the son of the sun-god, Baal. So while Baal the Father, remained in the Heavens, often represented by the sun, the mother and son continued on as physical beings. This is the source of many mother-son representations seen throughout history.

Tammuz, like his supposed father, became a hunter. When Tammuz was 40, he was killed during a freak accident by a wild pig. Ishtar proclaimed that Tammuz was now ascended to his father, Baal, and that the two of them would be with the worshippers in the sacred candle or lamp flame as Father, Son and Spirit. Ishtar, who was now worshipped as the "Mother of God and Queen of Heaven," continued to build upon this developing religion referred to as "Mysteries."

    She also proclaimed a period of sorrow each year prior to the anniversary of the death of Tammuz. It was called "Weeping for Tammuz," and it lasted for 40 days – one day for each year that Tammuz was alive. The concept was to deprive oneself of an earthly pleasure. During this time, no meat was to be eaten. Worshippers were to meditate upon the sacred mysteries of Baal and Tammuz, and to make the sign of the cross "+" in front of their hearts as they worshipped. The cross was the sign for Tammuz.

    This Babylonian sun worship tradition ensnared Yisrael (Ezekiel 8:14) in the past and continues to this present day, only now it is called Lent. Lent is simply a modified and modernized version of "Weeping for Tammuz." Those involved in the mysteries also ate sacred  cakes with the marking of a "+" or cross on the top. This is the origin of the wafers marked with the Tammuz "cross" or "+" which the Catholic religion uses during their Eucharist service.

    Every year, on the first Sunday after the first full moon after the spring equinox, a celebration was held. It was known as Ishtar's (Easter) Sunday, and was celebrated with rabbits and eggs, since it was a fertility rite. Ishtar also proclaimed that because Tammuz was killed by a pig, that a pig (ham) must be eaten on that Sunday.[55]

    So the Babylonian Easter celebration was determined by a tequfah – the vernal or spring equinox. Babylon is also where we see the origins of the Christ mass, later known as Christmas. It was celebrated on December 25, which at the time marked the tequfah known

as the winter solstice.

December 25 was deemed the birth date of Tammuz, and every other "christ" after him. Since this day was the shortest day of the year, it was associated with the "rebirth" of the sun. Therefore from Babylon onward, every culture that worshipped the sun attributed December 25 as the birth date of their "sun god."

This behavior was clearly displeasing to YHWH as we read. *"⁵ But YHWH came down to see the city and the tower which the sons of men had built. ⁶ And YHWH said, Indeed the people are one and they all have one language, and this is what they begin to do; now nothing that they propose to do will be withheld from them. ⁷ Come, let Us go down and there confuse their language, that they may not understand one another's speech." ⁸ So YHWH scattered them abroad from there over the face of all the earth, and they ceased building the city. ⁹ Therefore its name is called Babel, because there YHWH confused the language of all the earth; and from there YHWH scattered them abroad over the face of all the earth."* Beresheet 11:5-9.

So far, in the very beginning of the text we have seen a consistent pattern of mankind rebelling against the ways of YHWH. The first man and woman disobeyed and were expelled from the Garden. YHWH spared them from the judgment of immediate death. Mankind was permitted to exist for nearly 1,700 years until YHWH judged the planet. Once again, He was merciful, and allowed a remnant to live. Now at Babylon, the people had completely turned against YHWH.

As a result of Nimrod's rebellion and false worship at Babel, the people were disbursed and the languages were confused. The dispersion at the Tower of Babel happened during the days of Peleg when the earth was divided according to Beresheet 10:25. Mankind was

divided in such a way that they were prohibited from unifying and continuing the activities begun in ancient times.[56]

It would be centuries later that Babylon would develop into a world power sometimes referred to as neo-Babylon. While YHWH disbursed the people, He still permitted them to live. Interestingly, there are some who believe that this was also the time when the continents were broken apart and spread across the planet during a great cosmic disruption.[57]

So we can see with each progression of rebellion, disobedience and punishment, the earth experienced great upheavals as well. Just as man and the earth were connected from the beginning, that connection will continue to the end. Their fates are joined and as we look at prophecies concerning the future, we can expect the earth to experience cataclysmic events as judgment is poured out on mankind in the end.[58]

From the scattering of Babel, we see another development as the world is divided into Nations. Traditionally, the number seventy (70) is closely connected with "The Nations." This is because of the 70 descendents of Noah after the flood. While there was always a righteous line who followed the ways of YHWH, the Nations are typically considered to be Gentiles, or heathens, essentially because they practiced the false system of worship inherited from Babylon, sometimes referred to as "paganism."

It was in Babylon that we see man openly creating a form of systematic worship away from YHWH. This was not simply the corruption that occurred prior to the flood. It was outright rebellion against the Creator. Their actions constituted idolatry, and this was essentially the first recorded place where paganism was practiced.

Thus far, we have not defined the word "pagan" or "paganism." This is because it was important to first set the stage regarding Creation and the way set forth by YHWH. Essentially, paganism can be defined broadly or narrowly. In the most basic sense, paganism derives from the Latin "paganus" meaning "country dweller" or "rustic."[59]

So this term does not actually trace back to Babylon. It was originally a term ascribed to the religious practices of those in the rural areas of society where agriculture and the elements were the focus of people's attention. Those dependent upon harvests for their existence would rely upon the regular and predictable seasonal cycles. As a result, "nature" essentially became a religion for their way of life. They would look to the sun, the moon, the rain, the earth and the seasons as their life. They would pray to the elements and this became the focus of their worship – creation.

The term pagan eventually expanded to become "a blanket term, typically used to refer to non-Abrahamic, indigenous polytheistic religious traditions."[60] Most sun worship is polytheistic in the sense that it involves the worship of multiple deities. The dieties typically have unique personalities, traits and powers ascribed to them. I prefer an even broader definition which would encompass any religion that worships or promotes any "god" other than YHWH, or any path other than the way prescribed through the instructions in the Torah.

Contrary to some popular beliefs, YHWH is <u>not</u> a tolerant Elohim. He is one – echad. Various "gods" do <u>not</u> act out some divinely scripted drama that we call life, and YHWH is <u>not</u> a three person Elohim, known as "The Trinity." In fact, this may be a good time to discuss the popular Christian concept of the trinity, since it derives directly from Babylon.

Most who grew up in Christianity are probably familiar with the popular hymn "Holy, Holy, Holy" by Reginald Heber which twice concludes with the resounding chorus, "God in three persons, blessed trinity." That essentially sums up the Christian notion of the Trinity – "God in three persons." Of course, we have already seen that the term "god" is a generic title, and the song also refers to "Lord God Almighty."

The title "Lord," also spelled "LORD," is often used to replace the very Name of YHWH in most "Bibles," Hymns and other Christian texts. This is profoundly significant, because in Hebrew it is "baal" which was the name/title ascribed to Nimrod. By replacing the Name of YHWH with a title, it essentially violates the Third Commandment which literally forbids "bringing the Name of YHWH to naught."[61]

Once again, many religions refer to their "god" as "lord." Ecumenicals enjoy the term because it is non-offensive and universally used, but it is nonetheless a very generic and meaningless title, often used in false religions.

Indeed, if the Trinity is meant to apply to only "gods" and "lords," then it is essentially accurate, since the pagans refer to "gods," "lords" and "christs" which all have a place in pagan trinities. I have a problem when people attempt to apply the trinity notion of three persons to YHWH Elohim.

Clearly, as we already pointed out, there is a pluralistic nature to YHWH as He is unified – echad. His nature transcends anything that we can describe in our physical three or four dimensional existence.

Attempting to describe or limit the existence of YHWH to "three persons" is an idea that far predates Christianity, but was never considered by the Covenant people of YHWH - Yisrael.

The doctrine crept into Christianity as sun worshippers formed and molded the Christian religion. Christianity was essentially a combination of the belief in the Messiah, mixed with the "mysteries" of Babylon, to form a new state religion which would serve the political needs of the Roman Empire.

While the Trinity is a popular Christian doctrine and tradition, it is not an accurate Scriptural understanding of YHWH Elohim. Many stubbornly cling to this inherited tradition, and it is certainly possible to find ways to justify this belief if that is your desire. The important thing that you must ask yourself is whether you ever would have gleaned such an understanding from a strict reading of Scripture. Likely not, because it is pagan, and it derives from Babylon. The Trinity is not the only pagan idea found within the Christian religion as we shall see further in this discussion.

So for our definition of "pagan" we will be using a very basic and broad definition meaning: "heathen." Therefore, for the purposes of this discussion "paganism" will refer to any false religion practiced by the "pagans" or "heathens." This will include anyone who does not follow the narrow way prescribed by YHWH. This is a very intolerant definition, and rightly so. In this way, we will remain consistent with Scriptural thought which typically divides the world into two groups: 1) the righteous; and 2) the wicked. This categorization can also be divided between the Covenant people of Yisrael and all others, referred to as "the Nations," "the Heathens" or "the Gentiles."

This may seem strange to many Christians who have been taught that YHWH is finished with Yisrael and has replaced His "Old" Covenant with a "New" Covenant and a new people known as "The Church." Sadly, this is another false tradition that is discussed throughout the Walk in the Light series. YHWH has not changed His Covenant, nor has He changed His Ways. (Malachi 3:6).

YHWH does not condone or approve of worship that is contrary to His way. The universalist notion that the many religions of the world are merely different paths leading to the same "God" is completely false, and not supported by the Hebrew Scriptures. The Scriptures actually do teach that all paths lead to Elohim, but only the narrow path leads to immortality in paradise, all other paths lead to damnation in the Lake of Fire.

Noah was in Covenant with YHWH, and it is clear that some of his descendents followed the narrow way, while most did not. After the dispersion from Babylon we see that people were scattered throughout the world and new languages were given to them. This does not mean that they  forgot their false worship developed in Babylon. Indeed, they still worshipped their gods, only now they had different names as the languages were confused.

The people continued their pagan practices in their new locations, only now they had their own unique  languages and building materials as they implemented their religious systems. You have heard the phrase, "history repeats itself," and so it does. The same false gods and religions have been recycling and resurfacing since Nimrod and Babylon. This basic form of paganism was then spread throughout the world when Elohim confused the languages and separated the people. So what we see through history is the same sun god worship that began in Babylon being practiced throughout the earth in different cultures with essentially the same players, just different names – variations on a theme.

To this day, we find religious systems which include aspects of Babylonian worship that trace all the way back to Nimrod and the Tower of Babel. Of course, with time, each system then followed its own unique and individual progression to the point where each became somewhat unique and distinctive. As a result, their shared source is not always obvious.

Interestingly, we see step pyramids in Egypt, Mexico, Central and South America. We also see ziggurats throughout the Middle East and Africa as well as pagodas in the Far East. All of these structures are modeled on the Tower of Babel, and even share similar construction methods.[62] They  are all structures which point to the sun, and reflect the religious beliefs and systems of the people that built them.

 These pyramid shaped objects have relatives known as obelisks, otherwise known as sun pillars, minarets and steeples. Sadly, these objects which trace directly back to sun worship, are used today and litter the landscape of every major city in the world. While their modern day builders may be ignorant of

their original meaning, they are phallic symbols which derive from sun worship. They represent the phallis of Nimrod pointing to the sun.

As a result of the scattering from Babylon, the world population developed into different cultures, which developed their own variations in telling time. While mankind developed different calendars, YHWH never changed the one created at the beginning. This resulted in a continually expanding chasm that would develop between those who followed YHWH Elohim, and all others - the pagans. As in the days of Noah, YHWH sought a man that He could enter into Covenant with.

Living amidst the pagan environment that was spreading across the planet was a man named Abram. YHWH eventually brought Abram out of the region of Babylon, and made a Covenant with him. Through his journey and life, we can glean an understanding of the path of restoration – the path back to the ways of YHWH, and the way out of Babylon.

6

Out of Babylon

The man Abram, was born in the Land of Ur of the Chaldees. The city of Ur was located in southern Babylon. It was a sacred place known for moon worship. So Abram was born in the midst of a pagan society. He was led by his father Terah, but actually brought out of Babylon by YHWH. (Beresheet 11:31, 15:7). They moved to Haran in a region north and west of Babylon, generally known as Paddan Aram. Abram was later told to leave his country and his father's household and travel to the Land of Canaan, which was to the south.

YHWH gave the following promise to Abram:

"I will make you into a great nation and I will bless you; I will make your name great, and you will be a blessing. I will bless those who bless you, and whoever curses you I will curse; and all peoples on earth will be blessed through you."
Beresheet 12:2-3

Leaving his father's household was no small thing. It meant leaving the life that he knew and had labored to build. It meant leaving his family and the security of the position that he held in his land. It meant traveling through unknown lands and dwelling in those lands as a stranger.

The life of the man named Abram provides the

pattern for the journey of a Hebrew. A Hebrew is a person who desires to follow YHWH and join into a Covenant relationship with Him. So as we examine the life of Abram, we see the Plan of YHWH unfold. First we see him brought out of the source of sun worship. He came out of Babylon with his wife and some family and servants.

He journeyed to the land of Canaan, which was  filled with descendents of those who were previously disbursed from the Tower of Babel. These people had developed their own derivative "mystery" polytheistic religion. The Canaanites were an agricultural society and their religion revolved around their crops. So they were pagans in the "purest" sense of the word.

They believed that the seed, the father, would impregnate the womb of the earth, the mother. The fruit of the womb, the son, would be a male who would then father the next season cycle. Thus, the father and the son were intimately connected in this Canaanite Trinity. Some believe that this was actually the source of future Christian Trinitarian doctrine, although as we have already seen, the Trinity began in Babylon.[63]

It is speculated that the Canaanites actually originated the practices of demon-worship, occult rites, child sacrifice and cannibalism.[64] We know that they worshipped a god named Molech, which was intimately involved in the sacrifice of children. The people would sacrifice their firstborn to Moloch in the hope of receiving favor.

"The 12th century Rashi, commenting on Jeremiah 7:31 stated: 'Tophet is Moloch, which was made of brass; and they heated him from his lower parts; and his hands being stretched out, and made hot, they put the child between his hands, and it was burnt; when it vehemently cried out; but the priests beat a drum, that the father might not hear the voice of his son, and his heart might not be moved.'"[65]

In fact, in the region of Canaan, numerous bodies of children were discovered in the foundations of  buildings, proving without doubt that oblations of this character were common among Canaanites to strengthen the walls of homes and cities.[66] Their chief god was "baal" which means: "lord." Their primary goddess was "Astheroth" a derivative of Ishtar – Easter. We can see the Babylonian influence present in Canaan at the arrival of Abram. So this man who came out of one form of pagan religious system journeyed into another, arguably worse situation.

This was the land that YHWH promised to give him, along with great numbers of descendents. He dwelled in the midst of this pagan environment, although he did not participate in their conduct. He set up his own altar and called on the Name of YHWH. (Beresheet 13:4). He worshipped the Creator, YHWH Elohim, while those around him followed Babylonian traditions. He was essentially acting as a Priest to YHWH and was laying the groundwork for a future cleansing of this land, thought by many to have been the

loction of Eden.

The Scriptures record a period of famine, which resulted in Abram migrating to Egypt. Egypt was a very fertile land due to the Nile River. Many people would look to Egypt for sustenance during times of famine. Egypt was also a land immersed in their own unique form of polytheistic sun worship.

While in Egypt, the bride of Abram, named Sarai, was taken captive by the Pharaoh because of her beauty. YHWH was watching over Abram, and the Pharaoh was thereafter plagued until he released the bride, Sarai. Abram then left Egypt with great riches acquired from his stay in Egypt. This was a pattern that would be repeated by his descendents.

Another pattern involved Abram departing with a woman named Hagar (𐤏𐤂𐤔), or HaGer (𐤏𐤂𐤔). She would eventually bear him a son. Interestingly, her name literally means: "the stranger" in Hebrew. A stranger was a term often used to describe someone who was not in Covenant with YHWH. So Abram brought this "stranger" with him out of Egypt. By joining his family she would essentially enter into the Covenant household

Abram later returned to the land of promise, and was told that he would have descendents as numerous as the stars. Abram believed the promise and his belief was counted as righteousness. We can see a common trait in these Covenant men chosen by YHWH. They are given promises and they act upon those promises. They express their belief by their actions. They obey YHWH and become set apart from the heathens. They do not mix their worship of YHWH with the ways of the heathens. As a result of their belief, demonstrated by their obedience, YHWH considers them to be righteous.

Abram later asked for proof of the promises. Thus far, he had gone through a lot, but he still did not have a son and he was getting concerned that he had no heir to fulfill the promise. The Scriptures then provide a description of a very elaborate blood covenant ceremony prescribed by YHWH.

YHWH gave very specific instructions and Abram was required to follow them meticulously. Remember that the same attention to detail, and active participation, was required by Noah. Entering into Covenant with YHWH is not passive by any means – it requires action. It also requires blood, which is a concept foreign to most in modern society.

Abram was required to gather five different animals. He then took three of them, a heifer, a goat and a ram, and cut them in half. He set the pieces parallel to one another and then took the remaining two birds, a dove and a pigeon, and placed them across from one another. Thus there were 8 pieces total – 4 on each side with a channel of blood in between them.

Traditionally, the parties entering into a blood covenant would both pass between the pieces, and walk through the blood. This would indicate that they were both subject to the penalty of death if they broke the Covenant. This was not the case with Abram. Before he could walk between the pieces, he was placed into a deep sleep, a sort of symbolic death. This was the same condition that Adam was in when Hawah was taken from his side.

The Scriptures describe that while Abram was "dead," a fire and smoke, representing YHWH, passed through the pieces. After passing through the pieces, the Scriptures then record YHWH entering into a Covenant with Abram. The borders of a very large land grant are described, from the Nile to the Euphrates. (Beresheet 15:18-21).

This event indicated that YHWH alone would

suffer the penalty for the Covenant with Abram being broken. So this large land grant was essentially unconditional, but YHWH was going to have to pay the price. Since this was a blood covenant, that price would be death. This was unprecedented - a Covenant like no other.

We already saw that the local pagans were offering up their firstborn to their gods without any promise whatsoever. In fact, despite all of their sacrifices, the land would still fall under the curse of famine. This should have revealed that something was awry. With Abram, we see YHWH Elohim making very specific promises, and taking on the penalty if the Covenant is broken.

Now it is important to understand that Abram was uncircumcised at the time of this Covenant. He was described as a Hebrew, but he had not yet been circumcised. That would come later, but as was already stated, the life of Abram is a pattern of the walk of faith which is the Covenant path.

Those who are uncircumcised are typically called the Nations or the Gentiles. In this case we have a picture of YHWH entering into Covenant with the nations. In fact, YHWH actually told Abram that, *"in you all of the families of the Earth will be blessed."* (Beresheet 12:3).

This uncircumcised Hebrew then walked away from this event and had a son with Hagar (𐤏𐤂𐤅) - the stranger. It appeared that the promise would now be fulfilled through this son named Yishmael, but this was not to be.

Thirteen years later, when Yishmael was scheduled to enter into manhood, YHWH appeared to Abram and instructed him that He was not finished. When Abram was 99 years old, he was instructed to

walk perfect before YHWH. He was told that he would be the father of many nations – nations and kings would come out of him.

YHWH told Abram that his name was changed to Abraham, and he was instructed to circumcise himself and his household. This act was now a requirement of the Covenant, which would be marked in the flesh of all who were in the Covenant. At that time, the name of Sarai was changed to Sarah. Both Abram and Sarai had a hey (𐤄) added to their names. They were like a new Adam and Hawah with the breath of YHWH added to them. At this stage in the Covenant process they needed to be "filled with the Spirit." From this union would come the promised son who would be named Yitshaq.

Yitshaq would be the first covenant son who would be circumcised on the 8th day. This blood letting event on the 8th day connects with the previous blood covenant involving the 8 pieces. The picture was made complete later in the life of Yitshaq when Abraham is told to slaughter his "only son."

Abram was told that the Covenant would pass to Yitshaq and not Yishmael. So for all of those years Abram likely believed that Yishmael was the Promised Son. It was probably quite a shock to discover that there would be another. For the purposes of this discussion it is also significant to note that YHWH told Abraham that Yitshaq would be born at the Appointed Time, the moad next year. So this promise involved a child being born at an Appointed Time the following year. (Beresheet 18:14).

Now it should be noted that these words were spoken immediately prior to the judgment that was about to befall Sodom and Gomorrah. Since we are provided some hints that Lot was eating unleavened bread (Beresheet 19:3), this event likely occurred at the time known as Passover, and Unleavened Bread.

As we shall see, just as the righteous were delivered from Egypt hundreds of years later, Lot and his family were delivered from judgment during this important time. Thus, *"the Appointed Time next year"* in which Yitshaq was born would have been Passover. This is important, because Yitshaq, the promised son of the Covenant, is being connected with Passover, one of the times that YHWH prescribes for His Covenant people to meet with Him.

After Yitshaq was born and grown, Elohim said to Abraham: *"Take your son, your only son, Yitshaq, whom you love, and go to the region of Moriah. Sacrifice him there as a burnt offering on one of the mountains I will tell you about."* Beresheet 22:2.

This promised son was a miracle child who was given to Abraham and Sarah in their old age in order to fulfill the promise of great multitudes of descendents. YHWH was now telling Abraham to sacrifice him as a burnt offering, just like the inhabitants of the land did to their firstborn. This would involve slaughtering him, by shedding his blood and then burning him by fire.

I doubt that Abraham told Sarah. After all, this was her only child and only the pagans sacrificed their children. YHWH never required or condoned the sacrifice of people. She surely would have protested. Instead, early the next morning he arose and took Yitshaq and two servants. On the third day they arrived in the land of Moriah. Abraham told the two servants, *"stay here with the donkey, the young man and I will go yonder and worship, and we will come back to you."* Abraham placed the wood of the sacrifice on the shoulders of Yitshaq. Abraham took the fire for the burnt offering and a knife.

Yitshaq must have known that something was amiss. Abraham was probably not himself as he struggled to obey this difficult command. They typically would have brought their sacrifice with them, leading Yitshaq to ask the question: "We have the fire and the wood. Where is the lamb?" Abraham's response was: "Elohim Himself will provide the lamb for the burnt offering, my son." Beresheet 22:8. A direct translation from the Hebrew reads: "Elohim will provide Himself a lamb." This passage is often thought to mean that Elohim would be the One providing the lamb, which is true.

Another reading which has deeper meaning could reveal that Elohim would provide <u>Himself</u> as the Lamb. Now this makes perfect sense when we recall Who exactly passed through the cuttings of the Covenant, and Who would bear the penalty of the Covenant. The Covenant with Abraham, and this event would reveal how Elohim would provide the Lamb and provide Himself as the Lamb

When they came to the place where YHWH had said to make the offering, Abraham built an altar and laid out the wood on the altar. He then bound Yitshaq and laid him on the altar to sacrifice him. It is important to note that there is nothing to indicate that Yitshaq struggled or protested. He was a grown man while Abraham was quite old. According to the Book of Yasher, Yitshaq was 37 years old, so he obviously could have escaped, but it appears that he willingly laid down his life. (Yasher 22:41,53).[67] This would be a  pattern that would later be fulfilled by the Son of Elohim – the Messiah.

As Abraham was about to slaughter his son, he was stopped by the Messenger of YHWH and told not to touch his son. The Messenger then went on to state: "Now I know that you fear Elohim, because you have not withheld from me <u>your son, your only son</u>."

There was a sacrifice made that day, only it was not Yitshaq. It was a ram caught in a thicket by his horns. This ram in the thicket was then slaughtered and offered as a burnt offering by fire. This was the provision of YHWH, and the entire event provided a picture of how the Covenant with Abraham would culminate. Abraham called the place YHWH Yireh.

Some translations indicate that the meaning is: "In the Mountian of YHWH it shall be provided." While there certainly was provision, the word "yireh" (𐤄𐤀𐤓𐤉) comes from the root "ra'ah" which means: "to see, to consider, to discern." The question any reader should ask is: What shall be seen?

This moment was revealing how YHWH would provide the redemption and restoration of Creation through the Covenant with Abraham. It actually brings us back to the former Covenant, and makes the connection between the Word of YHWH and the Lamb of Elohim. This picture of the restoration provided by YHWH repeatedly emphasizes "your son, your only son." Obviously, Abram had a son named Yishmael, but Abraham had only one son – Yitshaq. This distinction is critical.

There is so much more going on in this passage than we can possibly see by simply reading the English. On the surface, we see a great promise that "the seed" of Abraham will be incredibly numerous and powerful and all the nations of the earth would be blessed because of the seed.

As with many Scripture passages, we can only understand the profound depth of the text by reading and studying the Hebrew. For instance, this entire passage is filled with the Aleph Taw (𐤕𐤀), which is a clear indication that it is a Messianic reference.

There are three times when Abraham is given

directions regarding *"your son, your only son,"* or Yitshaq. In each of those three references, there are three occurrences of the untranslated Aleph Taw (את). In Beresheet 22:9, the passage where it describes Abraham as laying the wood on the altar and binding Yitshaq, there are three occurrences of the untranslated Aleph Taw (את). Also in the following passage when Abraham was preparing to slay Yitshaq, there are three occurrences of the untranslated Aleph Taw (את).

This event, often referred to as "the Akeda," was a shadow picture of the fact that Elohim would provide a Lamb, His only Son. Some believe that Abraham simply obeyed and was willing to kill his son like the pagans offered their children to their gods.

This is neither a fair nor a complete understanding of the faith and righteousness expressed by Abraham through this event. Abraham told his servants, who had accompanied him, to stay with the donkey until he <u>and his son</u> returned. As a result, it is absolutely clear that Abraham believed his "only son" would be resurrected. Since the Covenant was promised to pass through the son, it was imperative that this "only son" live, even if he was offered as a sacrifice.

Therefore, the faith of Abraham was not primarily about the fact that he was willing to kill his promised son, since pagans regularly offered their children to their gods. The faith of Abraham was more fully expressed by his belief in the resurrection of his son. He specifically told the servants "we will come back to you." He clearly expected Yitshaq to live <u>after</u> being slaughtered.

Therefore, the Lamb of Elohim was destined to be slain, and the promise to Abraham that *"all nations would be blessed"* would extend through this Lamb. This is powerful information that can only fully be seen in the

Hebrew text.

Many fail to recognize the Messianic significance of this Covenant made with Abraham, which was proclaimed immediately after he offered his son. A substitute sacrifice was made, just as had been done for Adam and Hawah. YHWH had provided His Lamb in place of the Covenant Son. Indeed, this could have been the same place, "at the door of Eden" that the first blood was shed after the sin in the Garden.[68]

"[15] The messenger of YHWH called to Abraham from heaven a second time [16] and said, I swear by Myself, declares YHWH, that because you have done ×ƴ this thing and have not withheld your ×ƴ son ×ƴ your only son, [17] that in blessing I will bless and in multiplying I will multiply your ×ƴ seed as numerous as the stars in the heavens and as the sand on the seashore, and shall possess, your seed, ×ƴ the gates of their enemies, [18] and through your seed all nations on earth will be blessed, because you have obeyed Me." Beresheet 22:15-18.

The message could not be any clearer. The Covenant Son, born at the Appointed Time, would receive atonement by the shed blood of the Lamb of Elohim. To confirm this point, in this passage of Scripture, the word "son" is couched between two instances of the untranslated Aleph Taw (×ƴ). Likewise, when the Messenger refers to the seed, there are two occasions when the untranslated Aleph Taw (×ƴ) is right next to the word "seed."

This is, no doubt, a Messianic reference and it is interesting to note that the word "seed" (⊙ঀ𐤐) is a singular subject noun - it is not plural. While the seed of Abraham is often interpreted to mean his descendents, the text can also refer to one Seed. This is the same Seed described in Beresheet 3:15 as the promised Seed of Hawah that would crush the head of the nachash – or

"shining one."⁶⁹ This entire event points back to the Garden and reveals that the Covenant path is the way back to the Garden.

So we see from this example in the Covenant with Abraham that YHWH would offer up the Lamb of Elohim - His only Son. This offering would be specifically related to the Covenant. That is why Abraham called the place YHWH Yireh, because *"On the mountain of YHWH it will be seen."* Beresheet 22:14. On the mountain of YHWH it would be seen how the Lamb of Elohim would be provided.

While tradition holds that this is the same location where the House of YHWH was later erected by Solomon in Jerusalem, it is also very possible that this was on the Mount of Olives, on what is called the Miphkad Altar.⁷⁰ The location provided in the Scriptures is the general location, "in the land of Moriah," not Mount Moriah specifically. It is also highly likely that the Binding of Yitshaq occurred at the same Appointed Time that Yitshaq was born – Passover.

"In the Jewish tradition, the Binding of [Yitshaq] is also remembered on Passover. The *Akeda* is interpreted as a historical precedent with regard to the miracles associated with the holiday. Because [Yitshaq] was Abraham's first-born son, it is believed that [Elohim] spared the first-born Israelites over the first-born Egyptians because he remembered the Binding of [Yitshaq]. Similarly, there is an idea that the reason the blood of the lamb was spread over the door was to remember that just as the ram was sacrificed in the place of [Yitshaq], the lamb is being sacrificed to save the first-born Israelites. This idea comes from the *Mekhilta of Rabbi Ishmael*, which said 'And when I see the blood, I will pass over you. I see the blood of the Binding of [Yitshaq].'"⁷¹

After Abraham had offered the ram, in place of Yitshaq, we read the following: *"[15] The Messenger of YHWH called to Abraham from heaven a second time [16] and said, I swear by Myself, declares YHWH, that because you have done this and have not withheld your son, your only son, [17] I will surely bless you and make your descendents as numerous as the stars in the sky and as the sand on the seashore. Your descendents will take possession of the cities of their enemies, [18] and through your offspring all nations on earth will be blessed, because you have obeyed Me. [19] <u>Then Abraham returned to his servants, and they set off together for Beersheba. And Abraham stayed in Beersheba.</u>"* Beresheet 22:15-19.

This was a merging of the Covenants made with Abram and Abraham. YHWH had originally promised seed "as numerous as the dust of the Earth," prior to Abram entering into the Land. Later, when YHWH entered into Covenant with Abram, He promised seed "as numerous as the stars of the heavens." Now after offering up His only son, the promise was elevated to include numbers as great as the stars in the heavens <u>and</u> the sand on the seashore.

This was a joining of heaven and earth through the Covenant. Remember the second instance of the Aleph Taw (𐤕𐤀) in Beresheet 1:1. It was the sixth word out of seven Hebrew words, and it was preceded with the vav(𐤅) - a nail or a peg. It essentially connected "the heavens" (𐤅𐤔𐤌𐤉𐤌) and "the earth" (𐤅𐤀𐤓𐤑). So we see the Messiah at the center of this entire process of restoration through the Covenant.

Through this event, where Abraham was to bring his only son and kill him, we see how YHWH intended to pay the price of the Covenant made with Abram. YHWH would provide Himself a Lamb. This did not simply mean that YHWH would find His own lamb, it meant that YHWH Himself would be the lamb sacrifice

symbolized by the ram – the only Son of YHWH.

YHWH would allow the blood of His only Son to be shed, which is how all of the families of the earth would be blessed. It is through the Covenant process that YHWH would rectify the problem that plagued mankind since the Garden. He would provide new land, a new garden, which the families of the earth would be allowed to enter, if they walked the Covenant path that was blazed through the life of Abram, Abraham and his seed.

The key was that they would only become clean through the specific Covenant path revealed through Abraham. There was only one way, marked specifically by obedience to the ways of YHWH. It required YHWH actually leading an individual out of Babylon in order to be set apart from all forms of pagan worship.

Even though the Land of Canaan had been promised to Abraham through the Covenant of Circumcision, it was still filled with pagans, who practiced abominations. This seemed to create a problem for the promise that Abraham had received. For instance, where would he find a wife for this promised son?

Clearly, he was not going to have Yitshaq marry into a pagan culture. The answer was to seek out someone from his family. As a result, Abraham sent his trusted servant to accomplish the mission. The servant of Abraham did not go all the way back to Babylon, rather he went to Paddan Aram where he found Rebecca.

Yitshaq was eventually married to Rebecca, and the Covenant of Circumcision passed through the cutting of Yitshaq into Rebecca, who bore twins, Esau and Yaakob. Despite the fact that Esau was actually born first, Yaacob ultimately received the blessing of the firstborn through cunning and trickery.

Yaakob led a very interesting life, and a common

thread that we see in his life is deception. He left the land after deceiving Yitshaq, and receiving the birthright over his brother Esau. It is ironic that despite the fact that he obtained the birthright, he essentially became a fugitive. Like Abram, he had a promise, but would have to wait for the fulfillment.

He would need to follow the path of Abram. He fled to the place where the promise was first given to Abram, Paddan Aram - Haran. On the way to his Uncle Laban's, he had an encounter with YHWH at Beth El and anointed a stone pillar. He was later welcomed by his uncle, but was repeatedly deceived by him. Yaakob eventually married two dauthers of Laban, Leah and Rachel, and had twelve children - 11 sons and 1 daughter. He also obtained great wealth and possessions while living as a virtual slave in his uncle's home.

After twenty years, YHWH instructed Yaakob to leave, and he stealthily took his family to the Land of his inheritance. After three days, Laban discovered that Yaakob had left. Laban gave chase and confronted Yaakob. As it turns out, the favored wife of Yaakob named Rachel, the mother of Joseph, had stolen Laban's idols. She then lied about it and almost died because of her thievery.

You see, Yaakob had been living in a pagan environment all of the time he was indentured in his uncle's service. Laban worshipped false gods, represented by idols. This was made clear when the two resolved their confrontation through a covenant. The men distinguished between the Elohim of Abraham (the fear of Yitshaq) and "the god of Nahor." (See Beresheet 31). Laban never found his idols and they ended up getting carried back to the Promised Land. They became a problem that Yaakob needed to deal with.

Before crossing over into the Promised Land,

Yaakob wrestled with a mysterious Man until the "dawning of the day." As a result of that encounter he experienced a name change to "am Yisrael." Not only would he be called Yisrael, but he would become a people or community (am) called Yisrael. Upon crossing over into the Land of Promise, he camped at a place called Succot. It is important to take note of this place because it appears again, later in the history of Yisrael's descendents. It is actually an important Appointed Time.

Yisrael had one more son named Benjamin, who was the only child actually born in the Promised Land. His mother Rachel died giving childbirth. Rachel was also the mother of Joseph. The children grew, and it became very apparent that Joseph was the favored son of Yisrael.

In fact, Joseph actually had dreams that he was elevated above his brothers, and his parents. He dreamed that the sun, the moon and the eleven stars paid homage to him. These celestial bodies, given for signs, apparently represented his family. He also dreamed that he and his family were binding sheaves in the field. All of their sheaves stood up and bowed to Joseph's sheaf. Take special note that this would have occurred during the harvest, and both of these dreams have deep prophetic significance. (Beresheet 37).

As a result of all the favor shown to Joseph, his brothers became very jealous and sold him into slavery. He was taken to Egypt and went from a slave, to a prisoner, to the Viceroy of Egypt. He was set up to save the people from a devastating famine, which lasted 7 years. He prepared beforehand for 7 years and those preparations revolved around the harvests.

During these times of preparation, he married an Egyptian woman named Asenath. Her name means: "she belongs to Neith." Neith was a pagan Egyptian goddess.

Interestingly, she was the daughter of Potipherah priest of On. (see Beresheet 41:45, 50). The city of On, also known as Heliopolis, was a religious center dedicated to the worship of the sun god Ra. As with most major Egyptian cities, Heliopolis had its own unique myth concerning the Creation of the Universe.

In essence, it was believed that before anything existed or was created, there was chaos, darkness and endless, lifeless water, divinely personified as Nun. From this water, a mound of fertile earth emerged, and Atum, the solar creator god, appeared on the mound and "spit out" the deities Shu (air) and Tefnut (water). This pair of dieties procreated resulting in Geb (the earth) and Nut (the sky). Heliopolis is famous for worshipping the "group of nine," known as the *pesedjet* in Egyptian, including the dieties mentioned above as well as the offspring of Geb and Nut – Osiris, Isis, Seth and Nephthys.[72]

This was the family into which Joseph married, and we know that Joseph was grafted into Egyptian culture. He had an Egyptian name, Zaphnath-Paaneah. He looked, acted and spoke like an Egyptian, as shown by the fact that his brothers did not recognize him when they came to Egypt for food. This is clearly prophetic, as the offspring of Joseph are currently exiled throughout the world, blended into all of the pagan cultures – virtually unrecognizable. Some day soon this will change, but currently

people are not generally well versed in Scriptural prophecy and are not even anticipating this amazing event.

Through some very dramatic events during the

famine, Joseph was revealed to his brothers at the Appointed Time. He was reconciled with his family, and prepared for them to move to Egypt. The entire clan eventually moved out of the land of Canaan and into Egypt. The Scriptures record 70 "souls" or "beings" that came out of the loins of Yaakob, and presumably went with him into Egypt. (Beresheet 46:27).

7

Egypt

Interestingly, the 70 beings with Yaakob moved into a region of Egypt called Goshen, which actually fell within the Covenant boundaries described and promised to Abram. The Nile River was provided as the western boundary to the land promised to Abram, while the land of Canaan was promised to the seed of Abraham within the context of the Covenant of Circumcision. As we already saw, the number 70 carries great significance. It is typically associated with "the Nations" based upon the number of descendents from Noah.

Therefore, this sojourn into Egypt was being linked with a repopulation event within a Covenant, just as we saw with Noah. It reinforces the fact that that the Covenant with Abram was intended to draw the Nations into the Covenant. As we shall see, the number 70 is also intimately linked with time.[73] It was while the man Yisrael was in Egypt, before his death, that he gave an interesting prophecy over the children of Joseph. In particular, he declared that the youngest son Ephraim would become "a multitude of nations." (Beresheet 48:19). This is critical to understand as we continue to examine the unique role that Joseph plays in

the Covenant.

While in Egypt, the descendents of Yisrael were eventually afflicted and oppressed, just as foretold to Abram during the blood Covenant process. They were enslaved in a culture that was immersed in sun worship. In this culture, there were around 80 different gods with a mix of different relationships. One popular Trinity consisted of Osiris the Father, Isis the mother and Horus the son. As usual, the birth date of Horus was pegged to December 25 – the winter solstice.

These particular gods are significant because they continue to influence the Children of Yisrael after they finally leave Egypt. When the period of captivity was concluded, YHWH chose a man named Mosheh to help deliver them out of bondage. While Joseph was brought to Egypt as a slave and raised to power to get Yisrael into the land, Mosheh was born a slave and used to lead Yisrael out of the land.

The irony is that Mosheh was raised within the household of Pharoah. Just as Joseph had been grafted into the Egyptian power structure to bring Yisrael into Egypt, now Mosheh was grafted in to lead them out. This was accomplished in a very unique and interesting fashion.

The Scriptures describe a time when the Pharaoh of Egypt instructed two Hebrew midwives to kill males that were born to Hebrew women. The midwives refused to obey. They revered Elohim over Pharaoh, and they were blessed while the Yisraelites prospered. Later the Scriptures record: *"So Pharaoh commanded all his people, saying, 'Every son who is born you shall cast into the river, and*

every daughter you shall save alive.'" Shemot 1:22.

Apparently, Pharaoh saw the Hebrews as a threat and sought to weaken them by killing their male offspring. There was a reason that Pharaoh had the children thrown into the Nile River. These children were an offering to the river god Hapi. It was by no coincidence that YHWH sent a deliverer from those very waters.

Here is the account from the Scriptures. *"¹ And a man of the house of Levi went and took ×ץ a daughter of Levi. ² So the woman conceived and bore a son. And when she saw ×ץ that he was a beautiful child, she hid him three months. ³ But when she could no longer hide him, she took an ark of bulrushes for him, daubed it with asphalt and pitch, put therein ×ץ the child, and laid it in the reeds by the river's bank."* Shemot 2:1-3. Interestingly, in this passage which first describes the baby, there are three instances of the untranslated Aleph Taw (×ץ).

The Scriptures proceed to describe how this child avoided the death sentence issued by Pharaoh. *"⁵ Then the daughter of Pharaoh came down to bathe at the river. And her maidens walked along the riverside; and when she saw ×ץ the ark among the reeds, she sent ×ץ her maid to get it. ⁶ And when she opened it, she saw ×ץ the child, and behold, the baby wept. So she had compassion on him, and said, 'This is one of the Hebrews' children.'"* Shemot 2:5-6.

This passage also includes three instances of the untranslated Aleph Taw (×ץ), so by now, a person reading the Hebrew text would begin to realize that this baby was quite special. There are many others that follow in the subsequent text as it describes how Pharaoh's daughter proceeded to adopt the child and name him Mosheh.

There are two important questions that anyone would reasonably ask. The first is: Why would the mother of Mosheh place the child in the very river where the other Hebrew children were being killed? The second is: Why would the daughter of Pharaoh adopt a Hebrew slave baby that was supposed to be killed?

The answer to both questions is better understood when you realize why Pharaoh's daughter was likely bathing in the Nile. We are talking about a River that is generally heavy laden with silt and filled with large crocodiles. Not a very inviting place to take a bath. The princess could surely have had a nice, clean relaxing bath in the safety and security of the palace.

Some speculate that she was not taking a bath at all, but rather she was immersing herself in the sacred River because she was barren. She was immersing herself in the hope that Hapi, the fertility god, would give her a child. This would have been seen as an opportune time, since her father had provided plentiful offerings of Yisraelite children. Under these circumstances, you can imagine that the baby would have been considered to be an answer to prayer – a miracle child straight from the gods. What she did not realize was that this was actually an answer to the Yisraelites prayer for deliverance.

It is possible that Mosheh's mother was hoping for just that response. Any other way would have likely led to Mosheh being killed, along with the other Hebrew babies. How ironic since the method of disposing of the Hebrew children was to throw them into the Nile as an offering. Mosheh's mother surely knew the story of Noah being protected from the waters of judgment. Therefore, she made an ark for her son to escape Pharaoh's judgment.

Interestingly, according to Hebrew tradition in Sotah 12B, Mosheh was placed in the basket on the

Appointed Time of Shabuot. The Book of Jubilees 47:4 says that Mosheh remained in the ark for seven days at which time he was discovered by Pharaoh's daughter.

As with Noah – this Ark was intimately connected with the Covenant. It pointed to the fact that the man in this "Covenant House" would be used by YHWH as a mediator for His Covenant plan. This child was a son of the Covenant – circumcised on the 8th day no doubt. He was being prepared to lead the seed of Abraham into their inheritance. The two Ark events are essentially book ends to a process leading up to the gathering of a Covenant people called Yisrael.

This is where we begin to see some of the patterns come together. Remember, it was Abram who was told that his seed would go into bondage. When that Covenant was made Abram was uncircumcised, and he did not pass through the cuttings. It would be through their captivity in Egypt that the seed of Abraham would mix with the nations, the uncircumcised, and an incredible pattern will emerge. Through this promise, the nations would be brought out of Egypt and gathered to YHWH.[74]

Mosheh was, in fact, raised in the house of Pharaoh until he was eighteen years old. At that time, he killed an Egyptian who was mistreating another Hebrew. Mosheh thereafter fled Egypt and eventually arrived in Midian.

"The Midianites through their apparent religio-political connection with the Moabites are thought to have worshipped a multitude of gods, including Baal-peor and the Queen of Heaven, Ashteroth. An Egyptian temple of Hathor at Timna continued to be used during the Midianite occupation of the site. However, whether Hathor or some other deity was the object of devotion during this period is impossible to ascertain."[75]

Mosheh fled one pagan culture and entered into another, where he eventually met Zipporah at a well. Zipporah was the daughter of Jethro, a priest of Midian.⁷⁶ Like Joseph, he married into a pagan culture and he too had 2 sons. While Mosheh's life was very similar to Joseph's, it went in the opposite direction. According to some sources, after Mosheh left Egyptian royalty, he too was imprisoned, and ultimately ended up tending sheep.

When he was about 77 years old, Mosheh saw a bush that burned with fire, but was not consumed. Seder Olam 5 says the episode of the burning bush took place on Day 15 of Month 1. This was a significant Appointed Time called the Feast of Unleavened Bread. It is important to note that this event occurred on Mt. Horeb, described as the Mountain of Elohim. The Messenger of YHWH appeared in "a flame of fire" out of the midst of a bush. (Shemot 3:1-2).

Mosheh then proclaimed: "*I will turn aside now and see* ×ʋ *this great appearance (phenomenon).*" Shemot 3:3. Mosheh turned to see the Aleph Taw (×ʋ). The implication is that Mosheh actually met with the Messiah, the Messenger of YHWH.

"² *Elohim also said to Mosheh, I Am YHWH.* ³ *I appeared to Abraham, to Yitshaq and to Yaakov as El Shaddai, but by My Name I was not known to them.* ⁴ I also established ×ʋ My Covenant with them to give them ×ʋ the Land of Canaan, ×ʋ where they lived as aliens. ⁵ *Moreover, I have heard* ×ʋ *the groaning of the Yisraelites, whom the Egyptians are enslaving, and* I have remembered ×ʋ My Covenant. ⁶ *Therefore, say to the Yisraelites: I Am YHWH, and I will bring you out from under the yoke of the Egyptians. I will free you from being slaves to them, and I will redeem you with an outstretched arm and with mighty acts of judgment.* ⁷ I will take you as My own people, and I will be your Elohim. *Then you will know that I Am YHWH your Elohim, who*

brought you out from under the yoke of the Egyptians. ⁸ *And I will bring you to the Land I swore with uplifted hand to give to Abraham, to Yitshaq and to Yaakob. I will give it to you as a possession. I Am YHWH."* Shemot 6:2-8.

Mosheh was told that YHWH saw the suffering of the Yisraelites. YHWH then charged Mosheh to return to Egypt and deliver His people. Mosheh was apparently overwhelmed with the great task assigned to him. He immediately begged YHWH not to make him speak as he was instructed. He indicated that he was slow of speech and tongue. Amazingly, this former prince of Egypt and a man of many great deeds, personally chosen by YHWH Himself, was shy and afraid. This once strong and bold man was now unsure of himself and his ability to speak, so YHWH instructed Mosheh to use his brother Aaron (Aharon).⁷⁷

Mosheh and Aharon approached Pharaoh and attempted to obtain his permission to let the Yisraelites go into the desert to hold a festival to YHWH. The Scriptures detail the confrontation: *"¹ Afterward Mosheh and Aharon went to Pharaoh and said, This is what YHWH, the Elohim of Yisrael, says: 'Let My people go, so that they may hold a festival to Me in the desert.' ² Pharaoh said, 'Who is YHWH, that I should obey Him and let Yisrael go? I do not know YHWH and I will not let Yisrael go.' ³ Then they said, 'The Elohim of the Hebrews has met with us. Now let us take a three-day journey into the desert to offer sacrifices to YHWH our Elohim, or He may strike us with plagues or with the sword.'"* Shemot 5:1-3.

Now, as previously mentioned, Egypt was a polytheistic culture recognizing around 80 different gods. "Even Pharaoh was a god, always the son of Amon-Ra, ruling not merely by divine right but by divine birth, as a deity transiently tolerating the earth as his home. On his head was the falcon, symbol of Horus and totem of the tribe; from his forehead rose the *uraeus* or serpent, symbol of wisdom and life, and communicating magic virtues to the crown. The king was chief-priest of the faith, and led the great processions and ceremonies that celebrated the festivals of the gods. It was through this assumption of divine lineage and powers that he was able to rule so long with so little force."[78]

It is quite interesting to note that Pharoah, the ruler of a large portion of the civilized world, and a god  himself, did not know the Name of the Elohim of a large part of his population. That seems highly unlikely, and it just may have been Pharaoh's refusal to acknowledge YHWH. Whatever the case, that was about to change. Pharaoh would be forced to acknowledge YHWH, because YHWH prepared a great deliverance for His people so that the whole world would thereafter know His Name. YHWH had prepared a showdown - a demonstration of the power of the Elohim of Yisrael versus the gods of the Egyptians.

"[13] Then YHWH said to Mosheh, Get up early in the morning, confront Pharaoh and say to him, This is what YHWH, the Elohim of the Hebrews, says: Let My people go, so that they may worship Me, [14] or this time I will send the full force of My plagues against you and against your officials and your people, so you may know that there is no one like Me in all the earth. [15] For by now I could have stretched out My Hand and struck you and your people with a plague that would have wiped you off the earth. [16] <u>But I have raised you up for this very purpose, that I might show you My power and that My Name might be proclaimed in all the earth.</u>" Shemot 9:13-17.

Notice again that YHWH identified Himself as

"The Elohim of the Hebrews." Abram, being the first person called a Hebrew, represented a people who followed YHWH. In the Paleo script the word Hebrew is depicted as: ⌐ ⊕ ▢ ◯. A mechanical translation is "eye – house – head – hand." Could it be that a Hebrew is one who sees the house and knows and does the commandments, which are the rules of the house? There are many possible expansions and translations of this very important word, and Abram is the model for the definition. We actually look to his life for the meaning.

Abram was later circumcised and his name was changed to Abraham. So a Hebrew is one who enters into the household of YHWH by hearing and obeying, which is the Hebrew word "shema"(◯ᴹw). A Hebrew then enters into the blood Covenant, and becomes transformed into a new being. The Covenant of Circumcision leads one into the community of Yisrael (1⊻ ⊕w⌐). When you take the mark of circumcision, you are acknowledging that you belong to the royal family of El, that you walk straight in His path and He is your head. Therefore, Yisrael is essentially a community of Hebrews.

The household of Abram, and later Abraham, consisted of many people who were not his direct offspring. If they lived under his tent – they too were Hebrews if they followed his Elohim - YHWH.

YHWH brought the first Hebrew out of Babylon, and led him to the Promised Land. Now YHWH was calling a "multitude" of Hebrews out of Egypt to the Covenant Land. This is a pattern that will be repeated again in the future.

Therefore, it was YHWH, the Elohim of the Hebrews, Who had sent a representative to collect His people. It was now time for the Name of YHWH to be proclaimed in all the earth. The peoples of the earth had continued to practice their Babylonian derived religions to no avail. Egypt was the supreme power on earth at that time and identified their ruler with the Babylonian derived sun diety. Now YHWH would remove His people from that culture and set them apart. Pharaoh resisted and YHWH decimated this powerful nation through a series of plagues. Again, it is important to understand that this was the pattern previously revealed through Abram, and a pattern that will be repeated in the future.

YHWH eventually killed all of the firstborn of Egypt, who were not covered by the blood of the lamb, during the Passover, known as Pesach (חספ). This was in direct retaliation for what a Pharaoh had previously done to the Hebrew sons.

While pagans ritualistically offered their firstborn to their gods, the Pharaoh of Egypt had offered the Yisraelite males to his god. This was "the straw that broke the camel's back," so to speak, as far as YHWH was concerned. The firstborn of Yisrael belonged to Him, although He did not require or desire their sacrifice. He already revealed that through Abraham and Yitshaq. Now it was time for Egypt to pay the price through a series of successive plagues, culminating in the death of their firstborn.

It is important to note that the Yisraelites were not harmed by those plagues, because they were set apart from the Egyptians. The Passover was specifically orchestrated to provide them protection from the final plague – death of the firstborn. Those who obeyed the instructions were spared from death, while those who did not obey received the final plague.

Now we do not know precisely who obeyed and who did not obey. There was clearly a distinction made between Yisrael and Egypt on that night. The Yisraelites

were those who obeyed the instructions of YHWH delivered through Mosheh and Aharon, and the Egyptians were those who did not obey.

The primary distinction was not the land where you were born, they were all born in Egypt – thus they were technically all Egyptians by birth. The real question was whether or not they were in Covenant with YHWH. Those who are in Covenant with YHWH become citizens of the Kingdom of YHWH. This fact remains true to this day, and the distinguishing mark of those in the Kingdom is belief, demonstrated by obedience. Those who believe and obey the Covenant, including the Appointed Times, will be saved and delivered. Those who remain immersed in Babylonian traditions and sun worship will fall under judgment.

All the males who obeyed were circumcised, and every one who was part of Yisrael ate of the Passover lamb. (Shemot 12:43-49). All had to be within the Covenant of Circumcision which involved, not only the act of circumcision, but also belief in the promises of YHWH. (Debarim 30:6).

Every individual had to demonstrate their belief by following the instructions, called the Torah. YHWH was very specific about the fact that: *"the same Torah applies to the native-born and to the stranger (ger) living among you."* Shemot 12:49. There were not different rules for different people. Just as with the tents of Abraham, if you wanted to dwell within the Covenant, you obeyed the same rules of the house – no exceptions and no differences.

As a result, everyone who participated in the Passover was in "am Yisrael" - the people of Yisrael. It was the firstborn of "am Yisrael" who were delivered from death, while the firstborn of the Egyptians were killed. The households of all who obeyed - all that were

protected by the blood of the lamb - were delivered from death. But there was more to the promise than mere salvation from physical death of the firstborn. This was just the beginning of their journey of deliverance previously patterned by the life of Abraham. There was still much more to be completed at the Mountain of YHWH, after they were delivered out of Egypt.

8

Out of Egypt

Adam was originally connected to YHWH although that connection was broken through disobedience. YHWH had plans to reestablish that relationship with mankind through the union of marriage with those who obeyed. This restoration process was revealed through the life of Abraham, and would be fulfilled through his seed - the Children of Yisrael. The Children of Yisrael represented those in Covenant with YHWH, those who obey His commandments.

Included within those commandments were instructions concerning time, and the Appointed Times of YHWH. This recognition of the Creator's Calendar and proper keeping of His times would set them apart from the pagans and protect them from the judgment that would befall the pagans. This is a very important theme in the Scriptures. If you want to escape judgment you must be aware of the times and obedient to the commandments. The Appointed Times that Yisrael needed to obey to get out of Egypt were the Passover and Unleavened Bread, which both occurred in Month 1.

After the Passover meal at the beginning of Day 14, and the night of death, the Children of Yisrael plundered the Egyptians. They departed in a calm and organized fashion on Day 15, loaded with gold and silver.

Many of these items were likely jewelry, idols and religious artifacts.

You see the entire ordeal of deliverance was specifically intended as an afront against the gods of Egypt. The Scriptures record YHWH proclaiming: *"For I will pass through the land of Egypt on that night, and will strike all the firstborn in the land of Egypt, both man and beast; and against all the gods of Egypt I will execute judgment: I am YHWH."* Shemot 12:12.

Each of the ten plagues was intended to show that a god or gods were powerless against YHWH. The final act was devastating to an entire generation of Egyptians, especially Pharaoh. The plague of the firstborn killed the son of Pharaoh - "the son of god."[79] The plagues were intended so that all would know the Name of YHWH, and the world would recognize His supremacy over the false gods of the Egyptians. This is why YHWH Himself fought for His people. After decimating the Egyptian gods, the Yisraelites essentially stripped them away from the Egyptians. Of course, the Egyptians did not need them anymore since they had proven useless during the plagues. This may be one of the reasons they so readily gave them up.

It is critical to emphasize that the children of Yisrael were miraculously delivered from Egypt, not by themselves, but along with a mixed multitude of people. According to Shemot 12:37-38: *"[37] The children of Yisrael journeyed from Rameses to Succot, about six hundred thousand men on foot, besides children. [38] A mixed multitude went up with them also, and flocks and herds - a great deal of livestock."*

This is a very important and often overlooked fact. It was the children of Yisrael, along with this mixed multitude, who were redeemed. The Exodus from Egypt was an act of redemption, and this concept of redemption is essential to understand. It implies either ownership, right, or title to something or someone. It was because of this relationship, through the Covenant established with Abraham, that the Hebrews were redeemed. The price of redemption was the blood of the Lamb, which was demonstrated through the Passover. This redemption was for a reason higher than merely freeing slaves. The redemption was meant to restore that which had been lost in Eden.

After this great troop of people marched out of Ramses as a conquering army, the Scriptures record that they camped at a place called Succot. It is no coincidence that the first place that they camped was Succot, just as their father Yisrael had first camped at Succot when he returned to the Land.[80] These were not the same physical locations, but they obviously are meant to tell us something. Succot, as it turns out, is more than just a place – it is also a time. It is a very important Appointed Time, which we will read about further on in the discussion.

After leaving Succot, the Yisraelites then proceeded to different camps led by YHWH Who appeared as "a pillar of fire" by night and "a pillar of cloud" by day. This imagery should continue to remind the reader of when the smoking furnace and the lamp of fire passed through the cuttings of the Covenant made with Abram. This fire and cloud was YHWH fulfilling His promise. This was a Covenant procession.

Again, notice that just as the household of Abraham had originally contained numerous individuals who were not his physical descendents, so too this great assembly included the physical offspring of Yisrael as well as a mixed multitude of people.

The Scriptures record that the assembly was led to the edge of the Red Sea where they found themselves

trapped between water and the army of Pharaoh. "*Then Mosheh stretched out* ⵝⵄ *his hand over the sea; and YHWH caused* ⵝⵄ *the sea to go back by a strong east wind all that night, and made* ⵝⵄ *the sea into dry land, and the waters were divided.*" Shemot 14:21. In this passage there are three instances of the Aleph Taw (ⵝⵄ) related directly to the waters of the sea.

The waters have always symbolized judgment and cleansing. When YHWH previously flooded the planet He was judging the people for their sin while cleansing the planet from that sin. When the Yisraelites passed through the parted waters of the Red Sea, they literally passed through judgment and were cleansed. The very same waters that were used to cleanse this people were later used to judge Egypt. This act of passing through the waters was symbolic immersion or "tevila" sometimes called "mikvah."[81]

The tevila immersion would actually occur in a mikvah, which was a gathering together of waters. It is an important act for anyone identifying with the Covenant. It is an act of purification and cleansing. This act was not only meant to wash the body, but also to purify the soul. It was a recognition and reminder that we are tainted by sin and need to be clean before we can enter into the presence of a set apart Elohim.

At this point in their journey the Scriptures provide a very interesting time reference. "*[40] Now the sojourning of the children of Yisrael, who dwelt in Egypt, was four hundred and thirty years. [41] And it came to pass at the end of the four hundred and thirty years, even the selfsame day it came to pass, that all the hosts of YHWH went out from the land of Egypt. [42] It is a night to be much observed unto YHWH for bringing them out from the land of Egypt: this is that night of YHWH to be observed of all the children of Yisrael in their generations.*" Shemot 12:40-42.

Notice the reference to the "selfsame day." The text seems to indicate that they left on the very day that their sojourn began. This was not just some arbitrary day. Indeed, it was the seventh day of the Feast of Unleavened Bread which began on Day 15 of Month 1. This should make it clear that time is very important to YHWH. He is very precise and we should also strive to keep His times with absolute precision.

Also note the emphasis on the night. It is a night to be observed - that night of YHWH as they crossed through the Red Sea at night. It was in the morning of the seventh day of Unleavened Bread, on Day 21 of Month 1, that the Yisraelites, after having "crossed over" to the other side, witnessed the destruction of Pharaoah's army. This day is an "atzeret" – one of 2 days when Yisrael is commanded to assemble.

Although Yisrael left the city of Ramses on Day 15 of Month 1 according to Bemidbar 33:3, they only left the borders of the nation of Egypt when they crossed the Red Sea on Day 21 of Month 1 according to Shemot 12:41-42.

Now we also read the first specific reference to an Appointed Time, the time of Passover and Unleavened Bread. "*³ And Mosheh said unto the people, Remember this day, in which you came out from Egypt, out of the house of bondage; for by strength of hand YHWH brought you out from this place: there shall no leavened bread be eaten. ⁴ This day came you out in the month of the abib . . . . ⁸ And you shall show your son in that day, saying, This is done because of that which YHWH did unto me when I came forth out of Egypt. ⁹ And it shall be for a sign unto you upon your hand, and for a memorial between your eyes, that the Torah of YHWH may be in your mouth: for with a strong hand has YHWH brought you out of Egypt. ¹⁰ <u>You shall therefore keep this ordinance at its Appointed Time from year to year</u>.*" Shemot 13:3-4, 8-10.

So here Yisrael was given a specific command to observe these times as Appointed Times. The story is to be told and it will be "a sign upon your hand and for a memorial between your eyes." Anyone unfamiliar with the Shema would find this language to be quite strange. This is actually linking the observance of Passover with the Shema.[82] The word for "sign" is owt (×ℓ⊬) and it is the same word used for the various signs, or marks of the Covenant. Notice the Aleph Taw (×⊬) surrounding the vav (ℓ), which is a "nail" or "stake." The word for "memorial" is zikrone (⌐ℓ҈ⱲÞ), which also means "remember."

Before the Children of Yisrael left Egypt, YHWH gave Mosheh and Aharon a lesson in time. They were leaving a land of bondage and pagan sun worship. They were being separated, and time was a very significant issue to get straightened out. "*¹ And YHWH spoke unto Mosheh and Aharon in the land of Egypt, saying, ² This month shall be unto you the beginning of months: it shall be the first month of the year to you.*" Shemot 12:1-2.

The Hebrew word for month is chodesh (wՎH). It actually means: "to bring back, to make anew." There is no definite period of time established for a month other than the cycle of the moon. Unlike a week, which consists of seven full days, the months are not based upon a specific day count cycle. The months are intimately connected with the cycle of the moon.

A Hebrew month is defined as the moment of sunset the evening the moon's crescent first becomes potentially visible to the naked eye in Jerusalem. The ancients always looked for the visible crescent moon which was an owt (×ℓ⊬) or sign to

them.⁸³ They called the new moon "rosh chodesh" - literally "head of the renewal" or "head of the month." The text in Shemot 12 is specifically referencing a "renewed moon" which would occur when the first sliver of the moon is seen, marking the beginning of a month.⁸⁴ So we have YHWH, telling Mosheh and Aharon that "this new moon" shall be the beginning of new moons - it shall be the first new moon of the year or cycle (shanah).

We know that Yisrael observed the Passover on day 14 of month 1. They then departed from Ramses on day 15 and eventually crossed the Red Sea on Day 21. This seven day trek out of the land of Egypt occurred during a special Appointed Time called the Feast of Unleavened Bread. Yisrael was on the move for this seven day period, and did not have time for their bread to rise. How interesting that this event is commemorated by food. As we shall see, bread is symbolic of sustenance, and is a very important part of the Appointed Times.

After the Yisraelites were miraculously delivered from Egypt through the parting of the Red Sea, they were directed to the mountain where they would prepare themselves to enter into Covenant with YHWH. Throughout their trek to the mountain we are provided specific information concerning time, and we can discern when they eventually stood at the base of Mount Sinai in Arabia, and heard the voice of YHWH proclaim the Ten Words.⁸⁵

This day was no ordinary day. It was a very specific and special day. It was another Appointed Time, when YHWH spoke the Ten Words to Yisrael. Often referred to as the Ten Commandments, these Words stand apart from all others, because they were spoken by YHWH to all of Yisrael. The children of Yisrael could not bear to hear the Voice of YHWH and requested that

Mosheh be their mediator. (Shemot 20:19).

When they arrived at the mountain we read the following passage. "*³ Then Mosheh went up to Elohim, and YHWH called to him from the mountain and said, This is what you are to say to the house of Yaakob and what you are to tell the people of Yisrael: ⁴ You yourselves have seen what I did to Egypt, and how I carried you on eagles' wings and brought you to Myself. ⁵ Now if you obey Me fully and keep My Covenant, then out of all nations you will be My treasured possession. Although the whole earth is mine, ⁶ you will be for Me a kingdom of priests and a set apart nation. These are the words you are to speak to the Yisraelites.*" Shemot 19:3-6.

Notice the distinction between "the house of Yaakob" and "the people of Yisrael." The house of Yaakob was referring to all of the direct descendents of Yaakob, and the people of Yisrael were all those in Covenant with YHWH. Yaakob was the name of Yisrael before he entered into the fullness of the Covenant, before he fully became a Covenant people dwelling in the Land. Yisrael is the name representing the people in Covenant with YHWH.

Your genetics do not dictate your Covenant status – it is your heart. We shall soon see that the Covenant of Circumcision, which began in the male organ, will ultimately extend to the heart. Our willingness to obey is often a good representation of our hearts. It is interesting that YHWH chose this location on the male body for the sign. Remember according to the Babylonian myths this was the one part of Nimrod that could not be found. This, therefore, was an appropriate place to mark the sign, which distinguishes the Covenant people from the sun worshipping pagans. Yisrael was to be a Kingdom of priests, part of the royal family of YHWH.

Here is the mandate for these people – keep

(shamar) the Covenant. Guard it and protect it, just as Adam was to have done, and as Abraham had done. They needed to obey YHWH fully, not partially or half heartedly. If they did this then they would be a kingdom of priests, set apart from all other nations.

This was essentially a marriage proposal which Mosheh then brought to the elders and the people. Their response was unequivocal - "We will do everything YHWH has said." In other words - "I do." They accepted the proposal and were all told to get cleaned up for the ceremony. Even though they were part of a community, as individuals they all had to wash their clothes, wash their bodies - consecrate themselves like a bride preparing for her wedding. The ceremony would take place "on the third day." Then YHWH would come down from the mountain in the sight of all the people.

YHWH was now fulfilling the marriage Covenant aspect of the Abrahamic Covenant. The instructions, known as the Torah, remained at the center of the Covenant - like a Ketubah or a written marriage contract between a husband and a wife.[86]

As YHWH began to speak the terms of the Covenant, the people began to experience the awesome presence of YHWH and became afraid. "*[18] Now all the people saw ×ֶת the thunderings and ×ֶת the lightning flashes and ×ֶת the voice (sound) of the shofar, and ×ֶת the mountain smoking; and when the people saw it, they trembled and stood afar off. [19] Then they said to Mosheh, You speak with us, and we will hear; but let not Elohim speak with us, lest we die."* Shemot 20:18-19.

After Elohim had spoken what are referred to as the ten commandments, or ten words, the people could not take anymore. They were afraid of what they saw, they even "saw the sound." They asked Mosheh to listen

to the commandments, and then relay them to the people. This is very important, because they actually asked Mosheh to represent YHWH in their marital relationship. They asked a man to stand between them in their relationship with YHWH.

YHWH agreed to this request. So Mosheh, as the mediator of the Covenant, drew near the thick darkness where Elohim was. It was there in the thick darkness that YHWH gave the instructions to Yisrael regarding how they should live. This was essentially the instruction manual for an assembly of people taken out of a pagan civilization and chosen to dwell with the Creator of the Universe. These were the instructions for a Covenant people.

YHWH gave instructions on how to live with one another and how to deal fairly with people, including aliens and slaves. These were instructions for righteous and just living. YHWH ended with great promises concerning the Land that was previously promised to Abraham's seed. Interestingly, couched between the general list of instructions and the promise of the Land, they were given a schedule of appointments that they were supposed to keep.

Specifically, the Yisraelites were reminded of the Sabbath. They had already been instructed that the seventh day was set apart. It was a day when no work was done. They were also given three annual appointments when all of the men were to appear before YHWH.

"*14* Three times a year you shall celebrate a feast (hagag) unto Me. *15* ΧΫ́-the Feast of Unleavened Bread (hag hamatzot) you shall keep (shamar) seven days: eat unleavened bread (matza) as I commanded you, in the appointed time (moad) the month (chodesh) of the abib; for in it you came out from Egypt: and none shall appear before Me empty: *16* And

the Feast of the cutting (haqatsiyr), the firstfruits (bikkuri) of your labors, which you have sown in the field: and the Feast of Ingathering (awseef), which is in the end of the year, when you have gathered in your labors out of the field. ¹⁷ Three times in the year all your males shall appear before the Master YHWH." Shemot 23:14-17.

All three of these times are called Feasts, which is hag (∧ℍ) in Hebrew. It means: "festival" or "gathering." Notice that the three times are preceded by the Aleph Taw (✕ℓ), which is literally connected with the Feast of Unleavened Bread. In fact, it immediately precedes the Feast, which is when the Passover occurs. So we have a powerful connection between the Messiah and the Passover.

We are told that Mosheh spoke <u>all the Words</u> that YHWH had given him, and also <u>wrote down all the Words</u>. (Shemot 24:3-4). These Words were the instructions for a Covenant people to live with the Creator. They did not instinctively know how to please YHWH, so they were given very specific and straight forward instructions.

The people agreed to obey all of the Words and those instructions were not too difficult for the Yisraelites to obey as specifically indicated by Mosheh. (Debarim 30:11-14). For some reason, many people believe that YHWH gave Yisrael a burdensome set of rules and regulations that essentially put them into bondage. There are those who refer to Yisrael as being placed "under the law" as if YHWH delivered them from slavery in Egypt simply to make them His slaves.

Nothing could be further from the truth, and those who hold that view had better rethink their opinion of YHWH. He is not a cruel slave master as some would dare to portray Him. The Torah was a gift to Yisrael, and was meant to provide them with

abundant blessings. It was a treasure because it unlocked some of the mysteries of the universe. It showed them the way to abundant blessing and life. It showed them the Covenant path back to the Garden.

The Children of Yisrael entered into Covenant with YHWH. This Covenant was confirmed by blood, half of the blood was sprinkled on the altar and half was sprinkled on the people. (Shemot 24). Mosheh, Aharon, Nadab and Abihu, along with seventy elders of Yisrael then went up and *"saw the Elohim of Yisrael."* (Shemot 24:10). They ate and drank with Him in a very special place.

A very interesting event, shrouded with much mystery, then occurs. The Scriptures describe that Mosheh and his assistant Yahushua (Joshua)[87] rose up, and Mosheh went up to the Mountain of Elohim.

"15 And Mosheh went up into the mount, and a cloud covered the mount. 16 And the glory of YHWH abode upon Mount Sinai, and the cloud covered it six days: and the seventh day He called unto Mosheh out of the midst of the cloud. 17 And the sight of the glory of YHWH was like devouring fire on the top of the mount in the eyes of the children of Yisrael. 18 And Mosheh went into the midst of the cloud, and he went up into the mount, and Mosheh was in the mount forty (40) days and forty (40) nights." Shemot 24:15-18. It was on the seventh day that YHWH called out to Mosheh from the midst of the cloud, and this was the seventh day of the week.

Thereafter, YHWH gave Mosheh instructions concerning building His House, known as the Tabernacle, as well as all of the furnishings. He was also given the instructions for those who would serve in the House. When all of the instructions concerning the House were given, YHWH ended with this final instruction:

"*¹² And YHWH spoke to Mosheh, saying, ¹³ Speak thou also unto the children of Yisrael, saying, Verily My Sabbaths you shall keep: for it is a sign between Me and you throughout your generations; that you may know that I am YHWH that does set you apart. ¹⁴ You shall keep the Sabbath therefore; for it is set apart unto you: every one that defileth it shall surely be put to death: for whosoever does any work therein, that soul shall be cut off from among his people. ¹⁵ Six days may work be done; but in the seventh is the Sabbath of rest, set apart to YHWH: whosoever doeth any work in the Sabbath day, he shall surely be put to death. ¹⁶ Wherefore the children of Yisrael shall keep the Sabbath, to observe the Sabbath throughout their generations, for a perpetual Covenant. ¹⁷ It is a sign between Me and the children of Yisrael throughout the ages: for in six days YHWH made heaven and earth, and on the seventh day He rested, and was refreshed. ¹⁸ And He gave unto Mosheh, when He had made an end of communing with him upon Mount Sinai, two tables of testimony, tables of stone, written with the finger of Elohim.*" Shemot 31:12-18.

So the Sabbath cycle was referred to as a perpetual Covenant. The Sabbath was actually woven into the thread of Yisrael. Interestingly, the word Sabbath is mentioned six times, which is a number attributed to man. So we see that the Sabbath was actually made for man. We also see the creation of two tablets of testimony written on both sides with the finger of Elohim. (Shemot 32:15-16). The Words of the Covenant were literally "etched in stone."

This was a great moment. The Covenant relationship was sealed. It should have been a happy ending, but sadly, while Mosheh was on the mountain working out the Covenant, the Yisraelites were down below fornicating. When Mosheh saw what the Yisraelites were doing he broke the tablets. The

Covenant had been broken.

Remember, the children of Yisrael were out of Egypt, but they still carried many of the reminders of Egypt. This is why the First Commandment spoken by the Voice of YHWH was "*² I am YHWH your Elohim, who brought you out of the land of Egypt, out of the house of bondage. ³ You shall have no other gods before Me.*" Shemot 20:2-3. The phrase "before Me" is better translated "In My Face." In other words, YHWH  did not want to see any other gods in Yisrael. He alone was to be the object of their affection and worship.

The Yisraelites became impatient while Mosheh was on the Mountain for 40 days and 40 nights. The Yisraelites were down below staring at their idols, wanting to do something. That is where the idea of the golden calf materialized. Remember, in Egypt there were a multitude of gods and goddesses that symbolized different things on the earth and in the spirit realm.

One of the major cults in Egypt was the worship of Hathor. Hathor was one of the most commonly worshipped goddesses in Ancient Egypt, originally considered to be the mother of Horus, the falcon god. That title eventually went to Isis and Hathor was in later times regarded as his wife. Hathor was associated with love, fertility, sexuality, music, dance and alcohol. This was a goddess who knew how to party.

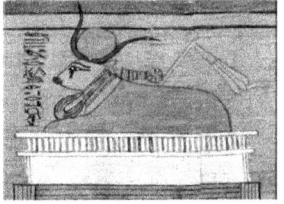"She was sometimes represented entirely anthropomorphically, in the form of a cow, or as a woman with cow's ears. When in human form, her headdress could be one of cow's horns with a solar disc, or a falcon on a perch. She was

also a sky goddess, and was regarded as a vast cow who straddled the heavens, with her four legs marking the four cardinal points."[88] She was honoured as the "Lady of Byblos" the source of the word "Bible."[89]

The Yisraelites wanted a party, so they invited Hathor and declared it "a Feast to YHWH." The problem was that it was not a feast prescribed or ordained by YHWH. YHWH had already given them the Appointed Times to observe, and this was not one of them. They also built an altar, and  made an idol in the manner that they had learned while in Mitsrayim. The golden calve was the child of Hathor and Apis, thus we see an example of a Babylonian derived trinity - father, mother, child worship which is predominate in pagan systems. They took what they were used to doing in a pagan society and began doing it to YHWH.

This was an abomination to YHWH. They were supposed to be a "holy" people, which means: "set apart."  They were not supposed to be worshiping like pagans, and saying that they were doing it for YHWH. They were mixing abominations in their worship, which is strictly prohibited. Sadly, this error was continually repeated by Yisrael, and this same error continues to this day in religions such as Christianity. Christianity claims to be offering pure worship to YHWH, but it does not. It has become mixed and polluted by pagan traditions derived from Babylon, some of which we will be examining further in this text.

Incredibly, the very altar constructed by the Children of Yisrael at the base of Mount Sinai has been found in Saudi Arabia, although they will never find the golden calf. That was ground up and fed to the pagan practicing multitude.[90] Not only has Mount Sinai been found, but so has the split rock from which water poured out for the people and livestock as they camped at the base of the Mountain.

Most people are taught that these locations are found in the Sinai Peninsula, which is nothing but a man-made tradition. Despite the fact that archaeology shows that the Red Sea crossing occurred at Nuweiba, Egypt across the Gulf of Aqaba into Saudi Arabia[91] people tend to cling to traditions over truth.[92]

While the Yisraelites had entered into a relationship with YHWH and reaped the rewards of deliverance, they committed idolatry, which was similar to adultery. They were unfaithful in their relationship with YHWH. They were running around naked, fornicating with Egyptian gods, which obviously made YHWH incensed.

It is no different than a man walking in on his fiancé while she is in the midst of an orgy. It was an unimaginable repulsive act of unfaithfulness. The deal was off. YHWH had no obligation to continue with the relationship, and who would blame Him if He simply smote the Yisraelites for their unfaithfulness. They had made gods of gold in direct contravention to the commandments of YHWH.

They had made sacrifices to their calf, but that was not the only blood that was shed that day. Three thousand died at the hands of the Levites. That day the Levites acted as the Hand of YHWH, and as a result, they were blessed and set apart. They would stand in the place of the firstborn of Yisrael. They would be

substitutes that would serve in the House of YHWH in place of the firstborn. This was a very significant event that will be discussed further in the text.

Mosheh thereafter returned to YHWH, and confessed the sins of Yisrael. He interceded and offered himself to be blotted out of the Scroll YHWH has written.[93] Mosheh essentially offered himself as an atonement for their sins. YHWH agreed to continue with the promises, but He assured Mosheh that those who sinned would be punished. YHWH struck Yisrael with a plague because of the calf Aharon made.

Things were different now. YHWH would fulfill His Word. He would allow them to go into the Land, but He said, "*I will not go with you, because you are a stiff necked people and I might destroy you on the way.*" Shemot 33:3. The party was over. The people were told to take off their ornaments, and YHWH would decide what to do with them. Mosheh spoke with YHWH and requested that the presence of YHWH be with them. YHWH replied "*My presence will go with you, and I will give you rest.*" Shemot 33:14.

Probably the most critical point in this entire process is the fact that the Yisraelites were given a second chance. Since the Covenant was broken, it needed to be renewed. This time, the man who mediated had to cut the stones and carry them up the mountain. Mosheh cut the new set of tablets and once more ascended the mountain. YHWH again inscribed the commandments, the same words that were inscribed upon the first tablets.

"*[1] And YHWH said unto Mosheh, Hew thee two tables of stone like unto the first: and I will write upon these tables the words that were in the first tables, which thou brakest. [2] And be ready in the morning, and come up in the morning unto mount Sinai, and present thyself there to Me in the top of the Mount. [3] And no man shall come up with thee,*

neither let any man be seen throughout all the Mount; neither let the flocks nor herds feed before that mount. *⁴ And he hewed two tables of stone like unto the first; and Mosheh rose up early in the morning, and went up unto mount Sinai, as YHWH had commanded him, and took in his hand the two tables of stone."* Shemot 34:1-4.

Mosheh was once again on the mountain for 40 days and 40 nights. This time the Scriptures specifically record that he was fasting. As the mediator of this renewed Covenant, he was now becoming the suffering servant, a role that would become increasingly important in a future renewal.

During this renewal process YHWH reiterated the three Appointed Times mentioned previously. These times are obviously significant to receive so much attention.

"¹⁸ The Feast of Unleavened Bread shalt thou keep. Seven days thou shalt eat unleavened bread, as I commanded thee, in the time of the month of the abib: for in the month of the abib you came out from Egypt. ¹⁹ All that opens the matrix is mine; and every firstling among your cattle, whether ox or sheep, that is male. ²⁰ But the firstling of an ass you shalt redeem with a lamb: and if you redeem him not, then shalt thou break his neck. All the firstborn of your sons you shall redeem. And none shall appear before Me empty. ²¹ Six days you shall work, but on the seventh day you shall rest: in earing time and in harvest you shall rest. ²² And you shall observe the Feast of Weeks, of the firstfruits of wheat harvest, and the Feast of Ingathering at the year's end. ²³ Three times in the year shall all your men children appear before the Master YHWH, the Elohi of Yisrael. ²⁴ For I will cast out the nations before thee, and enlarge your borders: neither shall any man desire your land, when you shall go up to appear before YHWH your Elohim three times in the year." Shemot 34:18-24.

So again, YHWH is reiterating that if they

wanted to be in His Covenant, they needed to observe His Appointed Times. The people had already improperly declared a feast at the wrong time, and in the wrong fashion. They could not just make up times as they had done with the golden calf. They could not worship Him as the pagans who worshipped false gods. They needed to be clean, set apart and they needed to do it His way.

After 40 days and 40 nights Mosheh descended from the mountain. His face actually radiated so that he needed to wear a veil over his face.[94] All tolled, there were three different times when Mosheh went up the mountain for 40 days and 40 nights.[95] These three times on the mountain, meeting with YHWH, are mirrored in the three times each year that we are to "appear before YHWH."

These 3 annual appointments are an intimate part of the Covenant process just as the 3 meetings between Mosheh and YHWH were critical to Covenant process. Something is birthed during these 3 annual times. So we can see that an important part of the Covenant process involved appointments that Yisrael needed to keep with YHWH.

After descending from the Mountain, Mosheh then went on to gather the offerings of materials to build the House, but first he reiterated the command concerning the Sabbath. He reminded them that it was a set apart day - qadosh (שׁוּדָק).

The first mention of an appointment was actually spoken by YHWH when He proclaimed the Ten Words. Commonly referred to as the Fourth Commandment it was given as follows: "[8] *Remember the Sabbath day, to keep it set apart.* [9] *Six days shall you labor, and do all your work:* [10] *But the seventh day is the Sabbath of YHWH your Elohim, in it you shall not do any work, you, nor your son, nor your*

daughter, your manservant, nor your maidservant, nor your cattle, nor your stranger that is within thy gates: ¹¹ For in six days YHWH made heaven and earth, the sea, and all that in them is, and rested the seventh day: wherefore YHWH blessed the Sabbath day, and set it apart." Shemot 20:8-11.

Notice that it is the Sabbath of YHWH. It belongs to Him. It was not newly established for Yisrael on that day. It was created at the beginning. This was not the first time that the Yisraelites were told about the Sabbath. Earlier in the journey out of Egypt, when they were given the promise of manna, they were also instructed to rest on the seventh day.[96] YHWH also ended His instructions with the Sabbath as seen in Shemot 31:12-17, so the Sabbath was firmly established as a very significant time.

So before Yisrael could begin building the House of YHWH, they needed to be reminded of the Sabbath. As YHWH rested after building all of Creation, they were to rest while building His House. They then went about building the House of YHWH. At the conclusion of the Book of Shemot we read that they set up the House on Day 1 of Month 1. There was not a complete explanation of this place, often called the Tabernacle. It literally means: "the tent of appointment." This was to be the place that they would meet with YHWH for their 3 appointments - their 3 annual Feasts.

These Feasts revolved around the Covenant Land, and it was important that they move into the Promised Land in order to fully walk in the Covenant path and keep the Covenant times. Sadly, as they were about to enter in, they received a bad report from 10 out of 12 "spies" who returned from a reconnaissance mission.

The people believed the bad reports and decided it was better to return to Egypt than confront the "giants" of the Land. As a result, the people would spend 40 years

in the wilderness until the generation of those who would have fought to take the Land died off.

Again, we see the mercy of YHWH. These people not only disobeyed, but they expressed a complete distrust in His ability to deliver to them the Land that He promised. He could have simply punished them for their disobedience, but He allowed them to live out their lives. It was not until they died, and a new generation was raised up, that their journey out of Egypt would be complete.

Leaving Egypt involved much more than simply crossing the Red Sea and leaving the physical boundaries of Egypt. It was an internal transformative process that continued in the wilderness. Through the wilderness experience, YHWH prepared a people who were wholly committed to His ways and ready to dwell with Him - the Covenant people Yisrael.

9

Yisrael

From the very beginning, in the Garden, it was revealed that YHWH desired a people who He could dwell with. A people He could call His own. A people who would obey him and follow His instructions. This was all about a relationship between the Creator and His Creation

Yisrael is actually referred to as "the planting of YHWH," and likened to a green olive tree. (Yirmeyahu 11:16-17). Under the leadership of Joshua, we see Yisrael become planted in the Promised Land. This was reminiscent of man being placed in the Garden. There are many who advocate that the Land of Yisrael was, in fact, where Eden was located and Jerusalem was the Garden. The pattern is certainly there, as well as the connection between obedience and remaining in the Land.

Since the Land was an integral part of the Covenant made with Abraham and confirmed at Sinai, it was vital that Yisrael actually enter into the Land of promise. They needed to be "planted" in the Garden of YHWH. As with Adam, they were to "tend" and "watch" the Garden. Failure to do so would result in the same punishment - expulsion. If you do not want to live in the Land, then you should not expect to enter into the Covenant. The Land and the Covenant are inseparable. That is why a generation died off in the wilderness

before Yisrael crossed the Jordan and entered in. That generation had rejected the Land.

Some erroneously try to differentiate or divide elements of the Covenant by stating that the Land was a part of the Covenant made with Abraham, and they are part of a different Covenant that does not include the Land. This is simply not possible. All Covenants made after Abraham were in essence, the same Covenant renewed.[97] You cannot be in a Covenant with YHWH that does not involve dwelling with Him. That is the point of His Covenant.

An important point to recognize is that only two of the fighting men from the generation that left Egypt in the Exodus actually crossed over into the Promised Land: Joshua and Caleb - two of the twelve who previously explored the land.

They were the two who gave a good report to the people and encouraged them to enter into the land - despite the presence of giants. They were prepared to fight for the Land. They were likely the ones who took the trouble to haul out a cluster of grapes as proof of the bounty that awaited them. The reason why these two were different is specifically detailed in the Scriptures: "*not one except Caleb son of Yephunneh the Kenizzite and Joshua son of Nun, for they followed YHWH wholeheartedly.*" Numbers (Bemidbar)[98] 32:12.

Notice that Caleb was not a native Yisraelite. The Scriptures record that his father was a Kenizzite yet they became part of Yisrael. Despite the fact that his father was from a foreign land, the Scriptures list Caleb as

being part of the Tribe of Judah. This means that at some point his family was "grafted in" to the tribe of Judah, properly known as Yahudah.[99]

This is how it worked when Yisrael camped after the Exodus. They divided into tribes and they camped around the Tabernacle. There was no "Tribe of the Mixed Multitude" - no "Tribe of the Nations." The mixed multitude was not separated from the other tribes, they became part of Yisrael just as Caleb's family joined Yisrael through the Tribe of Yahudah. Anyone who wanted to join with Yisrael was ultimately "grafted in" through a tribe.

Now look at Joshua son of Nun, whose true Hebrew name was Yahushua. His name was changed from Hoshea which means: "salvation" to Yahushua which means: "Yah is salvation." Yah is the short form of YHWH, so the name is a declaration that it is YHWH Who saves.

Yahushua was from the Tribe of Ephraim. The Tribe of Ephraim is extremely interesting because the name itself means: "doubly fruitful." Remember that Ephraim was the second son of Joseph (Yoseph).[100] He was born in Egypt along with his brother Manashah - unlike the other tribes of Yisrael. His mother Asenath was an Egyptian - the daughter of a pagan priest - just as Mosheh's wife was the daughter of a pagan priest.[101] Indeed, Yoseph, along with his 10 older brothers were born in Paddan Aram. Yisrael has always been mixed with the other nations.

Ephraim was the youngest son of Yoseph, yet he received the blessing and birthright of a firstborn son. He was adopted by his grandfather Yisrael, and elevated as a son. So we have this powerful picture of a child born into a pagan culture, and Yisrael then adopting him into the family, making him a tribe and blessing him - as a

firstborn son! (Beresheet 48).

We also see the two men - Caleb and Yahushua - representing Yahudah and Ephraim, both of whom were adopted into Yisrael in different ways. They were the only two fighting men from their generation to enter into the Land. How profound and encouraging for anyone born into paganism, finding themself outside of the Covenant. There is no need to fret, there is room for everyone who desires to obey.

If you still are not convinced, then read on. Before this new generation entered into the Promised Land, the Covenant was renewed at Moab. We read in Debarim 29:1 the following words. "*These are the terms of the Covenant YHWH commanded Mosheh to make with the Yisraelites in Moab, in addition to the Covenant He had made with them at Horeb.*" All of Yisrael was assembled, including sojourners in the midst of the assembly, to hear the words of the renewed Covenant.

"*¹⁰ All of you are standing today in the presence of YHWH your Elohim - your leaders and chief men, your elders and officials, and all the other men of Yisrael, ¹¹ together with your children and your wives, and the aliens living in your camps who chop your wood and carry your water. ¹² You are standing here in order to enter into a Covenant with YHWH your Elohim, a Covenant YHWH is making with you this day and sealing with an oath, ¹³ to confirm you this day as His people, that He may be your Elohim as He promised you and as He swore to your fathers, Abraham, Yitshaq and Yaakob. ¹⁴ I am making this Covenant, with its oath, not only with you ¹⁵ who are standing here with us today in the presence of YHWH our Elohim but also with those who are not here today.*" Debarim 29:10-15.

The Covenant was renewed with that new generation as well as with those who were not there. This points to a future people who would enter into the

same Covenant - which would again be renewed.

We have an example of this happening with Ruth who was, by no coincidence, a Moabite from the very land where this Covenant was renewed. The story of Ruth provides an incredible picture of a foreigner being grafted into Yisrael, and becoming an important part of the Messianic bloodline. Her famous words are the formula for becoming grafted in to Yisrael: *"For wherever you go, I will go; and wherever you lodge, I will lodge; Your people shall be my people, and your Elohim, my Elohim."* Ruth 1:16. Through this story we see a vivid example of redemption.

While Mosheh led Yisrael in the wilderness, it was Yahushua (Joshua) who would lead them into their inheritance. Yahushua (Joshua), who had been at the side of Mosheh when he went up the mountain. Yahushua (Joshua) who along with Caleb, spied out the Land and brought back a good report. As previously indicated, his original name was Hoshea son of Nun. We are told of his name change immediately before he entered into the Land with the eleven other spies. The change involved adding the Name of YHWH - which has great significance.

We know that Abram left a pagan land and crossed over to join into Covenant with YHWH where he ultimately became a "new" man named Abraham. Yaakob left the Land as one man and returned a different person with his tribes and a new name - Yisrael. So too, Hoshea left Egypt as one man and entered into the Land as a different being. Hoshea left Egypt a slave and entered the land as a conquering leader - Yahushua.

Therefore, it is important that we experience a "transformation" on our Covenant journey. We must walk in the "newness" and "fullness" that YHWH has in store for us before we enter into the Promised Land.

Before entering into the Land, the Yisraelites received a Covenant refresher and renewal in Moab. They had previously committed idolatry and they had been warned. "You shall not bow down to their gods or serve them or do after their works; but you shall utterly overthrow them and break down their pillars and images." Shemot 23:24.

The Yisraelites were supposed to live holy, set apart lives according to the Torah – their wedding contract. They were supposed to stay true to their Husband YHWH, and not commit spiritual idolatry with other gods – which would constitute adultery.

In other words, as the Bride of YHWH, if they wanted to live in His House (Garden) – the Land – then they needed to remain faithful to Him and His ways. Under the leadership of Yahushua (Joshua), Yisrael was finally permitted to enter into the Land, which was divided up between the Tribes. Here is the instruction provided in Moab for cleansing the Land.

"*1* These are the statutes and judgments which you shall be careful to observe in the Land which YHWH Elohim of your fathers is giving you to possess, all the days that you live on the earth. *2* <u>You shall utterly destroy all the places where the nations which you shall dispossess served their gods, on the high mountains and on the hills and under every green tree. *3* And you shall destroy their altars, break their sacred pillars, and burn their wooden images with fire; you shall cut down the carved images of their gods and destroy their names from that place. *4* You shall not worship YHWH your Elohim with such things.</u> *5* But you shall seek the place where YHWH your Elohim chooses, out of all your tribes, to put His Name for His dwelling place;

and there you shall go. ⁶ There you shall take your burnt offerings, your sacrifices, your tithes, the heave offerings of your hand, your vowed offerings, your freewill offerings, and the firstborn of your herds and flocks. ⁷ And there you shall eat before YHWH your Elohim, and you shall rejoice in all to which you have put your hand, you and your households, in which YHWH your Elohim has blessed you. ⁸ <u>You shall not at all do as we are doing here today - every man doing whatever is right in his own eyes</u> ⁹ for as yet you have not come to the rest and the inheritance which YHWH your Elohim is giving you. ¹⁰ But when you cross over the Jordan and dwell in the Land which YHWH your Elohim is giving you to inherit, and He gives you rest from all your enemies round about, so that you dwell in safety, ¹¹ then there will be the place where YHWH your Elohim chooses to make His Name abide. There you shall bring all that I command you: your burnt offerings, your sacrifices, your tithes, the heave offerings of your hand, and all your choice offerings which you vow to YHWH. ¹² And you shall rejoice before YHWH your Elohim, you and your sons and your daughters, your male and female servants, and the Levite who is within your gates, since he has no portion nor inheritance with you. ¹³ Take heed to yourself that you do not offer your burnt offerings in every place that you see; ¹⁴ but in the place which YHWH chooses, in one of your tribes, there you shall offer your burnt offerings, and there you shall do all that I command you." Debarim 12:1-14.

So YHWH was very specific as to how and where He was to be worshipped. He was even concerned when He was to be worshipped. It is also clear that the Yisraelites were not to worship Him as the pagans worshipped their gods, and Yisrael was to remove all traces of worship from the Promised Land.

They were also instructed not to set up poles and pillars in order to worship false gods. "^{21} You shall not plant for yourself any tree, as a wooden image, near the altar which you build for yourself to YHWH your Elohim. ^{22} You shall not set up a sacred pillar, which YHWH your Elohim hates." Debarim 16:21-22. The point was very clear – "do not act like the pagans if you want to live in My House."

Yisrael would be surrounded by heathens. They were supposed to be set apart, and through their obedience they would be a light to the world. As they shined the light of YHWH to the Nations they would draw men unto YHWH.

Just as they had passed through the waters of the Red Sea when they left Egypt, they passed through the waters of the Jordan as they entered into the Land. These events were supposed to represent a washing of the Assembly – a corporate immersion.

The Book of Yahushua (Joshua) describes their entry into the Land. It is pertinent to note that after crossing the Jordan, they circumcised all of the males. These were, after all, the Covenant people. They then ate the Covenant meal – the Passover at Gilgal.

Once they had taken care of those Covenant requirements they set their eyes on the pagan gods of the land. First on the list was Jericho, or rather Yeracho. Named after the moon (yerach), it was a walled city that was the center of Canaanite moon worship. Interestingly, Yisrael is sometimes represented by the moon, which reflects the light of the Sun, so this was

YHWH setting things straight.[102] Just as He had done with the Egyptian gods, once again, YHWH would fight the battle against the pagan gods.

The Scriptures record that Yisrael settled into the Land and then renewed the Covenant again at Mount Gilboa near Shechem. These renewals did not involve new covenants, they were the same Covenant. This is something that Christianity fails to recognize, erroneously believing that the Messiah came and entered into a "New" covenant - which He did not do. He simply "renewed" the Covenant with Yisrael, which had been done many times in the past. He followed a pattern which had been established by Mosheh and Yahushua.

Despite renewing the Covenant, the tribes were constantly struggling within themselves, between each other, with their leaders, with their neighbors and with YHWH. While Yisrael remained tribal in structure, they were bound by a common system of worship with the High Priest as their spiritual leader. This failed to unify all of the tribes and they often looked for a leader who would function in a role known as a "Judge."[103]

Sadly, during this period of Judges, we read that men were repeatedly doing whatever *"seemed right in his own eyes."* Yisrael was specifically warned not to do this. (Debarim 12:8). This lead to division, strife and separation from YHWH. It meant that they did not submit themselves to the spiritual leadership, but worshipped YHWH however they saw fit. This is a recipe for disaster as we saw at Sinai. They also repeatedly strayed away from YHWH, and fell into the pagan practices of the Gentile nations around them.

From the time that they conquered the Land under the leadership of Yahushua, there was a period of approximately 350 years that elapsed until YHWH would raise up a leader who would unite the tribes as a

cohesive nation. The people eventually cried out for a king which was inevitable, and even foretold by Mosheh. (Debarim 17:14).

At that time Samuel (Shemuel)[104] was the undisputed authority figure in Yisrael. Shemuel was a unique individual who was a nazarite from the tribe of Ephraim. He was dedicated to YHWH by his mother Hannah and, in essence, adopted by Eli the High Priest. This must have been the case because he served as a priest and only a Cohen or a Levite could serve in the Mishkan.[105]

It was Shemuel who attended to the Mishkan after the death of Eli, since his two sons Hophni and Phinehas died in a battle against the Philistines. It was Shemuel who had the authority from YHWH to annoint the first King of the Kingdom of Yisrael. How fascinating that this very unique man from the tribe of Ephraim would stand in the transition between the priest and the King.

Shemuel anointed Shaul, who was from the tribe of Benyamin. Benyamin was the only one of the 12 sons of Yisrael that was born in the Land, and the tribe of Benyamin was the smallest amongst the tribes. This tribe was nearly decimated after the sin of Gibeah. (see Judges 19-20). This tribe was located geographically between Yoseph, the largest tribe and Yahudah. Yoseph and Benyamin were the two youngest sons of Yisrael and they shared the same mother – Rachel.

The reign of Shaul did not last long because he did not diligently obey the commandments. Here is what Shemuel told Shaul: "[13] *You have done foolishly. <u>You have not kept the commandment of YHWH your Elohim, which He commanded you.</u> For now YHWH would have established your kingdom over Yisrael throughout the age.* [14] *But now your kingdom shall not continue. YHWH has sought for Himself a*

man after His own heart, and YHWH has commanded him to be commander over His people, because you have not kept what YHWH commanded you." 1 Shemuel 13:13-14.

Shaul failed just as Adam had failed. He did not keep, guard, watch over and protect (shamar) the commandments.[106] Therefore, YHWH found a man like Yahushua and Caleb - a man who would follow Him with his whole heart. David was a giant slayer as were Yahushua and Caleb. He trusted in his Elohim and we know from the Psalms (Tehillim)[107] that he loved the Torah. These are the character traits of a man who YHWH will allow to lead His people - Yisrael.

David was the youngest child of Jesse (Yeshai) and was born and raised in Bethlehem. The reign of King David is looked upon as the Golden Years of Yisrael. He made mistakes, but his heart for YHWH never wavered. As a result, YHWH covenanted with David that the throne would never depart from his offspring. David was responsible for moving the capital of the Kingdom to Jerusalem.

David established his throne in Jerusalem, and endeavored to build a House for YHWH. Up until then the Tabernacle made in the wilderness was still being used and moved to various locations. David set his heart to build a permanent house.[108]

At the direction of Gad, David purchased the threshing floor of Araunah, along with oxen to slaughter.[109] There he built an altar to YHWH, and it was chosen as the location of the House of YHWH. This draws the connection between the harvests of the Land, and the place where the people of Yisrael would assemble.

A threshing floor is a specially flattened surface made either of rock or beaten earth where the farmer would thresh the grain harvest. The threshing floor was

either owned by the entire village or by a single family. It was usually located outside the village in a place exposed to the wind.[110]

Once the grain was threshed, a process of separating it from the stalks, usually through beating, it needed to be separated from the chaff through a process known as winnowing. The fact that the location of the House of YHWH was a threshing floor has profound implications when you consider that the Appointed Times, known as the moadim, were centered around the harvests.[111]

YHWH had already provided the Appointed Times to Yisrael, and specifically told them to come to one place – the place where He put His Name. In other words, where His House was located. Those Appointed Times revolved around the harvest seasons so the people would bring their offerings to the threshing floor of YHWH. Essentially, through this process of obedience, they would offer themselves to be threshed by Him.

While David purchased the land, he was not permitted to build the House because he had blood on his hands. He was responsible for making the plans and preparations for building the House, as well as developing the songs, the instruments and other aspects of the worship service.[112]

After the reign of King David, things deteriorated very rapidly. His son, Solomon (Shlomo),[113] built and dedicated the House of YHWH. He also built other great structures and he accrued incredible wealth. He was known for his great wisdom, but sadly he fell into serious idolatry at the end of his life.

Read how his heart turned away from YHWH: *"¹ But King Shlomo loved many foreign women, as well as the daughter of Pharaoh: women of the Moabites, Ammonites, Edomites, Sidonians, and Hittites - ² from the nations of whom*

YHWH had said to the children of Yisrael, 'You shall not intermarry with them, nor they with you. Surely they will turn away your hearts after their gods.' Shlomo clung to these in love. ³ And he had seven hundred wives, princesses, and three hundred concubines; and his wives turned away his heart. ⁴ <u>For it was so, when Shlomo was old, that his wives turned his heart after other gods; and his heart was not loyal to YHWH his Elohim, as was the heart of his father David.</u> ⁵ <u>For Shlomo went after Ashtoreth the goddess of the Sidonians, and after Milcom the abomination of the Ammonites.</u> ⁶ <u>Shlomo did evil in the sight of YHWH, and did not fully follow YHWH, as did his father David.</u> ⁷ <u>Then Shlomo built a high place for Chemosh the abomination of Moab, on the hill that is east of Jerusalem, and for Molech the abomination of the people of Ammon.</u> ⁸ And he did likewise for all his foreign wives, who burned incense and sacrificed to their gods. ⁹ So YHWH became angry with Shlomo, because his heart had turned from YHWH Elohim of Yisrael, who had appeared to him twice, ¹⁰ and had commanded him concerning this thing, that he should not go after other gods; but he did not keep what YHWH had commanded. ¹¹ <u>Therefore YHWH said to Shlomo, because you have done this, and have not kept My Covenant and My statutes, which I have commanded you, I will surely tear the kingdom away from you and give it to your servant.</u> ¹² Nevertheless I will not do it in your days, for the sake of your father David; I will tear it out of the hand of your son. ¹³ However <u>I will not tear away the whole kingdom; I will give one tribe to your son for the sake of My servant David, and for the sake of Jerusalem which I have chosen.</u>" 1 Kings 11:1-13.

So a man who began his reign renowned for his wisdom ended up an idolater. He failed to keep (shamar) the commandments which separated him from the One Who had blessed him so greatly. He did exactly what Yisrael was instructed not to do. He participated in the abominable practice of the pagans. He worshipped

Ashtoreth - Easter, as well as Milcom. He also built "high places" for Milcom, Chemosh and Molech.

The Scriptures are very clear that it was his disobedience which led to his demise. The Torah specifically forbids kings from obtaining great wealth or taking many wives. (Debarim 17:16-17) They were supposed to prepare their own Torah Scroll to remind them to live and rule according to the instructions of YHWH. (Debarim 17:18).

Shlomo was provided with everything he needed to be a great king, but he failed miserably and ended up being involved in abominable conduct, some of the worst pagan rituals that existed, including the sacrifice of children. He blatantly disobeyed the commandments and the Kingdom would suffer as a result. Before his death, it was prophesied by Ahiyah of Shiloh that the Kingdom would be torn apart.

The prophet confronted the servant of Shlomo, Jeroboam, as he was leaving Jerusalem. Ahiyah took a new cloak and tore it into 12 pieces. He told Jeroboam to take 10 pieces and spoke the following to him:

"*31 See, I am going to tear the kingdom out of Shlomo's hand and give you ten tribes. 32 But for the sake of My servant David and the city of Jerusalem, which I have chosen out of all the tribes of Yisrael, he will have one tribe. 33 I will do this because they have forsaken Me and worshiped Ashtoreth the goddess of the Sidonians, Chemosh the god of the Moabites, and Molech the god of the Ammonites, and have not walked in My ways, nor done what is right in My eyes, nor kept My statutes and laws as David, Shlomo's father, did. 34 But I will not take the whole kingdom out of Shlomo's hand; I have made him ruler all the days of his life for the sake of David My servant, whom I chose and who observed My*

commands and statutes. *³⁵ I will take the kingdom from his son's hands and give you ten tribes. ³⁶ I will give one tribe to his son so that David My servant may always have a lamp before Me in Jerusalem, the city where I chose to put My Name. ³⁷ However, as for you, I will take you, and you will rule over all that your heart desires; you will be king over Yisrael. ³⁸ If you do whatever I command you and walk in My ways and do what is right in My eyes by keeping My statutes and commands, as David My servant did, I will be with you. I will build you a dynasty as enduring as the one I built for David and will give Yisrael to you. ³⁹ I will humble David's descendents because of this, but not for many days.*" 1 Kings (Melakim) 11:31-39.

  This was an incredible prophecy given to Jeroboam - an Ephraimite. The Scriptures record that Jeroboam was a mighty man of valour - he was a powerful man. Shlomo recognized this and placed him in charge of the whole labor force of the House of Yoseph, but Jeroboam rebelled against Shlomo. His people were being oppressed and YHWH chose Jeroboam to punish Shlomo. He also gave Jeroboam great promises if he would only do what Shlomo failed to do - be like David - obey and guard (shamar) the commands, walk in His ways and do what was right.[114]

  After the death of King Shlomo, the prophecy given by Ahiyah came to pass. The House of Yisrael, also known as the Northern Kingdom, petitioned Shlomo's son, King Rehoboam, essentially asking for tax relief. In the past, King Shlomo, had put a heavy burden on the people amassing great wealth and building mighty structures.

  Instead of taking the advice of the elders, Rehoboam took the advice of his young friends and

responded to the apparent reasonable request by stating: "*My father laid on you a heavy yoke; I will make it even heavier. My father scourged you with whips; I will scourge you with scorpions.*" 1 Kings (Melakim) 12:11.

His "unwise" response resulted in a split in the Kingdom of Yisrael. The House of Yisrael, which consisted of the Ten Northern Tribes, aligned with Jeroboam son of Nebat. The House of Yahudah, which consisted of the Southern Tribes, aligned with Rehoboam. While the House of Yahudah maintained the worship of YHWH in Jerusalem the Northern Tribes set up their own false worship system. Ironically, that is how things started to go bad for the House of Yisrael.

Apparently, Jeroboam feared that if the House of Yisrael continued to go to Jerusalem they would eventually join up with the House of Yahudah and reunite the Kingdom of Yisrael. This notion was unfounded, self serving and contrary to the promise given to him by YHWH. Therefore, after seeking some bad advice he set up pagan worship in the north.

"[26] *Jeroboam thought to himself, The kingdom will now likely revert to the house of David.* [27] *If these people go up to offer sacrifices at the temple of YHWH in Jerusalem, they will again give their allegiance to their master, Rehoboam king of Yahudah. They will kill me and return to King Rehoboam.* [28] *After seeking advice, the king made two golden calves.* He said to the people, 'It is too much for you to go up to Jerusalem. Here are your gods, O Yisrael, who brought you up out of Egypt.' [29] One he set up in Bethel, and the other in Dan. [30] And this thing became a sin; the people went even as far as Dan to worship the one there. [31] *Jeroboam built shrines on high places and appointed priests from all sorts of people, even though they were not Levites. ³² He instituted a festival on the fifteenth day of the eighth month, like the festival held in Yahudah, and offered sacrifices on the altar. This he did in Bethel, sacrificing to the calves he had made. And at Bethel he also installed priests at the high places he had made. ³³ On the fifteenth day of the eighth month, a month of his own choosing, he offered sacrifices on the altar he had built at Bethel. So he instituted the festival for the Yisraelites and went up to the altar to make offerings."* 1 Kings (Melakim) 12:26-33.

This is really quite incredible because Jereboam was already promised a perpetual throne like David's, if he would simply obey.

He was specifically given his kingdom as a direct result of the fact that Shlomo worshipped pagan gods, and set up "high places" for them to be worshipped. Now, instead of worshipping the gods of the neighboring tribes, he once again set up images of the Egyptian gods. He had previously sought refuge in Egypt after the prophecy given by Ahiyah. That is likely the reason for him choosing golden calves.

Instead of trusting the word of YHWH, he tried to hold onto power using his own intellect and setting up his own system of worship – in direct contravention to the ways of YHWH! Jeroboam not only established new places of worship, he also established different appointed times and set up a false priesthood.[115]

The sin of Jeroboam was even worse than the sin of his predecessors at Sinai. Despite warnings, Jeroboam refused to repent and therefore, as a result of this great sin, the House of Yisreal was scheduled for punishment. It was not a mystery that they would be punished,

Mosheh had told them long ago, but they apparently did not remember or they just did not care.

As you can probably imagine, not everyone in this new breakaway kingdom was pleased with the idolatry that was introduced by Jeroboam. While everyone must have surely appreciated the tax relief, they needed to choose whether the trade was worth it or not – they had a choice to make.

The Scriptures record the following: *"¹³ And from all their territories the priests and the Levites who were in all Yisrael took their stand with him. ¹⁴ <u>For the Levites left their common-lands and their possessions and came to Yahudah and Jerusalem, for Jeroboam and his sons had rejected them from serving as priests to YHWH.</u> ¹⁵ Then he appointed for himself priests for the high places, for the goat and the calf idols which he had made. ¹⁶ <u>And after them, those from all the tribes of Yisrael, such as set their heart to seek YHWH Elohim of Yisrael, came to Jerusalem to sacrifice to YHWH Elohim of their fathers. ¹⁷ So they strengthened the kingdom of Yahudah,</u> and made Rehoboam the son of Shlomo strong for three years, because they walked in the way of David and Shlomo for three years."* 2 Chronicles 11:13-17

So we see that at least the Levites from the Northern Kingdom left and went to dwell with Yahudah. While others from the Northern Kingdom *"came to Jerusalem to sacrifice"* we do not know for sure if they moved there. We can safely assume from the language that the statement: *"they strengthened the kingdom of Yahudah"* means that they were added to the kingdom by moving to Judea. Therefore, the Southern Kingdom was a mixture of all of the tribes, although primarily Yahudah, Benyamin and Levi.

As we read from Scriptures, neither king followed good advice and both kingdoms ended up falling away from YHWH. As a result of their sins, both

kingdoms ended up receiving the promised curses of YHWH, which are found within the Torah.

Since they were divided and acting independently of one another, YHWH treated them differently. They committed different sins and were given different punishments. The House of Yisrael would be punished first, while the House of Yahudah staved off judgment as they traversed in and out of idolatry throughout the succession of many kings. Both ended up suffering the judgment foretold by Mosheh, which was expulsion from the Land.

10

Out of Yisrael

The Kingdom of Yisrael was divided after the reign of only two kings. The Ten Northern Tribes, known as the House of Yisrael, split from the Kingdom and developed their own unique form of worship derived from Egypt. The Scriptures reveal that the Southern Tribes, known as the House of Yahudah also strayed from YHWH and chased after foreign gods.

The House of Yisrael toyed with the calendar and the Appointed Times, which ultimately led to their demise. They made the same mistake as their ancestors at Sinai, only they multiplied the sin. The first king of the House of Yisrael was Jeroboam I, and he actually ordained a festival in Month 8 exactly one month after the Festival ordained by YHWH in Month 7. According to 1 Melakim 12:32-33, he also set up golden calves and sacrificed to them on an altar that he made at Bethel on Day 15 of Month 8.

The House of Yisrael continued 209 years until they were completely removed from the Land of Yisrael by the Assyrians through 5 successive captivities that occurred between 723 BCE and 714 BCE.* They have been in exile ever since that time.[116]

The House of Yahudah ended up falling into paganism, but in a different way. They built booths on the Temple Mount and mixed the worship of false gods

with the worship of YHWH. They turned the Temple Mount into a veritable Pantheon. The Prophets Ezekiel (Yehezqel)[117] and Yirmeyahu describe the abominations they committed. They set up pagan statues and images; they made cakes and burned incense to "The Queen of Heaven;" they poured out drink offerings to pagan gods; they participated in the pagan practice of "weeping for Tammuz" and they prayed to the sun. All of this conduct traces straight back to Babylon.

Let us read what the prophets exposed regarding the House of Yahudah.

"*¹ And it came to pass in the sixth year, in the sixth month, on the fifth day of the month, as I sat in my house with the elders of Yahudah sitting before me, that the hand of the Master YHWH fell upon me there. ² Then I looked, and there was a likeness, like the appearance of fire - from the appearance of His waist and downward, fire; and from His waist and upward, like the appearance of brightness, like the color of amber. ³ He stretched out the form of a hand, and took me by a lock of my hair; and the Spirit lifted me up between earth and heaven, and brought me in visions of Elohim to Jerusalem, to the door of the north gate of the inner court, where the seat of the image of jealousy was, which provokes to jealousy. ⁴ And behold, the glory of the Elohim of Yisrael was there, like the vision that I saw in the plain. ⁵ Then He said to me, 'Son of man, lift your eyes now toward the north.' So I lifted my eyes toward the north, and there, <u>north of the altar gate, was this image of jealousy in the entrance.</u> ⁶ Furthermore He said to me, 'Son of man, do you see what they are doing, the great abominations that the House of Yisrael commits here, to make Me go far away from My sanctuary? Now turn again, you will see greater abominations.' ⁷ So He brought me to* the door of the court; and when I looked, there was a hole in the wall. ⁸ Then He said to me, 'Son of man, dig into the wall' and when I dug into the wall, there was a door. ⁹ And He said to me, 'Go in, and see the wicked abominations which they are doing there.' ¹⁰ <u>So I went in and saw, and there - every sort of creeping thing, abominable beasts, and all the idols of the House of Yisrael, portrayed all around on the walls.</u> ¹¹ And there stood before them seventy men of the elders of the House of Yisrael, and in their midst stood Jaazaniah the son of Shaphan. Each man had a censer in his hand, and a thick cloud of incense went up. ¹² Then He said to me, '<u>Son of man, have you seen what the elders of the House of Yisrael do in the dark, every man in the room of his idols</u>? For they say, 'YHWH does not see us, YHWH has forsaken the land. ¹³ And He said to me, 'Turn again, and you will see greater abominations that they are doing.' ¹⁴ So He brought me to the door of the north gate of YHWH's House; and to my dismay, women were sitting there weeping for Tammuz. ¹⁵

Then He said to me, 'Have you seen this, O son of man? Turn again, you will see greater abominations than these.' ¹⁶ So He brought me into the inner court of YHWH's House; and there, at the door of the Temple of YHWH, between the porch and the altar, were about twenty-five men with their backs toward the Temple of YHWH and their faces toward the east, and they were worshiping the sun toward the east. ¹⁷

And He said to me, 'Have you seen this, O son of man? Is it a trivial thing to the House of Yahudah to commit the abominations which they commit here? For they have filled the Land with violence; then they have returned to provoke Me to anger. Indeed they put the branch to their nose. ¹⁸ Therefore I also will act in fury. My eye will not spare nor will I have pity; and

though they cry in My ears with a loud voice, I will not hear them.'" Yehezqel 8:1-18.

Of particular note is the specificity involving the date of the prophecy. These dates are given to reveal that YHWH is very concerned about time, as His people should be. Yehezqel knew what time it was on the Creator's Calendar and so should we. The people had lost touch with time and with YHWH. All of the deeds of the House of Yisrael and Yahudah were seen, exposed and revealed by YHWH. Their deeds resulted in angering YHWH.

Read the warnings given by Yirmeyahu:

"¹ The word that came to Yirmeyahu from YHWH, saying, ² Stand in the gate of YHWH's House, and proclaim there this word, and say, 'Hear the word of YHWH, all you of Yahudah who enter in at these gates to worship YHWH!' ³ Thus says YHWH of hosts, the Elohim of Yisrael: 'Amend your ways and your doings, and I will cause you to dwell in this place. ⁴ Do not trust in these lying words, saying, The Temple of YHWH, the Temple of YHWH, the Temple of YHWH are these. ⁵ For if you thoroughly amend your ways and your doings, if you thoroughly execute judgment between a man and his neighbor, ⁶ if you do not oppress the stranger, the fatherless, and the widow, and do not shed innocent blood in this place, or walk after other gods to your hurt, ⁷ then I will cause you to dwell in this place, in the Land that I gave to your fathers throughout the ages and to eternity. ⁸ Behold, you trust in lying words that cannot profit. ⁹ Will you steal, murder, commit adultery, swear falsely, <u>burn incense to Baal, and walk after other gods whom you do not know</u>, ¹⁰ and then come and stand before Me in this house which is called by My Name, and say, 'We are delivered to do all these abominations?' ¹¹ Has this House, which is called by My Name, become a den of thieves in your eyes? Behold, I, even I, have seen it," says YHWH. ¹² But go now to My place which was in Shiloh,

where I set My Name at the first, and see what I did to it because of the wickedness of My people Yisrael. [13] And now, because you have done all these works," says YHWH, and I spoke to you, rising up early and speaking, but you did not hear, and I called you, but you did not answer, [14] therefore I will do to the House which is called by My Name, in which you trust, and to this place which I gave to you and your fathers, as I have done to Shiloh. [15] And I will cast you out of My sight, as I have cast out all your brethren - the whole posterity of Ephraim. [16] Therefore do not pray for this people, nor lift up a cry or prayer for them, nor make intercession to Me; for I will not hear you. [17] Do you not see what they do in the cities of Yahudah and in the streets of Jerusalem? [18] <u>The children gather wood, the fathers kindle the fire, and the women knead dough, to make cakes for the queen of heaven; and they pour out drink offerings to other gods</u>, that they may provoke Me to anger. [19] Do they provoke Me to anger? says YHWH. Do they not provoke themselves, to the shame of their own faces? [20] Therefore thus says the the Master YHWH: Behold, My anger and My fury will be poured out on this place - on man and on beast, on the trees of the field and on the fruit of the ground. And it will burn and not be quenched. [21] Thus says YHWH of hosts, the Elohim of Yisrael: Add your burnt offerings to your sacrifices and eat meat. [22] For I did not speak to your fathers, or command them in the day that I brought them out of the land of Egypt, concerning burnt offerings or sacrifices. [23] But this is what I commanded them, saying, <u>Obey My voice, and I will be your Elohim, and you shall be My people. And walk in all the ways that I have commanded you, that it may be well with you.</u> [24] Yet they did not obey or incline their ear, but followed the counsels and the dictates of their evil hearts, and went backward and not forward. [25] Since the day that your fathers came out of the land of Egypt until this day, I have even sent to you all My servants the prophets, daily rising up early and sending them. [26] Yet

they did not obey Me or incline their ear, but stiffened their neck. They did worse than their fathers. ²⁷ Therefore you shall speak all these words to them, but they will not obey you. You shall also call to them, but they will not answer you. ²⁸ So you shall say to them, <u>This is a nation that does not obey the voice of YHWH their Elohim nor receive correction. Truth has perished and has been cut off from their mouth.</u> ²⁹ Cut off your hair and cast it away, and take up a lamentation on the desolate heights; for YHWH has rejected and forsaken the generation of His wrath. ³⁰ <u>For the children of Yahudah have done evil in My sight, says YHWH. They have set their abominations in the House which is called by My Name, to pollute it.</u> ³¹ <u>And they have built the high places of Tophet, which is in the Valley of the Son of Hinnom, to burn their sons and their daughters in the fire, which I did not command, nor did it come into My heart.</u> ³² Therefore behold, the days are coming, says YHWH, when it will no more be called Tophet, or the Valley of the Son of Hinnom, but the Valley of Slaughter; for they will bury in Tophet until there is no room. ³³ The corpses of this people will be food for the birds of the heaven and for the beasts of the earth. And no one will frighten them away. ³⁴ Then I will cause to cease from the cities of Yahudah and from the streets of Jerusalem the voice of mirth and the voice of gladness, the voice of the bridegroom and the voice of the bride. For the land shall be desolate." Yirmeyahu 7:1-34.

The House of Yahudah was supposed to learn from what happened to the Northern Tribes – the House of Yisrael. They were supposed to turn away from their wicked ways, and turn back to YHWH. They placed their trust in the Temple building instead of the One Who dwelled therein. Despite these warnings, the people remained defiant. They refused to obey the commandments of YHWH. They continued

to worship other gods. They burned incense to the pagan gods and baked cakes to the "queen of heaven" and poured out drink offerings to her. (See Yirmeyahu 44).

As was previously mentioned, the title "Queen of Heaven" was taken on by Semiramis, also known as Ishtar in Babylon. This fertility goddess was known as Astarte in Canaan, and is currently recognized as Easter in most of the world today. So the House of Yahudah was involved in Babylonian sun worship, and they were doing it in the exact place they were supposed to be worshipping YHWH. They were mixing their worship. They were going to "The House of the Lord" as many Christians do today, but they were involved in Babylonian sun worship.

A person may be shocked to read about such conduct, and bewildered at how these people could so blatantly violate the commandments of YHWH. Your first impression might be to assume that they were willfully and defiantly rebelling against YHWH, but that might not be correct.

Often times, the decline is slow and unrecognizeable. People are prone to compromise the truth, especially when it occurs in small increments extended over time. So these people might have inherited many false traditions over the years, unwittingly believing that they were perfectly acceptable.

When a prophet would appear and tell them to repent, they could barely comprehend what he or she was saying. They had become so deluded and blinded by their traditions, which had become so ingrained, that they could not discern the difference between their traditions and the truth. We will soon see that this is exactly the condition of many people in modern society who believe that they are following truth, when they are actually following lies that are leading them away from the

Garden and straight to Gehenna.[118]

The House of Yahudah failed to heed the warnings and also fell away from YHWH. After lasting 324 years, the House of Yahudah was almost completely removed from the Land by the Babylonians through 7 successive captivities that occurred between 618 BCE and 595 BCE.* Those who were exiled to Babylon, in the last captivity in 595 BCE, remained in captivity for a period of seventy years. While in Babylon, the House of Yahudah developed many traditions and even came out with a new language.[119]

They gave names to each month – something YHWH never commanded them to do. They even named the fourth month Tammuz! This was the same Tammuz that originated in Babylon, and this name for month 4 is used by some in Judaism to this very day. Tammuz was the son of Nimrod and Semaramis. He is part of trinitarian sun worship and because of that fact, it is highly inappropriate and even blasphemous to give the fourth Scriptural month that name.[120]

So even after being punished for their Babylonian activities by Neo-Babylon, the House of Yahudah continued to pay homage to their "sun god" by naming a month after him. But we are getting ahead of ourselves, because it is important to spend more time looking at the different exiles experienced by this divided Kingdom, this divided and fractured Bride of YHWH.

As a result of the various abominations of Yisrael and Yahudah - both Houses were removed from the Land and were disbursed throughout the world. Since they wanted to worship like pagans, they were scattered

throughout pagan cultures. YHWH was not going to let them commit these acts in His Land, and in His House. No Husband would knowingly allow his wife to commit adultery in their marital home, or in their marriage bed.

So through 12 combined exiles, the Yisraelites were taken out of the Land. All of the House of Yisrael was removed. They were scattered throughout the earth, at the height of the Assyrian Empire. So we see the House of Yisrael being dispersed throughout Assyria between 723 - 714 BCE. By 624 BCE the Assyrian Empire had been conquered by the Babylonians. You can read about the removal of the House of Yisrael in 2 Melakim 17.

The exile of the House of Yahudah was a bit different. They were attacked and exiled by the 10th Dynasty of Babylon - sometimes referred to as "New" Babylon, or "Neo" Babylon. Not everyone was removed. Those who remained were called "bad figs" by YHWH. The "good figs" were the ones removed, and taken to Babylon. They would be allowed to return after an exile of between 70 - 93 years. The nation that removed them would also eventually be punished by YHWH and come to an end.

In fact, the Kingdom of Babylon came to an end on the very night the Babylonians were feasting and profaning the Set Apart objects from the House of YHWH. Once again, if you want to anger YHWH, just mix the things that He considers set apart, with the things that He considers profane. This is what the House of Yisrael had done, followed by the House of Yahudah. Their actions resulted in punishment, and now Babylon would be punished as was previously prophesied by Yirmeyahu.

It was the Prophet Daniel, who was in exile in Babylon, who actually interpreted the handwriting on

the wall concerning that judgment. As a result, Daniel was immediately elevated as the third highest in the Kingdom of Babylon. The reason why he was the third, was because Nabonidus and his son, Belshazzar, were co-regents at that time. They shared the rulership of the Kingdom of Babylon.

Daniel's promotion in the Babylonian Kingdom only lasted for a couple of hours. For on the very same night the handwriting on the wall appeared, Cyrus the Great of Medo-Persia conquered Babylon and Belshazzar was slain according to Daniel 5:30-31. *"³⁰ That very night Belshazzar, king of the Chaldeans, was slain. ³¹ And Darius the Mede received the kingdom, being about sixty-two years old."*

It is recorded in Herodotus 1/191 that Babylon was taken by surprise when the Babylonians were feasting. The Medo-Persians stealthily gained access to the city of Babylon and were able to literally open the city gates from within the city. This fulfilled the prophecy of Yeshayahu 45:1-7.

"¹ Thus says YHWH to His anointed, to Cyrus, whose right hand I have held - to subdue nations before him and loose the armor of kings, to open before him the double doors, so that the gates will not be shut: ² I will go before you and make the crooked places straight; I will break in pieces the gates of bronze and cut the bars of iron. ³ I will give you the treasures of darkness and hidden riches of secret places, that you may know that I, YHWH, Who call you by your name, Am the Elohim of Yisrael. ⁴ For Yaakob My servant's sake, and Yisrael My elect, I have even called you by your name; I have named you, though you have not known Me. ⁵ I am YHWH, and there is no other; There is no Elohim besides Me. I will gird you, though you have not known Me, ⁶ That they may know from the rising of the sun to its setting that there is none besides Me. I am YHWH, and there is no other; ⁷ I form

the light and create darkness, I make peace and create calamity; I, YHWH, do all these things."

Daniel became a favored court official of Cyrus the Great, and was then made overseer of the entire Kingdom of Babylon. This angered some of Daniel's colleagues who conspired to have him thrown into the lion's den. But Daniel survived, and Cyrus the Great praised and extolled the Name of YHWH Elohim.

Daniel understood when Babylon was conquered in 541 BCE that it fulfilled the 70 year prophecy of Yirmeyahu 25:11-12. Daniel knew this in 540 BCE in the first year of Cyrus the Great as King of Babylon. *"[1] In the first year of Darius the son of Ahasuerus, of the lineage of the Medes, who was made king over the realm of the Chaldeans - [2] in the first year of his reign I, Daniel, understood by the scrolls the number of the years specified by the Word of YHWH through Yirmeyahu the prophet, that He would accomplish seventy years in the desolations of Jerusalem."* Daniel 9:1-2.

All of these events were perfectly timed, and precision is something very important to YHWH. Daniel knew this, and that is why he was focused on the return of Yahudah, among other historical events. We will examine his life as it relates to some very specific and important times in the plan of YHWH.

11

Daniel

Daniel was a very unique and interesting individual. In fact, the book of Daniel is unique from all of the other texts in the Tanak. While it is filled with prophecies, in the Hebrew Scriptures it is generally included with The Writings. In most modern editions of the Scriptures, it is located in The Prophets. Therefore, this rich text straddles both The Writings and The Prophets.

Daniel was from the Southern Kingdom, the House of Yahudah, which was conquered by the Babylonians. The beginning of the text of Daniel tells how Daniel was taken as a young man in the first Babylonian captivity in 618 BCE. Read the following account at the beginning of text:

"[1] *In the third year of the reign of Jehoiakim king of Yahudah, Nebuchadnezzar king of Babylon came to Jerusalem and besieged it.* [2] *And YHWH gave Jehoiakim king of Yahudah into his hand, with some of the articles of the House of Elohim, which he carried into the land of Shinar to the house of his god; and he brought the articles into the treasure house of his god.* [3] *Then the king instructed Ashpenaz, the master of his eunuchs, to bring some of the children of Yisrael and some of the king's descendents and some of the nobles,* [4] *young men in whom there was no blemish, but good-looking, gifted in all wisdom, possessing knowledge and quick to understand, who had ability to serve in the king's palace, and whom they might* teach the language and literature of the Chaldeans. ⁵ And the king appointed for them a daily provision of the king's delicacies and of the wine which he drank, and three years of training for them, so that at the end of that time they might serve before the king. ⁶ Among these were some from Yahudah: Daniel, Hananiah, Mishael and Azariah. ⁷ The chief official gave them new names: to Daniel, the name Belteshazzar; to Hananiah, Shadrach; to Mishael, Meshach; and to Azariah, Abednego." Daniel 1:1-7.

Daniel was from the tribe of Yahudah and descended from nobility. It is important to remember that Daniel was taken into captivity by the Babylonians about 100 years after the northern Kingdom of Yisrael had been taken in the Assyrian captivity. The House of Yahudah was also found to be unfaithful, and the prophet Yirmeyahu prophesied the following: "¹¹ this whole Land shall be a desolation and an astonishment, and these nations shall serve the king of Babylon seventy (70) years. ¹² Then it willcome to pass, when seventy (70) years are completed, that I will punish the king of Babylon and that nation, the land of the Chaldeans, for their iniquity, says YHWH; and I will make it a perpetual desolation." Yirmeyahu 25:11-12.

We have already mentioned this prophecy which concerned <u>the punishment of Babylon</u> after the passage of seventy (70) years. There was another seventy (70) year prophecy concerning <u>the return of Yahudah</u> after the passage of seventy (70) years. "For *thus says YHWH: After seventy (70) years are completed at Babylon, I will visit you and perform My good word toward you, and cause you to return to this place.*" Yirmeyahu 29:10.

These two prophecies are often considered to be the same, but they are not. They are two separate and distinct seventy (70) year prophecies. One deals with the punishment of Babylon, while the other deals with the return of the House of Yahudah from exile.

The Kingdom of Yahudah was indeed conquered by the Babylonian King Nebuchadnezzar after a series of sieges and exiles that culminated in the destruction of Jerusalem. The last three kings of the House of Yahudah were all taken captive including Jehoiakim, Jehoiachin and Zedekiah. Also, many of the royal family and nobility were forced into Nebuchadnezzar's service. Nebuchadnezzar conquered Yahudah over a period of twenty four (24) years, in which the people of Yahudah were taken captive at seven different times. In the very first captivity in 618 BCE*, four young men from Yahudah were taken named Daniel, Hananiah, Mishael and Azariah.

As previously mentioned, the Babylonian kingdom ruled by Nebuchadnezzar was not the same Babylon that was founded by Nimrod centuries earlier. Some scholars refer to this empire as the 10th Dynasty of Babylon, or the Neo Babylonian Empire. New or not, it still contained the same pagan roots as old Babylon.

Interestingly, the names of the four young Hebrew men mentioned in Daniel 1:6-7 all contained the Name of YHWH, or the title Elohim. These young Hebrew men were identified with the Mighty One Who they served. Once they entered into Babylon they became immersed in the pagan culture which included their food, their calendar, their language and their religion. The young men were even given new names attributed to the gods of the land.

The goal was to break the connection and remembrance of their Elohim, and assimilate them into the pagan culture. This is the underlying purpose of any system opposed to YHWH – to distract and draw people

away from the one True Elohim, particularly His Name and His Torah.

The name Daniel (𐤃𐤍𐤉𐤀𐤋) means: "El is my judge" in Hebrew. His new name Belteshazzar means: "Bel protects his life." Bel Marduk was originally the patron deity of the City of Babylon and eventually became the supreme deity of Babylonia, the sun god. Bel Marduk was credited with bringing order to an otherwise chaotic universe, and his exploits are described in the ancient text known as the Enuma Elish.

The name Haniniyah (𐤇𐤍𐤍𐤉𐤄) means: "Yah has favored" in Hebrew. His new name Shadrach means: "command of Aku." Aku was the Sumerian moon god. The name Mishael (𐤌𐤉𐤔𐤀𐤋) means: "Who is El" in Hebrew. His new name Meshach means: "Who is Aku" and it was clearly in direct opposition to his Hebrew name.

The name Azaryah (𐤏𐤆𐤓𐤉𐤄) means: "Yah has helped" in Hebrew. His new name Abednego means: "Servent of Nego." Nego, also known as Nebo and Nabu, was the Babylonian god of wisdom, and worshipped as the son of Marduk. Thus he was the "son of god" to the Babylonians. His mother was a moon goddess Sarpanit, often depicted as being pregnant, and is considered to be the same goddess as Easter (Ishtar).

So here we see the Babylonian Trinity with different names and attributes in Neo Babylon. Imagine being a Torah observant Yisraelite who serves YHWH, given a name exalting an abominable pagan god. Again, the objective was to snuff out the remembrance of the god of the captives, in this case YHWH, and enforce the worship of the victor's gods. It did not work.

Despite the fact that these individuals were captives, the Scriptures record that Daniel greatly excelled in Babylon. "[17] *As for these four young men, Elohim gave them knowledge and skill in all literature and wisdom; and Daniel had understanding in all visions and dreams. [18] Now at the end of the days, when the king had said that they should be brought in, the chief of the eunuchs brought them in before Nebuchadnezzar. [19] Then the king interviewed them, and among them all none was found like Daniel, Hananiah, Mishael, and Azariah; therefore they served before the king. [20] And in all matters of wisdom and understanding about which the king examined them, he found them ten times better than all the magicians and astrologers who were in all his realm. [21] Thus Daniel continued until the first year of King Cyrus."* Daniel 1:17-21.

In the tradition of Yoseph, Daniel was taken to a foreign power and served in the court of the King. He also had the ability to interpret dreams and visions, although in the case of Daniel – he was also able to tell the king what he had dreamed – not just interpret the dreams.

As a result of his skills, Daniel was greatly elevated in the Babylonian Empire. He experienced great favor, esteem and power. He was given the governorship of the province of Babylon, as well as the head-inspectorship of the sacerdotal caste, which consisted of the scholars, educators and scientists, including the astrologers, astronomers, magicians, sorcerers, priests and the like, also known as Magi or wise men.

Later, after Cyrus the Great conquered the Babylonians, Daniel continued his administratorship in the Medo-Persian Empire as well. In fact, Daniel continued his career as a court official until the first of King Cyrus, who was the first king of the Persian Empire as just mentioned in Daniel 1:21. He was given the unique responsibility of being the principal administrator of three world empires - not something many people can put on their resume. One of the titles

given to Daniel was Rab HarTumaya - the Chief of the Magicians. When he continued in this role, a Hebrew from nobility functioning in a traditional hereditary Median priesthood, it resulted in the plot which got him thrown in the lion's den from which he was miraculously delivered. (see Daniel 6).

Daniel was immersed in a culture that worshipped gods, and sons of gods, and he was actually in charge of the pagan priests. Again, this is very similar to what we saw with Yoseph. These patriarchs did not try to change the cultures in which they lived, yet they remained true to their principles. Daniel, and some of his fellow Yahudim, however, stand out in that they set themselves apart from the pagans who surrounded them.

A good example of that can be found in the incident involving Daniel being thrown into the Lion's Den. Daniel had refused to stop openly petitioning YHWH despite an edict signed by King Darius. He was supposed to be eaten by the lions, but YHWH protected him and he was not harmed. (see Daniel 6).

In another instance, Shadrach, Meshach and Abednego refused to worship the idol of gold set up by the King. They were thrown into a blazing furnace, but they too survived unharmed. Their testimony to the King was as follows:

"^{16} O Nebuchadnezzar, we do not need to defend ourselves before you in this matter. ^{17} If we are thrown into the blazing furnace, the Elohim we serve is able to save us from it, and He will rescue us from your hand, O king. ^{18} But even if He does not, we want you to know, O king, that we will not serve your gods or worship the image of gold you have set up." Daniel 3:16-18.

The three were thrown in the fire, but they were not harmed. A fourth figure appeared in the fire and the King proclaimed: "Look . . . I see four men loose, walking in the midst of the fire; and they are not hurt, and the form of the fourth is like the Son of Elohim." Daniel 3:25.

As a result of this event, the King exalted Shadrach, Meshach and Adednego as well as their Elohim. There was no other Elohim that could deliver from fire. While YHWH once judged the planet by water, He will one day judge by fire. Only YHWH will be able to deliver His people from the fiery judgment that is soon coming upon this planet. (Yeshayahu 66).

Along with the recognition and elevation of YHWH in the Babylonian Kingdom, it must have been known that there was a seventy (70) year judgment pronounced over the King of Babylon that was looming on the horizon. This leads to another significant event previously mentioned involving the Babylonian King named Belshazzar, who reigned during that period of time when the punishment was scheduled to occur.

For many years scholars could not confirm the existence of any such King in the Babylonian records. "It was not until 1853 CE that archaeological evidence was unearthed which indicated that Belshazzar was a co-regent and son of Nabonidus. Nabonidus was considered to be reigning alone as the last king of Babylon by secular historians until that time. This find, a small tablet currently located in the Yale Babylonian collection, provided archaeological evidence for the story of Belshazzar in Daniel 5:1-31.

Belshazzar was made co-regent of his father Nabonidus in the third year of Nabonidus. Father and son ruled together until Babylon was conquered by the Medo-Persian empire. Nabonidus ruled from Tema as King, while Belshazzar ruled from Babylon as a crown

prince. This perfectly agrees with the account in Daniel 5:16 where Belshazzar offered to make Daniel the third highest ruler in the Kingdom if he could interpret the writing on the wall."[121]

With that understanding, let us examine the incident. "*[1] King Belshazzar gave a great banquet for a thousand of his nobles and drank wine with them. [2] While Belshazzar was drinking his wine, he gave orders to bring in the gold and silver goblets that Nebuchadnezzar his father had taken from the Temple in Jerusalem, so that the king and his nobles, his wives and his concubines might drink from them. [3] So they brought in the gold goblets that had been taken from the temple of Elohim in Jerusalem, and the king and his nobles, his wives and his concubines drank from them. [4] As they drank the wine, they praised the gods of gold and silver, of bronze, iron, wood and stone. [5] Suddenly the fingers of a man's hand appeared and wrote on the plaster of the wall, near the lampstand in the royal palace. The king watched the hand as it wrote. [6] His face turned pale and he was so frightened that his knees knocked together and his legs gave way.*" Daniel 5:1-6.

The banquet being described was a huge affair with a very specific purpose. It seems quite apparent that the purpose of this feast was to defy the Elohim of Yisrael. Not only were the implements of the Temple profaned, false gods were praised while the implements were being used. Interestingly, the predecessors of Belshazzar had a healthy respect for YHWH, a lesson he should have learned.

This was made abundantly clear when Daniel was eventually called to interpret the handwriting, after no one else in the Kingdom was able to do so. Here is what he told the King: "*[18] O king, the Most High Elah gave your father Nebuchadnezzar sovereignty and greatness and glory and splendor. [19] Because of the high position He gave him, all the peoples and nations and men of every language dreaded and* feared him. Those the king wanted to put to death, he put to death; those he wanted to spare, he spared; those he wanted to promote, he promoted; and those he wanted to humble, he humbled. ²⁰ But when his heart became arrogant and hardened with pride, he was deposed from his royal throne and stripped of his glory. ²¹ He was driven away from people and given the mind of an animal; he lived with the wild donkeys and ate grass like cattle; and his body was drenched with the dew of heaven, until he acknowledged that the Most High Elah is sovereign over the kingdoms of men and sets over them anyone He wishes. ²² But you his son, O Belshazzar, have not humbled yourself, though you knew all this. ²³ Instead, you have set yourself up against the Master of heaven. You had the goblets from His Temple brought to you, and you and your nobles, your wives and your concubines drank wine from them. You praised the gods of silver and gold, of bronze, iron, wood and stone, which cannot see or hear or understand. But you did not honor the Elohim who holds in His Hand your life and all your ways. ²⁴ Therefore He sent the Hand that wrote the inscription. ²⁵ This is the inscription that was written: MENE, MENE, TEKEL, PARSIN. ²⁶ This is what these words mean: Mene: Elohim has numbered the days of your reign and brought it to an end. ²⁷ Tekel: You have been weighed on the scales and found wanting. ²⁸ Peres: Your kingdom is divided and given to the Medes and Persians. ²⁹ Then at Belshazzar's command, Daniel was clothed in purple, a gold chain was placed around his neck, and he was proclaimed the third highest ruler in the kingdom. ³⁰ That very night Belshazzar, king of the Babylonians, was slain, ³¹ and Darius the Mede took over the kingdom, at the age of sixty- two." Daniel 5:18-31.

It appears that Belshazzar might have been holding this particular feast because he believed that the seventy (70) year prophecy of Yirmeyahu 29:10 had not been fulfilled. This prophecy stated that after seventy (70) years of captivity for Yahudah were accomplished,

YHWH would cause Yahudah to return to Jerusalem. Belshazzar determined that this prophecy had not been fulfilled, and thereby decided there was no reason to fear YHWH.

However, YHWH never had any intention of fulfilling the prophecy of Yirmeyahu 29:10 at this time. Rather, it was the design of YHWH to fulfill the prophecy of Yirmeyahu 25:12-14 in which, after seventy (70) years of Yahudah's captivity, YHWH would punish Babylon.[122]

While much of the focus of Scriptures and prophecy involves Yisrael, it must be understood that all nations and people will be judged by YHWH for their conduct. YHWH does not condone the actions of the pagan nations such as Egypt and Babylon. While He may use them to effect His will, they will ultimately receive punishment for their deeds. This is the focus of the Book of Revelation, when final judgment is rendered upon the nations of the planet.

Now let us read what YHWH, through Yirmeyahu, specifically prophesied to Babylon: "*[12] When the seventy (70) years are fulfilled, I will punish the king of Babylon and his nation, the land of the Babylonians, for their guilt, declares YHWH, and will make it desolate throughout the ages. [13] I will bring upon that land all the things I have spoken against it, all that are written in this scroll and prophesied by Yirmeyahu against all the nations. [14] They themselves will be enslaved by many nations and great kings; I will repay them according to their deeds and the work of their hands."* Yirmeyahu 25:12-14.

The prophecy indicated that after Yahudah served for seventy (70) years, the King of Babylon would be punished. Since there were seven (7) different captivities which began in seven (7) different years over a twenty-four (24) year period, according to Daniel 1:1

and Yirmeyahu 52:30, there were several ways which YHWH could fulfill His word.

Belshazzar may not have been aware of the prophecy of Yirmeyahu 25:12-14, or he may have been applying an incorrect start date for the seventy (70) year prophecy. That prophecy was obviously fulfilled when Belshazzar was overthrown, and his defeat was directly related to punishment by YHWH on Nabonidus. This reveals how precise YHWH is concerning His times. Failure to understand His time can lead to serious consequences, particularly if you choose to defy His commandments.

At this point it should be clear that there were two distinct seventy (70) year prophecies given through Yirmeyahu. The one involving the punishment of Babylon was fulfilled after the interpretation of the handwriting by Daniel. The other, concerning the return of Yahudah, had obviously not yet occurred. As a result, we later read how Daniel pondered the matter of the second seventy (70) year prophecy.

He knew that the prophecy had been given, and therefore the matter should be discernable. He had witnessed the fulfillment of the first seventy (70) year prophecy, and he wanted to know when the second seventy (70) years would be concluded which would mark the end of the punishment of the House of Yahudah.

This is the hallmark of Daniel - time and the precise foreknowledge of the occurrence of important specific events. We read about his important inquiry concerning the seventy (70) years in Chapter 9 of the Book of Daniel which begins as follows: "[1] *In the first year of Darius son of Ahasuerus (a Mede by descent), who was made ruler over the Babylonian kingdom* [2] *in the first year of his reign, I, Daniel, understood from the Scriptures, according*

to the Word of YHWH given to Yirmeyahu the prophet, that the desolation of Jerusalem would last seventy years. ³ So I turned to YHWH Elohim and pleaded with Him in prayer and petition, in fasting, and in sackcloth and ashes." Daniel 9:1-3.

    The Medo-Persians were now in control of the Babylonian Kingdom. We are told that it was during the first year of Darius the Mede, son of Ahasuerus, that Daniel made this plea to YHWH. Daniel "understood" that what he had just observed was a fulfillment of Yirmeyahu's prophecy, and he wanted to know when his people would return. Daniel proceded to confess to YHWH, and acknowledge, that the punishments which beset his people were a direct result of their failure to obey the Torah of YHWH, and because of their failure to repent. Daniel then petitioned YHWH not to delay restoring His people and Jerusalem.

    Daniel recounts the following answer to his petition: "²⁰ Now while I was speaking, praying, and confessing my sin and the sin of my people Yisrael, and presenting my supplication before YHWH my Elohay for the set apart mountain of my Elohay, ²¹ Yes, while I was speaking in prayer, the man Gabriel, whom I had seen in the vision at the beginning, being caused to fly swiftly, reached me about the time of the evening offering. ²² And he informed me, and talked with me, and said, O Daniel, I have now come forth to give you skill to understand. ²³ At the beginning of your supplications the command went out, and I have come to tell you, for you are greatly beloved; therefore consider the matter, and understand the vision: ²⁴ Seventy weeks are determined for your people and for your set apart city, to finish the transgression, to make an end of sins, to make reconciliation for iniquity, to bring in the righteous ages, to seal up vision and prophecy, and to anoint the Most Set Apart. ²⁵ Know therefore and understand, that from the going forth of the command to restore and build Jerusalem until Messiah the Prince, there shall be seven weeks and sixty-two weeks; the street shall be built again, and the wall, even in troublesome times. ²⁶ And after the sixty-two weeks Messiah shall be cut off, but not for Himself; and the people of the prince who is to come shall destroy the city and the sanctuary. The end of it shall be with a flood, and till the end of the war desolations are determined. ²⁷ Then He shall confirm a covenant with many for one week; but in the middle of the week He shall bring an end to that which is perpetual. And on the wing of abominations shall be one who makes desolate, even until the consummation, which is determined, is poured out on the desolate." Daniel 9:20-27.

We know that the evening offering occurred immediately after sunset, so Daniel continued to offer up prayer and praise at this important time of day despite the absence of a Temple. When the messenger Gabriel appeared, he gave Daniel skill to understand. Then he provided Daniel, not only a time frame for the appearance of the Messiah, but a detailed list of items that the Messiah was to accomplish. This was intimately connected with the restoration of Jerusalem intended by YHWH.

He provided Daniel with a framework of seventy (70) "weeks" in which these matters would be concluded. In Hebrew we read shabuyim shabuyim (). If you took away all vowel markings these words are exactly the same. The text actually reads "seventy sevens." These periods of sevens are then further divided into seven "weeks," sixty two "weeks" and one "week" providing a total of seventy "weeks."

People have poured over these numbers for millennia wondering about their meaning. There are a variety of issues that need to be resolved to understand this passage, including the starting point. In other words, What was the command? Was it the command from YHWH to Gabriel to answer Daniel's petition or was it

the command from a man? Some other very important questions are: When did Daniel receive the prophecy? When was the first year of Darius son of Ahasuerus in Daniel 9:1? And when did the decree go forth to restore and build Jerusalem in Daniel 9:25?

Also how do we deal with these various periods of time? Are they the same lengths or are they different? It is generally understood that the "weeks" are seven (7) year periods, but if Gabriel had wanted to give Daniel a number of years he could have simply told him 49 years, 436 years and 7 years. He was obviously telling Daniel a mystery that needed skill to understand. What takes understanding is the fact that these seven year periods were not just arbitrary seven (7) year periods - some were likely Shemitah years, or Shemitah cycles.

The command concerning the Shemitah year is provided in the Torah. "*¹⁰ For six years you are to sow your fields and harvest the crops, ¹¹ but during the seventh year let the Land lie unplowed and unused. Then the poor among your people may get food from it, and the wild animals may eat what they leave. Do the same with your vineyard and your olive grove.*" Shemot 23:10-11 (see also Debarim 15).

Every seventh year the Yisraelites were supposed to let the Land rest. Thus, there was a Sabbath for the Land every seven years. Just as the seven day count began at creation, so too did the seven (7) year Shemitah count. The Shemitah year would begin on the first day of the seventh month on Yom Teruah, which marks the beginning of physical Creation. From this day until the following Yom Teruah there would be no official harvest.

This cycle of seven years is repeated seven times, and then a Jubilee Year is counted. These 50 years form the Jubilee Cycle. At the end of the seventh Shemitah year, there are 9 more days than the typical Civil Year

until Day 10 of Month 7, which is the Appointed Time of Yom Kippur - the Day of Atonement. A Civil Year typically begins on Day 1 of Month 7 in the first 49 years of the Jubilee Cycle, but in the 50th year, the Civil Year begins on Yom Kippur. This is the distinguishing feature of the Jubilee Year - it begins on Yom Kippur.

Amazingly, Yisrael failed to obey the command concerning the Shemitah year, and that was the reason why Yahudah was in exile for seventy (70) years. YHWH was giving His Land the rest that He commanded. (2 Chronicles 36:21).

These Shemitah cycles are intimately connected with, and determined by, the Jubilee Cycle. "^{3} For six years sow your fields, and for six years prune your vineyards and gather their crops. ^{4} But in the seventh year the Land is to have a Sabbath of rest, a Sabbath to YHWH. Do not sow your fields or prune your vineyards. ^{5} Do not reap what grows of itself or harvest the grapes of your untended vines. The Land is to have a year of rest. ^{6} Whatever the Land yields during the Sabbath year will be food for you - for yourself, your manservant and maidservant, and the hired worker and temporary resident who live among you, ^{7} as well as for your livestock and the wild animals in your land. Whatever the Land produces may be eaten. ^{8} Count off seven Sabbaths of years - seven times seven years - so that the seven Sabbaths of years amount to a period of forty-nine years. ^{9} Then have the shofar sounded everywhere on the tenth day of the seventh month; on the Day of Atonement sound the shofar throughout your Land. ^{10} Consecrate the fiftieth year and proclaim liberty throughout the land to all its inhabitants. It shall be a Jubilee for you; each one of you is to return to his family property and each to his own clan. ^{11} The fiftieth year shall be a Jubilee for you; do not sow and do not reap what grows of itself or harvest the untended vines. ^{12} For it is a Jubilee and is to be set apart for you; eat only what is taken directly from the fields."

Vayiqra 25:3-12.

The imagery of the Jubilee is reminiscent of the Feast of Shabuot, sometimes referred to as Pentecost. Shabuot involves this same count in days, and it occurs every year to remind us of the Jubilee. This is why it is critical to participate in, and observe the Appointed Times of YHWH if you desire to discern His times and His prophesied events.

With that foundation being laid, let us now look at various aspects of the seventy (70) week prophecy and see if we can discern just what and when Gabriel is referring to. First, we will view the information from the perspective that this is a purely Messianic prophecy, then we will look at another alternative.

From the information given to Daniel by Gabriel, we discern that there is a command issued "to restore and rebuild Jerusalem." We further know that from the issuance of that command until Messiah the prince shall be seven sevens and sixty two sevens. As previously mentioned, these sevens may actually be referring to Shemitah cycles. We are further told that "after *the sixty-two weeks Messiah shall be cut off, but not for Himself.*" Sometime after the Messiah is "cut off" the city and the Temple would be destroyed.

For the clock to begin, we need to look for the specific word or decree that was issued concerning restoring and rebuilding Jerusalem, not simply the Temple. This would obviously be linked with the end of the seventy (70) year period of exile, which was the very reason why Daniel was praying in the first place.

There is very specific information in the Scriptures concerning a governmental decree which seems to meet the criteria. We read in Ezra the following account:

"*¹ Now in the first year of Cyrus king of Persia,*

that the Word of YHWH by the mouth of Yirmeyahu might be fulfilled, YHWH stirred up the spirit of Cyrus king of Persia, so that he made a proclamation throughout all his kingdom, and also put it in writing, saying, ² 'Thus says Cyrus king of Persia: All the kingdoms of the Earth YHWH Elohim of heaven has given me. And He has commanded me to build Him a House at Jerusalem which is in Yahudah. ³ Who is among you of all His people? May his Elohim be with him, and let him go up to Jerusalem which is in Yahudah, and build the House of YHWH, Elohim of Yisrael (He is Elohim), which is in Jerusalem. ⁴ And whoever is left in any place where he dwells, let the men of his place help him with silver and gold, with goods and livestock, besides the freewill offerings for the House of Elohim which is in Jerusalem. ⁵ Then the heads of the fathers' Houses of Yahudah and Benjamin, and the priests and the Levites, with all whose spirits Elohim had moved, arose to go up and build the House of YHWH which is in Jerusalem. ⁶ And all those who were around them encouraged them with articles of silver and gold, with goods and livestock, and with precious things, besides all that was willingly offered. ⁷ King Cyrus also brought out the articles of the house of YHWH, which Nebuchadnezzar had taken from Jerusalem and put in the temple of his gods; ⁸ and Cyrus king of Persia brought them out by the hand of Mithredath the treasurer, and counted them out to Sheshbazzar the prince of Yahudah." Ezra 1:1-8.

  This decree of Cyrus to return and rebuild the House was issued in the first year of his reign. What an amazing event, the King of a pagan nation declared YHWH to be Elohim. He then took on the responsibility of rebuilding the House of YHWH,

returning all of the treasures which had been taken from the House and allowing the captives of Yahudah to return to their Land.

Notice that it was only those from the Tribes of Yahudah, Benjamin and the Levites who returned, because these were the Tribes that constituted the House of Yahudah which had been taken captive by the Babylonians. The other tribes from the House of Yisrael had been removed from the Land by the Assyrians, who moved them into the regions of the north. They were not scheduled to return to the Land as their punishment was not completed according to the prophet Yehezqel.[123]

The issuance of the decree of Cyrus was no doubt a wonderful part of the fulfillment of the second seventy (70) year prophecy which allowed the Yahudim to return. Regardless, they still had a long and difficult road ahead of them. Over time, the decree lost its force, until it was later found by Darius, the successor of Cyrus who reissued the decree and advanced funds to finish the House.

As a result of these different decrees and because of the funding problems, the rebuilding of the Altar and the Temple experienced great delays and was fraught with difficulties. Seventy years passed from the original decree to rebuild the Second Temple by Cyrus in 526 BCE,* to its completion under Darius in 456 BCE.* It was during this period that we read certain prophets such as Haggai and Zekaryah giving encouragement and direction to those who returned.

We know from historical records that while the original decree was given in the first year of Cyrus, there were numerous subsequent decrees that followed. So the question is which one of those decrees, if any, would start the count on Daniel's seventy weeks.

The answer is none, because all of them were tied

specifically with the Temple, but the decree we are looking for involved rebuilding Jerusalem. There was a decree that was issued after the Persians took control of the Medo-Persian Empire. This decree was issued by the Persian King Artaxerxes in the seventh year of his reign in 456 BCE. Here is the decree as provided in the text of Ezra.

"*7* Some of the children of Yisrael, including priests, Levites, singers, gatekeepers and Temple servants, also came up to Jerusalem in the seventh year of King Artaxerxes. *8* Ezra arrived in Jerusalem in the fifth month of the seventh year of the king. *9* He had begun his journey from Babylon on the first day of the first month, and he arrived in Jerusalem on the first day of the fifth month, for the gracious Hand of his Elohim was on him. *10* For Ezra had devoted himself to the study and observance of the Torah of YHWH, and to teaching its statutes and ordinances in Yisrael. *11* This is a copy of the letter King Artaxerxes had given to Ezra the priest and teacher, a man learned in the words of the commands and decrees of YHWH for Yisrael: *12* Artaxerxes, king of kings, To Ezra the priest, a teacher of the Torah of the Elah of heaven: Greetings. *13* Now I decree that any of the Yisraelites in my kingdom, including priests and Levites, who wish to go to Jerusalem with you, may go. *14* You are sent by the king and his seven advisers to inquire about Yahudah and Jerusalem with regard to the Torah of your Elah, which is in your hand. *15* Moreover, you are to take with you the silver and gold that the king and his advisers have freely given to the Elah of Yisrael, whose dwelling is in Jerusalem, *16* together with all the silver and gold you may obtain from the province of Babylon, as well as the freewill offerings of the people and priests for the Temple of their Elah in Jerusalem. *17*

With this money be sure to buy bulls, rams and male lambs, together with their grain offerings and drink offerings, and sacrifice them on the altar of the Temple of your Elah in Jerusalem. [18] You and your brother Yahudim may then do whatever seems best with the rest of the silver and gold, in accordance with the will of your Elah. [19] Deliver to the Elah of Jerusalem all the articles entrusted to you for worship in the Temple of your Elah. [20] And anything else needed for the Temple of your Elah that you may have occasion to supply, you may provide from the royal treasury. [21] Now I, King Artaxerxes, order all the treasurers of Trans-Euphrates to provide with diligence whatever Ezra the priest, a teacher of the Torah of the Elah of heaven, may ask of you - [22] up to a hundred talents of silver, a hundred cors of wheat, a hundred baths of wine, a hundred baths of olive oil, and salt without limit. [23] Whatever the Elah of heaven has prescribed, let it be done with diligence for the Temple of the Elah of heaven. Why should there be wrath against the realm of the king and of his sons? [24] You are also to know that you have no authority to impose taxes, tribute or duty on any of the priests, Levites, singers, gatekeepers, Temple servants or other workers at this house of Elah. [25] And you, Ezra, in accordance with the wisdom of your Elah, which you possess, appoint magistrates and judges to administer justice to all the people of Trans-Euphrates - all who know the laws of your Elah. And you are to teach any who do not know them. [26] Whoever does not obey the laws of your Elah and the law of the king must surely be punished by death, banishment, confiscation of property, or imprisonment." Ezra 7:7-26.

Despite the fact that the Temple had been rebuilt, and Ezra had returned with the Levitical priesthood to

reinstate the Temple service, problems soon besieged the new Jewish province. It was constantly under attack both politically and militarily. This is why we read about Nehemiah requesting help from Artexerxes 13 years later in 443 BCE. One day the King noticed that the countenance of Nehemiah, his cup bearer, was down and he inquired regarding the problem. Nehemiah responded concerning the difficulties that his people were experiencing in Jerusalem.

"*¹ And it came to pass in the month of Nisan, <u>in the twentieth year of King Artaxerxes</u>, when wine was before him, that I took the wine and gave it to the king. Now I had never been sad in his presence before. ² Therefore the king said to me, Why is your face sad, since you are not sick? This is nothing but sorrow of heart. So I became dreadfully afraid, ³ and said to the king, May the king live forever! Why should my face not be sad, when the city, the place of my fathers' tombs, lies waste, and its gates are burned with fire? ⁴ Then the king said to me, What do you request? So I prayed to the Elohim of heaven. ⁵ And I said to the king, If it pleases the king, and if your servant has found favor in your sight, <u>I ask that you send me to Yahudah, to the city of my fathers' tombs, that I may rebuild it</u>. ⁶ Then the king, with the queen sitting beside him, asked me, How long will your journey take, and when will you get back? It pleased the king to send me; so I set a time. ⁷ I also said to him, If it pleases the king, may I have letters to the governors of Trans-Euphrates, so that they will provide me safe-conduct until I arrive in Yahudah? ⁸ And may I have a letter to Asaph, keeper of the king's forest, so he will give me timber to make beams for the gates of the citadel by the Temple and for the city wall and for the residence I will occupy? And because the gracious hand of my Elohim was upon me, the king granted my requests. ⁹ So I went to the governors of Trans-Euphrates and gave them the king's letters. The king had also sent army officers and cavalry with me.*" Nehemiah 2:1-9.

From the decree to rebuild Jerusalem until Messiah the Prince, Daniel was told there would be seven (7) weeks and sixty-two (62) weeks (Daniel 9:25). "*^{25} Know and understand this: From the issuing of the decree to restore and rebuild Jerusalem until the Messiah the Prince, there will be seven sevens and sixty two sevens. It will be rebuilt with streets and a trench, but in times of trouble. ^{26} After the sixty-two sevens, the Anointed One will be cut off and will have nothing.*" Daniel 9:25-26.

The fact that these two divisions are mentioned separately could lead one to reasonably assume that they are different time periods. They could either be different measurements of time, or they simply might not be continuous.

Daniel was looking for the restoration of the City of Jerusalem, which obviously included the House of YHWH. He was asking about a literal rebuilding of the city, and he was given a literal time frame. This count historically began in the 20th year of Artaxerxes according to Nehemiah 2:1-8.

The double dated Elephantine Letters indicate that Artaxerxes began to reign over Egypt in 465 BCE.[124] However, Artaxerxes began to reign over the Persian Empire two years later in 463 BCE in the year that his father Xerxes died.

Therefore, the 20th year of Artexerxes would have been in 445 BCE as King of Egypt, or 443 BCE as King of the entire Persian Empire, and this would have been the time frame in which the count began.*

There have been a multitude of attempts to explain this prophecy since it was first given to Daniel. As historians and scholars have failed to perfectly understand the chronology of the Medo-Persian and Persian Empires, a solid historical foundation has not been laid from which to interpret the prophecy.

What can be said with certainty is that sixty-two (62) Shemitah cycles (62x7=434 years), with eight (8) intervening Jubilee years, covers a span of 442 civil years (434 years + 8 years = 442 years). All scholars would agree that 442 years, reckoned from the 20th of Artaxerxes in 443 BCE, would bring one to around the turn of the time when we would anticipate seeing the Messiah in 2 BCE.[125]

If we look at the prophecy in Daniel, we see that it states, "after *the sixty-two (62) weeks Moshiach will be cut off.*" Daniel 9:26. The Hebrew text uses the word "karath" (✕ ⳗ ⳉ) for "cut off." The word "karath" means "cut" or "covenant." Through the Prophets, YHWH revealed His plan to restore the Kingdom by His Servant, His Right Arm - the Messiah. The Covenant made with Abraham, and mediated by Mosheh at Sinai, had been broken by Yisrael.

Through the Covenant made with Abraham, we see that the One Who passed through the pieces was subject to the penalty of death. The death of that One would atone just as was shown through the pattern of Abraham and Yitshaq. YHWH would provide the Lamb, His only Son, who would be cut off during Passover.

After the Covenant made with Abraham was renewed by the blood of the Lamb – the Messiah – the prophetic patterns provided by the Levitical Priesthood and the Temple sacrifices had been fulfilled. As a result, the sacrifices and the offerings of the Levitical Priesthood ceased, in order to fulfill the prophecy in Daniel 9:27.

Therefore, the information given to Daniel was good news coupled with bad news. It started with a decree to return and rebuild, followed by the Messiah, but then the Messiah would be cut off and the City and

the Temple would be destroyed. Using a variety of methods of calculating this great mystery, we are repeatedly directed to not only the turn of a century, but also the turn of a millennium, and the beginning of a new age – the Age of the Messiah.

Armed with all of this information, we will now examine that time period leading up to the Age of the Messiah as described in Daniel. Interestingly, the Hebrew Scriptures are silent during this period of history, a very significant time before the Messiah was scheduled to appear. While we can read about the return of the House of Yahudah through the books of Ezra, Nehemiah and Esther and some of the Prophets, none reach into the time of Messiah as given to Daniel.

We can read in the texts known as the Maccabees,[126] of a time after the Persian kingdom had been defeated by another world power, but they do not shed any historical light into the time period that people would be looking for Messiah.

Interestingly, besides being told when the Messiah would come, Daniel was also shown the successive empires that would rule that region of the world – one of them being the Macedonian Empire under Alexander the Great.

Alexander is important because he is responsible for bringing about a transformation of the societies which he conquered. He essentially spread, merged and adapted pagan religions and cultures in a way never before done. To a certain extent, you could say that through his achievements, he was undoing what YHWH had done at Babylon. He was reconnecting the disbursed pagan cultures and unifying them through a common language, a common political system and a common religious system. This process was known as Hellenism.

12

Hellenism

As was already discussed, Daniel was a unique individual. He was alive and taken captive when the House of Yahudah was conquered by the Babylonians and removed from the Land. He was also alive when the Medo-Persians defeated the Babylonians, and he was alive when the Persians permitted the House of Yahudah to return to the Land.

Like Yoseph, he was forcibly brought to a great nation as a slave, and rose to power within that Empire. Both Yoseph and Daniel were given visions, and they both were able to interpret visions of the kings, which led to their success. The similarities between these two men are no coincidence, and they both have deep Messianic significance. Remember that the greatest achievement in Yoseph's rise was his ability to interpret dreams involving seven year periods.[127]

The life of Yoseph provides many patterns for the Messiah, while Daniel was unique because he was given specific dates concerning the coming of the Messiah. He lived to see world dominance transfer from the Babylonian Empire to the Medo-Persian Empire, and from the Medo-Persian Empire to the Persian Empire. And he was given a vision in which he saw the transfer of power from the Persian Empire to the Macedonian Empire. In his vision he saw the Macedonian Empire

divided into four smaller empires. He also saw the emergence of the Roman Empire – an empire that would influence the world right up until the second coming of the Messiah.

Here is the vision given to Daniel concerning future world powers to come. "⁵ . . . *suddenly a goat with a prominent horn between his eyes came from the west, crossing the whole earth without touching the ground.* ⁶ *He came toward the two-horned ram I had seen standing beside the canal and charged at him in great rage.* ⁷ *I saw him attack the ram furiously, striking the ram and shattering his two horns. The ram was powerless to stand against him; the goat knocked him to the ground and trampled on him, and none could rescue the ram from his power.* ⁸ *The goat became very great, but at the height of his power his large horn was broken off, and in its place four prominent horns grew up toward the four winds of heaven.*" Daniel 8:5-8.

The next world power in the vision given to Daniel was described as a goat, and the interpretation of the vision was, once again, given by Gabriel as follows: "²¹ *The he-goat is the king of Greece; and the great horn between his eyes is the first king.* ²² *As for the horn that was broken, in place of which four others arose, four kingdoms shall arise from his nation, but will not have the same power.*" Daniel 8:21-22.

The "he goat" was none other than Alexander the Great. Alexander was unique because of the profound impact that he had upon the cultures that he conquered. He did not simply defeat a population and dominate them, rather he merged them into the collective Grecian culture through a process called Hellenization.

As a result, a conquered people could continue to worship their own gods, and they would also be introduced to foreign gods. Sometimes similar gods would be merged, and what we see occurring is a sort of

reversal of what happened at Babel. Mankind was reuniting under a common language and unified pagan culture with a pantheon of gods.

Hellenism was the ultimate tolerant system because it embraced new and different religions, and included them under the umbrella of this new Grecian culture. Prior to Alexander there was no unified Greece. Rather, in the Mediterranean region, there were different city states which were each known as a polis. The people of these city states were unique, although they also had much in common. At times they would unify for a common purpose, such as a common enemy, while at other times they would fight among each other.

Alexander III was born at Pelia in the year 356 BCE. He was a Macedonian, the son of Philip II who was king, or rather Basileus, of Macedon. Alexander succeeded his father to the throne in 336 BCE at the age of 20 and died in Babylon in 323 BCE at the age of 32. In his brief 12 year reign, he managed to conquer and transform the civilized world as we know it. His father, Philip, had previously succeeded in uniting most of the mainland city states of Greece under Macedonian hegemony in the League of Corinth.  This set the stage for Alexander to lead the unified armies of this Grecian coalition after quelling various internal revolts. With this experienced army under his command, Alexander was able to conquer the Persian King Darius III and the entire Persian Empire at the Battle of Guagamela in 330 BCE.

While Alexander is considered to be one of the greatest military commanders in history, it was his impact upon culture that would have the most lasting and enduring legacy. While his father was clearly the

influence on his military abilities and accomplishments, it can be strongly argued that his mother, Olympias of Epirus, was responsible for his cultural impact.

While the Epirites descended from the same Hellenic tribes, they lived in smaller rural villages rather than the polis city states of the Southern Greeks. Religion was a powerful cultural force for the Epirites with Zeus at the center of it all. The religious impact of Epirus was significant due to the presence of the shrine and the oracle of Dodona, which was regarded as second only to the oracle at Delphi.

It is important to understand that the so-called Greek gods were derived from various fables, myths and stories which were quite varied, and they lack any degree of uniformity. There were numerous gods and goddesses all with different origins and characteristics. One such god with varied and mixed historical accounts was Dionysus.

Olympias was "said to be a priestess of Dionysus who led her followers in orgiastic rites in which snakes apparently played a major part. One ancient author wrote of her habit of taking tame snakes out of baskets of ivy and 'allowing them to curl themselves around the thyrsis of the woman so as to terrify the men.' It is said that Phillip eventually became so nervous about his wife's religious observances that his affection cooled, and he 'seldom came to sleep with her.'"[128]

Some believe that Dionysus was a late arrival into Greek mythology due to the minimal references by Homer, and his absence from the Olympian Pantheon. Nevertheless, his worhip was quite influential in the Greek culture, especially when he became the patron god of the theater, which

likely boosted his popularity and influence. Also, the fact that his worship was closely linked to wine and drunkenness did not hurt his appeal.

Dionysus was considered to be the son of Zeus. Zeus was the chief god in the Greek pantheon and his mother was a mortal woman named Semele. Thus Dionysus was a son of god, born from a mortal woman. He was associated with fertility rites and particularly wine. He was later morphed into the Roman god Bacchus, who is displayed as dying on a cross. Adherents to Dionysian worship would become intoxicated and partake in sexual orgies. "Dionysus was a savior god who . . . died and rose from the dead. The Dionysians believed in rewards in Heaven and punishments in Hell. They believed in salvation through repentance and baptism for the remission of sins. They practiced the rituals of communion and baptism."[129]

Alexander was inspired by the writings of Homer, and we see that these writings became a framework for the Hellenistic religious systems, as well as later writers such as Plutarch, who wrote about The Contendings of Horus and Seth. Many older myths were morphed and renamed into Hellenism, and of course this is at the core of Hellenistic culture – "The Collective."

Thus Hellenization involved a blending of Grecian culture with other cultures in the middle and near east. A major part of the Grecian culture which was spread included their pagan system of worship, and it was through this syncretism that the Canaanite god Baal, the Egyptian god Amon, and the Persian god Ahura Mazda became identified with the Greek sun god Zeus and the Roman sun god Jupiter. Likewise, the Canaanite goddess Astarte (also known as Easter) and the Persian goddess Anahita (also known as Anaitis) became identified with the Greek goddess Aphrodite or the

Roman goddess Venus. Through this blending process, many similarities developed between the gods and goddesses of the pagan cultures, parallels developed which led to continuity and consistency. What eventually emerged was a religious melting pot with religious tolerance and general acceptance of all gods. This was essentially a unification of the Babylonian hybrid religions that had previously been scattered throughout the world.

Because of Alexander's affection for Homer and the popular mythologies, his invasion of Asia minor was considered to be another Trojan War. "[T]he first thing Alexander did at Troy was to pay an act of homage to Achilles, who was initially his heroic prototype. Later, Heracles, a hero who became a god in virtue of his achievements, filled this role. Alexander was also connected to Dionysus, whom the Greeks believed came from Asia and who became 'the god' of the Greek expansion into the middle east, receiving the greatest amount of personal devotion in the Hellenistic kingdoms. Alexander held a Dionysiac celebration at Nysa where, according to tradition, Dionysus was born. This religious emphasis was characteristic of Alexander. He gave his own adhesion to Zeus, and religious acts . . . were not antiquarian features for him."[130]

Thus, it could be said that the cult of Dionysus was one of the chief beneficiaries of Alexander's expansionism. As Alexander went on to conquer the Persians and expand his empire, he spread Hellenism and Dionysus worship throughout the Mediterranean and beyond, although Dionysus  certainly was not the only Greek god promulgated through Hellenism.

Hellenistic cultures could aptly be described as pagan or polytheistic. They included a variety of gods who all had various personalities and "specialties" if you will. In typical pagan fashion, these gods represented different aspects of the spiritual and the natural realm, and had various strengths and powers, as well as weaknesses.

Greek mythology could actually be described as one big mythical soap opera involving love affairs, wars, feasts, triumph and tragedy all acted out by an array of gods, goddesses and some select men and women.

Temples, altars and shrines were littered throughout the Greek territory, as well as those lands which were conquered by them. Therefore, along with the Greek language and culture went their gods, which were easily adaptable to the local gods of the conquered people who were primarily polytheistic and pagan themselves.

This especially posed a problem for those from the House of Yahudah who had previously returned to rebuild the Temple and Jerusalem. After all, they were considered to be "atheists" because they worshipped only one Elohim - YHWH. As a result, they were considered to be "without the gods." Polytheism, which is the belief in many gods, stands diametrically opposed to monotheism, which is the belief in a single god.

The Yahudim had only one Temple in one city, which was the House of YHWH. This stands in stark contrast to the Hellenists who had a variety of temples for a variety of gods in all of their communities, especially the larger cities. Not all of the Yahudim were able to resist the influence of Hellenism, which spread into the Land of Yahudah through the expansionism of Alexander. Many were attracted and influenced by its allure.

This was similar to how much of the modern world is currently drawn to aspects of western culture such as music, television, movies, sports and entertainment - amusement. In fact, it could be said that it was the Greeks who invented "amusement" – a word of Greek origin. For the rulers of pagans needed various diversions for their pagan subjects, in order that they would continue to function productively as willing "slaves" to their masters within pagan society.

Amusement was the answer, for it kept the pagan "slaves" from thinking too much. It also was an opportunity to indoctrinate the masses into pagan ideology. This is the purpose of amusement to this very day, and modern societies have mastered the art of amusement by deceiving people into thinking that they are free, when most of the world is deluded and living an illusion, a veritable artificial reality created by society.

You see "muse" means "to think" and "a" means "no." Amusement therefore is activity which requires "no thinking." Hopefully, if you are still reading this book, you will not find it amusing. For the purpose of this book is to make you think. Sadly, many find religion to be boring and feel the need to be amused or entertained when they attend a religious event. Indeed, modern religion has actually indoctrinated many into paganism through the observance of various Babylonian derived traditions by keeping adherents amused instead of filled with truth.

Aside from the various temples dedicated to the worship of the various gods, a typical Hellenized community would also include a "gymnasium" where people would exercise and compete in the nude. The name comes from the Greek term *gymnos* meaning "naked." The primary purpose for being in a gymnasium was to be exercising in the nude, and it would therefore

become very apparent who was an uncircumcised Gentile and who was a circumcised Yisraelite. People would also socialize and discuss philosophy in the adjoining baths.

The gymnasiums were directly linked to pagan temple worship, which typically involved fornication, sacrifices and eating. Therefore, the gymnasiums and pagan temples in Hellenistic cultures became the center of most social activity.

We see the convergence of religion and athletics in the Olympic games, which were enhanced and expanded throughout Hellenized cultures. They are rooted in paganism, and their very core was religious in nature. They were held every four years, on the second or third full moon after the summer solstice, not unlike those held in modern times. They were actually a religious festival held at major temple sites, and they derive their name from the most famous goddess Olympia.

The activities would all occur in and around pagan temples and shrines, and the various athletic contests were interspersed with sacrifices and ceremonies honoring Zeus, the sun god, and Pelops, the hero and mythical king of Olympia. All of the athletes trained and competed naked, offering their bodies to the glory of Zeus. Before the games began, a priest would sacrifice a bull in front of all of the participants who took an oath to Zeus. These games were so pervasive that they even affected the Temple service in Jerusalem, as priests neglected their duties to view and participate in the activities.

During the apex of Greek influence, the priests of the Jerusalem Temple would sometimes leave the sacrifices half-burned on the altar to rush off to a stadium to compete in the Greek games.

We actually read about this conduct in the Book of Maccabees: ' . . . the priests were no longer intent upon  their service at the altar. Despising the sanctuary and neglecting the sacrifices, they hastened to take part in the unlawful proceedings in the wrestling arena after the call to the discus, disdaining the honors prized by their fathers and putting the highest value upon Greek forms of prestige.' (2 Maccabees 4:14-15 RSV).[131]

It should be evident that Hellenism, and its accompanying lifestyle, is generally offensive to the Torah and those who follow YHWH. It is important to understand this culture which permeated the Promised Land after Alexander the Great conquered the Land. It not only influenced the Yaduhim who lived in the Land, but also the majority who did not return to the Land from exile.

As a result, despite the miraculous decrees from the Persian Kings to return and rebuild, the Yahudim,  the Temple, and the City of Jerusalem, were in a very bad state spiritually from Hellenism. This cultural phenomenon affected and infiltrated the Yahudim throughout the Mediterranean region where they had been exiled. This occurred during the life of Alexander and beyond. While Alexander lived a very brief life, his impact was far reaching in both time and space.

On or about June 12, 323 BCE, Alexander died in the palace of Nebuchadnezzar II, in Babylon. This was quite appropriate because, one could argue, he was responsible for completing the cycle, which had begun in Babylon thousands of years earlier. While sun worship

had been scattered and languages had been confused originally at Babylon, Alexander had begun a process of merging these varied pagan traditions under one umbrella and one language – the Greek Language.

After the death of Alexander and the assassination of his supposed successor Perdiccas in 321 BCE, the united Maccedonean Kingdom, that he had so amazingly united, collapsed. This kingdom entered into a 40 year period of war between the successors, known as the *Diadochi*. This conflict eventually resulted in the Hellenistic world settling into 4 stable power blocks: 1) the Ptolemaic kingdom of Egypt, 2) the Seleucid Empire in the east, 3) the kingdom of Pergamon in Asia minor, and 4) Macedon – precisely as foretold to Daniel.

Not all of the successors continued the Hellenistic policies of Alexander, although the Seleucid Empire that ruled over the Land of Yisrael aggressively continued the Hellenization of their territory. The Seleucids experienced significant conflict with the Ptolemies to the west and the Parthians to the east, as well as other tribes and surrounding powers. The Kingdom experienced a decline until a brief resurgence when Antiochus III the Great took the throne in 222 BCE.

His son, Seleucus IV Philopator reigned from 187 BCE to 176 BCE until he was assassinated. Seleucus' younger brother, Antiochus IV Epiphanes, seized the throne and reigned from 176 BCE to 166 BCE. It was during the reign of Antiochus IV Epiphanes that some dramatic events occurred in the Land. Epiphanes means: "manifest" and he claimed to be the earthly manifestation of Zeus.

By that time, many of the Yahudim in the Land had become enamored by the Grecian lifestyle to such an extent, that they learned the Greek language and took on the Greek attire. This conduct would have been

considered "unclean" by most followers of YHWH, since both the language and the dress were so intimately associated with paganism. Nevertheless, many "converted" to this lifestyle and were called Hellenists. While many did this voluntarily, Antiochus IV chose to forcibly Hellenize, or rather "de-judaize" the remaining Yahudim in his kingdom.

He proceeded with his efforts through the assistance of an individual named Jason, who sought the position of High Priest when Antiochus came to power. Jason was a Hellenized Yahudi who became High Priest in 176 BCE. "He transformed Jerusalem into a Greek City, with Greek schools and gymnasiums where traditionally young athletes exercised nude (a Greek athletic practice). Even some of the young priests at Jerusalem took up the Greek language, athletic sports, and manner of dress: ' . . . he (Jason) founded a gymnasium right under the citadel, and he induced the noblest of the young men to wear the Greek hat. There was . . . an extreme of Hellenization and increase in the adoption of foreign ways . . .' (2 Maccabees 4:12-13 RSV).[132]

Jason went so far as to send money to Antiochus to offer sacrifices to the Greek god Hercules in the city of Tyre. At that time, Hercules was a popular Greek deity in the Land of Yisrael. Interestingly, Hercules was considered to be a demi-god who was the result of the union between the god Zeus and the mortal woman Alcmene. After his death, the legends teach that Hercules became a god.

"In [175 BCE]* Menelaus supplanted Jason by offering Antiochus IV more money for the position of high priest. Menelaus' original name was Onias, but, like Jason, because of his love for the Greek culture changed his name to Menelaus. Menelaus and the sons of Tobias went to King Antiochus. According to Josephus, they told the king that 'they were desirous to leave the laws of their country {the law of Moses}, and their Jewish way of living, and to follow the king's laws (ie. the religion of Dionysus), and the Greek way of living (ie. Greek philosophy).' Antiochus made Menelaus the high priest. In [169 BCE],* while Antiochus was campaigning in Egypt, Jason heard a false rumor that Antiochus [IV] had died and thus he attempted to regain by force his former position of the high priest. Jason and his supporters conquered Jerusalem, with the exception of the citadel, and murdered many supporters of his rival, the high priest Menelaus: '. . . Jason took no less than a thousand men and suddenly made an assault upon the city. When the troops upon the wall had been forced back and at last the city was being taken, Menelaus took refuge in the citadel.' (2  Macabees 5:5 RSV). In response to this riot, when Antiochus came back from Egypt in [169 BCE]* he took Jerusalem by storm and proceeded to enforce the Hellenization of the Jews. He forcefully established the religion of Dionysus: ' . . . king Antiochus wrote to his whole kingdom, that all should be one people, and every one [of the Yahudim] should leave his laws [the Torah] . . . many . . . of the Israelites consented to his religion . . . For the king had sent letters by messengers to Jerusalem and the cities of Judah that they should . . . forbid burnt offerings, and sacrifice [to Elohim] . . . set up altars, and groves, and chapels of (Dionysian) idols, and sacrifice swine's flesh, and unclean beasts: That they should also leave their children uncircumcised . . . forget the [Torah of Mosheh], and change all the (religious) ordinances . . . And he appointed inspectors over all the people and commanded the cities of Judah to offer sacrifices, city by

city. Many of the people, everyone who forsook the law, joined them . . .' (1 Maccabees 1:41-49, 51-51 RSV) Many people forsook the [Torah of Mosheh] and joined the mysteries of Dionysus."[133]

From this point on we see that those in the Land needed to make a choice – obey the King or obey the Torah of YHWH. Worship the predominate pagan "son of god" known as Dionysus, or worship YHWH. Things continued to escalate until Antiochus raised a statue of Zeus above the Altar in the Temple of YHWH – the Temple that had been rebuilt by Zerubabbel after the return of the Yahudim from their Babylonian exile.

One year earlier, Antiochus IV had proceeded to slaughter a pig on the Altar which is an outright abomination. The slaughter of pigs was a Dionysian practice, and we can see the influence that Dionysus worship had in this flagrant act. Antiochus IV then commanded that the Yahudim offer worship there.

According to 1 Maccabees 1:54, Antiochus set up a horrible thing on the Altar in year 145 of the Syrian Kingdom. This date equates with the year 170 BCE.* 1 Maccabees 4:52-54 clearly indicates that this event occurred on Day 25 of Month 9, which equates with Sunday, December 21, 170 BCE* on the proleptic Julian Calendar.

This was more than the faithful Yahudim could take. The Yahudim revolted under the leadership of Mattathias Maccabee and his sons. The Yahudim regained control of the City of Jerusalem in 167 BCE* and the Temple was thereafter cleansed, which is where the celebration of Hanukah derives.

After three years of fighting with the Seleucids, the Yahudim were granted freedom of religion and political autonomy by Antiochus V in 165 BCE.* This condition continued for 27 years until Antiochus VII

Sidetes invaded Judea in 138 BCE.* During this period of Hasmonean rule, the Kingdom and priesthood remained very political in nature, and rivalry developed between two factions known as the Sadduceess and the Pharisees.

Roman influence in the region came about as a result of the conquests of a military commander of the Roman Republic known as Pompey the Great. In 64 BCE, the Yahudim were suffering from internal power struggles after the death of King Alexander Jannaeus which threatened the stability of their kingdom. The King's sons, Hyrcanus and Aristobulus, as well as other political and religious factions, all vied for the crown, and eventually sought mediation from Pompey.

Pompey endorsed Hyrcanus, but Aristobulus and his followers waited to resist the decision. While Pompey was busy in a minor campaign against the Nabataeans, Aristobulus seized Jerusalem. This resulted in Pompey conquering Jerusalem in the spring of 64 BCE, whereupon he made Hyrcanus the high priest and established Judea as a client state of Rome.

Despite this new status, Judea remained independent of Roman authority as long as they maintained order and allegiance to Rome. In 47 BCE, Julius Caesar arrived in Judea and the Yahudim were granted various benefits owing to the uniqueness of their monotheistic religion, and Hyrcanus was officially made the King or Ethnarch. In 44 BCE,* Julius Caesar even respected the Yahudim enough that he decreed they did not have to pay tribute because it was a Sabbath Year.[134]

Antipater Idumean was granted the first Roman title of the area. He was appointed as procurator. It was his responsibility to see to the day to day management of Roman interests and oversee the province. He was assassinated soon after his appointment and his son, Herod, took his place. Parthian invasions from Syria

then set up Antigonus II on the throne, but Herod garnered the intervention of the Roman Senate and was confirmed as Ethnarch in 37 BCE.

Herod was a brutal man who, upon taking power, executed forty-five of the Sanhedrin (the governing body of the Yahudim) and arrested Antigonus II, the King of the Yahudim who was later beheaded. Herod maintained a disdain for the Yahudim descendents having royal blood, but despite his brutality and disinterest in customs of the Yahudim, he was careful not to infringe too far upon the traditions of the people.

He found it vital to his own survival to seek the approval of the masses, but the overwhelming reason for his success was the administration of force to suppress open opposition. The Yahudim exercised limited self-rule as it related to their religious practices. The Sanhedrin was maintained under Herod as a sort of religious council to oversee the affairs of faith and religious law.

Upon the death of Herod in 1 BCE,* the Roman emperor, Augustus, was faced with a difficult decision. He initially appointed Herod's sons as rulers of smaller districts within the larger kingdom, but was eventually forced to place Judea under the direct control of Roman Prefects, who were in turn responsible to the Governor of Syria. Pontius Pilate was the Prefect between the years 27 CE and 37 CE.[135]

Things were quite tenuous under Roman rule. The "King" was not really a king at all but a ruler who derived his power from the Roman Empire, and shared power with other Roman authorities. Herod and his sons were Idumean, which means that they were not from the tribe of Yahudah. Rather, the "Kingly" line was now established with descendents of Edom who were, in turn, descended from Esau - Yaakov's brother.

The High Priesthood had become a political position which could be bought. In 23 BCE,* the Temple service had fallen into the hands of a sect of Yahudim referred to as the Sadducees, who claimed their descendency from the Zadokites. There were two other primary sects known as the Pharisees and the Essenes. All of these sects had different interpretations of the Torah, as well as unique traditions and customs which each developed to adapt to their very precarious existence in the Land. There were also many other smaller factions with varying practices and customs.

Up to this point, despite the corruption in the Priesthood and the Throne, Yahudah had maintained a ruling body known as the Sanhedrin. This body consisted of elders from the Land who may or may not have belonged to one of the differing sects. It was through the Sanhedrin that matters of Torah were discussed and ruled upon. It was the religious Court and deciding body of the Yahudim.

An interesting and important event occurred prior to the time when the Prefect Pontius Pilate was appointed. "According to Josephus (Antiquities 17:13) around the year [6 CE],* the son and successor to King Herod, a man named Herod Archelaus, was dethroned and banished to Vienna, a city of Gaul. He was replaced, not by a Jewish king, but by a Roman Procurator named Caponius. The legal power of the Sanhedrin was then immediately restricted. With the ascension of Caponius, the Sanhedrin lost their ability to adjudicate capital cases. This was the normal policy toward all the nations under the yoke of the Romans. The province of Judea had, however, been spared from this policy up to this point. However, Caesar Augustus had had enough of the [Yahudim] and finally removed the judicial authority from them at the ascension of Caponius. This transfer of power was recorded by Josephus. 'And now Archelaus' part of Judea was reduced into a province, and Caponius, one of the equestrian order of the Romans, was sent as a procurator, having the power of life and death put into his hands by Caesar!' The power of the Sanhedrin to adjudicate capital cases was immediately removed. In the minds of the . . . leadership, this event signified the removal of the scepter or national identity of the tribe of [Yahudah]!"[136]

This directly impacts a prophecy given by Yaakob in Beresheet 49:10 which states: *"The scepter shall not depart from Yahudah, nor a lawgiver from between his feet, until Shiloh comes; and to Him shall be the obedience of the people."* If Shiloh referred to the Messiah, as many interpret the text, then that would mean that the Messiah must have been born before this event occurred, before 6 CE.

Daniel had prophesied in Daniel 9:25 that there would be sixty-two (62) Shemitah cycles, or 442 years until Messiah the Prince, which points to around 2 BCE. The Roman Empire was also prophesied to have a significant impact upon the Land and Jerusalem at that time. (Daniel 2:40-43 see also Daniel 9:26).

Due to all of the prophecies in the Tanak about a coming Messiah, and especially because of Daniel's prophecy, those who remained faithful to YHWH around the turn of the millennium were anxiously anticipating their Messiah. During this period, the Yahudim were a divided and conquered people, living under the control of, and in the midst of a pagan culture. Their own leadership was corrupted and dysfunctional. This was the environment into which the Messiah would come and be cut off, as foretold by Gabriel.

This chapter has been a brief lesson in history, but it is important information to understand, as the

culmination of these events all pointed to a specific place and time. No discussion of pagan holidays and traditions would be complete without mentioning the influence of Hellenism, because that was the time and culture when YHWH chose to send His Son – the Messiah.

13

The Messiah

As we look at the time when the Messiah was anticipated to appear, the condition of the Kingdom of Yisrael could not be much worse. The Kingdom had been divided into two competing "houses." Both had fallen away from YHWH because they strayed from His commandments. They failed to walk the straight path and insisted upon chasing after pagan gods, customs and traditions. As a result of their defiance, they both received separate and unique punishments.

The House of Yisrael was completely displaced from their Land by the Assyrians. They were relocated throughout that empire, which was later conquered by the Babylonians and the Medes. They were scattered to the "four corners" of the earth, and assimilated into various cultures – eventually they completely lost their identity and became, in essence, Gentiles. By the time that the Messiah arrived, they were considered to be "the lost sheep of the House of Yisrael." They were wandering without a shepherd. They needed to be found and brought back into the fold.

The House of Yahudah, on the other hand, was conquered and exiled by the Babylonians who were later conquered by the Medo-Persians. In their exile, they largely maintained their identity as Tribes, and it is important to understand that not all of the Yahudim

were exiled from the Land. Some remained, although it does not appear that they maintained any cohesive governmental structure, and they were greatly encroached upon by their surrounding neighbors.

Historical and archaeological evidence shows that the Yahudim who were exiled to Babylonia assimilated into that culture, but maintained a distinctively Hebrew identity. Many retained Hebrew names, they signed and witnessed contracts, they gave and received inheritances and some even operated in governmental positions. It appears that they lived and functioned as Hebrews and even had their own city called "Al Yahudah" – this was a far different exile than that of the House of Yisrael.

So while the House of Yisrael was completely removed from the Land and seemingly "lost" in history, the House of Yahudah was exiled until the time of their prophesied return. When it was time for their return, they knew who they were, they knew where they were and they knew where they needed to go.

The promise of return from the Babylonian exile was fulfilled, as prophesied, and some of the descendents of those who were exiled returned to the Land. We read about this return primarily in the accounts of Haggai, Zechariah, Nehemiah and Ezra. It is important to recognize that only the House of Yahudah was given the promise of return within seventy years, and only a remnant of the House of Yahudah was returned from exile.

Many attempt to imply that the House of Yisrael somehow snuck back in along the way and resettled into their tribal territories, but that is simply not the case.[137] The duration of the punishment for the House of Yisrael was destined to be much longer, as we shall soon see. In fact, the House of Yisrael's conduct was so severe, that she was actually divorced from YHWH. (see Yirmeyahu

3:1-14).

    While Yirmeyahu revealed a seventy year exile for Yahudah, the prophet Yehezqel also prophesied another set of punishments for both houses. Yehezqel actually demonstrated the different periods as he was commanded to lie on his left side for three hundred and ninety days, and his right side for forty days. The time that he laid on his left side represented a day for every year of sin committed by the House of Yisrael, and the time that he laid on his right side represented a day for every year of sin committed by the House of Yahudah. (see Yehezqel 4).

    Interestingly, Mosheh provided that YHWH would multiply the punishment seven times if they fell away and did not repent and return. (Vayiqra 24:24). The formula for this multiplication is set forth in Vayiqra 24, and we know from the Scriptures that the House of Yisrael incurred the penalty due to their defiant conduct. As a result, the House of Yisrael would be in exile for 390 years times 7 or 2,730 years. If you add that number to the approximate Assyrian span of exiles extending from 723-714 BCE,* you can see that the exile of the House of Yisrael or "The Time of the Gentiles" is drawing to an end. This has very profound prophetic implications.

    The restoration of the divided Kingdom of Yisrael could not occur until the sins of both Houses were dealt with according to the Torah. The Bride of YHWH must be clean – "without spot or blemish." (see Ephesians 5:27). Atonement was needed for the entire Commonwealth of Yisrael, as a prerequisite for Elohim to be married to His people. This marriage was foretold by the prophet Yeshayahu, who links Messianic prophecies with the marriage of the Bride to the Land and to Elohim.

"¹ For Zion's sake I will not keep silent, for Jerusalem's

sake I will not remain quiet, till her righteousness shines out like the dawn, her salvation like a blazing torch. ² The nations will see your righteousness, and all kings your glory; you will be called by a new name that the mouth of YHWH will bestow. ³ You will be a crown of splendor in YHWH's hand, a royal diadem in the hand of your Elohim. ⁴ No longer will they call you Forsaken, or call your Land Desolate. But you will be called Hephzibah (My delight is in her), and your land Beulah (Married); for YHWH will take delight in you, and your Land married. ⁵ As a young man marries a maiden, so will your sons marry you; as a bridegroom rejoices over his bride, so will your Elohim rejoice over you." Yeshayahu 62:1-5.

This was why Yisrael needed the Messiah. The Messiah was aluded to all throughout the Scriptures, as we saw with the Aleph Taw (✕ʊ). The pattern of Abraham and Yitshaq revealed that YHWH would send His Son to die as the Lamb of Elohim. While in captivity, Daniel had been visited by the Messenger Gabriel. He was provided very specific time frames for the coming of the Messiah, which required an understanding of the Calendar of YHWH. The Messiah came into the world amidst the Hellenistic influence in the Land of Yisrael.

While some of the House of Yahudah had returned, most remained scattered. All maintained their identity, but they were challenged in their adaptation due to the cultural influence of Hellenism. Some of the Yahudim completely conformed to the pagan customs and traditions of Hellenistic society. These Yahudim were referred to as Hellenists.

Others attempted to remain set apart and maintain autonomous lives, but this proved difficult while under the control of the Greeks and later the Romans. As we already saw, even the priesthood had been influenced and corrupted by pagan culture that

encompassed the Land.

Many during this era sought the Messiah as a solution to the predicament. They thought they needed a political leader who could free them from the powers that reigned over them. What they really needed was One sent from YHWH Who could deliver them from their perpetual cycle of sin and cleanse them from that sin.

It turns out that the Messiah did indeed come, exactly as foretold. The Messiah Yahushua was born at the beginning of Day 1 of Month 7, or September 11, 3 BCE at around 6:00 pm on the Gregorian dating calendar. It was the Appointed Time of Yom Teruah, which began at the setting of the sun, and the sighting of the renewed moon. That was the moment of His birth, when He came out of the water of the womb - accompanied by the resounding blast of shofars throughout the Land.

We know this because it was also the moment when a great sign occured in the heavens announcing the Birth of The Messiah. *"¹ And there appeared a great sign in heaven; a woman clothed with the sun, and the moon under her feet, and upon her head a crown of twelve stars: ² And she being with child cried, travailing in birth, and pained to be delivered."* 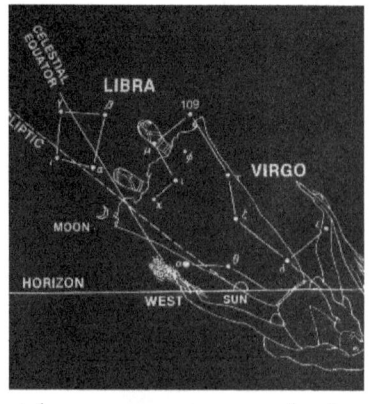 Revelation 12:1-2. Anyone with a computer and the appropriate astronomical software can see this event as it occured over 2,000 years ago.[138]

The Prophet Yeshayahu alluded to this sign involving a virgin giving birth (Yeshayahu 7:14). This event occured in Bethlehem, the City of David. It did not occur in Jerusalem, nor did it need to occur in Jerusalem, because this was not a Pilgrimage Feast. So the Messiah was born at the Appointed Time of Yom Teruah, once again emphasizing the importance of the Appointed Times. His parents surely stayed in the vicinity for Yom Kippur on Day 10 of Month 1, and then, just 2 weeks after the Word of YHWH became flesh, He tabernacled with mankind in Jerusalem during Succot (see Yahanan 1:14).

His Name was Yahushua, the same name as the patriarch often called Joshua. The message was clear that He would gather the Covenant people from their servitude and free them from their slavery. It would be different than people expected. He spent much of His time teaching the Torah and correcting the religious leaders who were following their traditions, and neglecting the purity of the Torah. The people were being taught traditions of men as if they were commandments of Elohim, and Yahushua had to teach the truth to the people.

Religious traditions are quite powerful and they often actually lead people away from the truth. (see Mattityahu 15:1-3). Yahushua rebuked the teachers for their vanity - teaching people traditions and doctrines, as if they were actually commandments. "*[7] Howbeit in vain do they worship me, teaching for doctrines the commandments of men . . . [9] Full well you reject the commandment of Elohim, that you may keep your own tradition . . . [13] Making the word of Elohim of none effect through your tradition, which you have delivered: and many such like things do you.*" Mark 7:7, 9, 13.

Interestingly, when not in Jerusalem for the Appointed Times, He spent most of His time in the North, which was called "Galilee of the Nations." This was the region that the House of Yisrael had once occupied. The Assyrians later removed and replaced them with people from all over their Empire. Yahushua

was sending a message loud and clear. He came for the nations, particularly for the "lost sheep of the House of Yisrael" that had been scattered throughout the nations. (Mattityahu 15:24).

As a result of the sins of the House of Yisrael, the north was heavily influenced by pagan practices. Yahushua thus spent His time confronting many of the pagan gods of the region. He turned water into wine at the wedding in Cana. His first recorded miracle was a direct affront to the popular pagan god Dionysus. We already discussed the affinity that Alexander had with Dionysus, the Greek god of fertility and wine.

Remember that Dionysus was a son of Zeus, a "son of god," and a "christ" in the Grecian culture. He had a mortal mother, and was known for turning water into wine. Interestingly, Dionysus, also known as Bacchus, was allegedly born on December 25. This is the case with many pagan "sons of god," beginning with Tammuz in Babylon. Interestingly, Dionysus/Bacchus has been depicted as  being crucified on a cross, a tradition later adopted by Christianity concerning their christ. This god, Dionysus, was a false "savior," and Yahushua took special note to confront this cult.

Yahushua also made a direct affront to Dionysus when He allowed demons to enter into a herd of pigs.  Those pigs were likely being raised for pagan worship at the nearby Decapolis City of Hippos. Recent archaeological discoveries, which this author was directly involved with, have found large wine producing facilities attached to the Hellenistic compound at Hippos, linking

Dionysus with that pagan city. Pigs were ritually slaughtered during the worship of Dionysus. When this herd of pigs drowned, it surely caused a problem with the Dionysian worship. (see Mattityahu 8; Mark 5; Luke 8).

Yahushua demonstrated His authority over the spirit realm by commanding demons. He demonsrated His authority over the elements when He walked on water, healed the sick and multiplied food. Ultimately, He demonstrated His authority over death through His resurrection on Day 17 of Month 1 in 34 CE.[139]

His death and resurrection was an integral part of the Abrahamic Covenant. It was a fulfillment of the pattern revealed through the Akeda. It was needed to restore the Kingdom of Yisrael and reunite the Bride of YHWH - Yisrael. Messiah did not come to establish a new Covenant, or create a new religion called Christianity. He came to fulfill various prophecies, and "renew" the Covenant with the House of Yisrael and the House of Yahudah. (see Yirmeyahu 31; Mattityahu 26; Mark 14; Luke 22).

Remember that while the House of Yahudah was present at the "Last Supper," which is the Covenant meal of the Passover Seder, the House of Yisrael was still in exile because of their idolatry. Yahushua stated that He came for the lost sheep of the House of Yisrael. (see Mattityahu 10:6; 15:24). So while He walked in the Land and taught the Yahudim, His real purpose was to reach the scattered tribes of the House of Yisrael, and bring them back in the flock - the restored Kingdom of Yisrael.

This was why He sent the Spirit on the Appointed Time of Shabuot. The Set Apart Spirit would empower His disciples (talmidim) to carry this great message of hope to the Nations. He called them to become fishers of men, in fulfillment of the prophecy

given by Yirmeyahu concerning a greater regathering than what had occurred in Egypt. (see Yirmeyahu 16).

So while many expected a Messiah Who would be a great political leader, that hope would have to wait. The current task of the Messiah was to reestablish the Kingdom through the Covenant. To do this, the sins of the Bride needed to be atoned, and the Bride needed to be prepared and regathered.

Just as Yisrael had once grown into a Nation while in Egyptian bondage, the same pattern was now occurring throughout the world. Yisrael was and remains scattered throughout the world, being prepared and readied for an even greater deliverance that will occur at the end of the Age. This is why Yahushua appeared before Yahanan and gave him the vision of "the Day of YHWH," which is included in the Book of Revelation. It was essentially an instruction manual for the end of the Age that Yahanan was born into.

So while the Talmidim of Yahushua were busy spreading the Good News to those who were scattered, a new battle was raging, as the truth was continually opposed by many of the Yahudim. Incredibly, after Yahushua was resurrected, a great rift occurred in the already fractured and splintered Assembly of Yahudah. While many believed the testimony of Yahushua, there were many who opposed the truth. This ultimately caused deep and lasting division, which was all part of the plan of restoration, just as the previous division of the Kingdom of Yisrael had been part of the plan.

14

Division

After the resurrection of Yahushua the focus for all Yisraelites remained in Jerusalem, whether or not they believed that Yahushua was the promised Messiah. That was until the year 70 CE, when the Second Temple and Jerusalem were completely razed by the Romans. This exacerbated the division that was occurring between the Yahudim who did not believe in Yahushua, and those who did.

The unbelieving Yahudim who survived the destruction of Jerusalem were predominantly from the Pharisaic Sect. Under the leadership of Yohanan ben Zakkai, they established a headquarters and council at Jamnia, also known as Yavne. They essentially formed the new religion of Rabbinic Judaism, which established the Rabbis as leading authority figures, rather than the descendents of Aharon. They also developed a curse against the followers of Yahushua, who they called "The Minim."[140]

Those in Judaism later ended up changing the times, by developing a calculated calendar under Hillel II. So the Appointed Times, which are critical to the worship of YHWH, were changed by Hillel II under the authority of Julian the Apostate in 359 CE.

This "Jewish" calendar approximates months and years in a fashion that does not accurately represent the

precise motions of the lunar cycle within the solar cycle, which the rabbis readily admit.[141] However, the adherents of Rabbinic Judaism follow this man-made calendar to this very day.

    The followers of Yahushua took a different course. Since they were being cursed by their Yahudim brethren in the Synagogues, they eventually separated and started to see many "Gentiles" also come to believe in Yahushua. What started as a trickle soon became a flood of conversions. Essentially, there were numerous pagans converting to a belief in Yahushua. This essentially involved being grafted into Yisrael, through the authority of Yahushua. The issue of spiritual authority was a major reason for their separation, since the unbelieving Yahudim did not accept the authority of Yahushua. They demanded their own conversion procedure, which involved a specific circumcision ritual above and beyond the circumcision required in the Torah.

    The influx of Gentile converts into the Assembly often resulted in pagans bringing their pagan habits and traditions into the congregation. This led to a variety of sects and beliefs being spread about among the followers of Yahushua. This opened the door for a major event around 325 CE, when the sun worshipping Roman Emperor Constantine founded the Christian religion, essentially hijacking and transforming the faith in Yahushua. This new religion rejected the Appointed Times, and adopted pagan festival dates as their "Holy Days."

    These events, among others, expanded the division between the newly formed religions of Judasim and Christianity. So through their division, both Judaism and Christianity strayed from the true Scriptural Appointed Times reserved for the Covenant people -

Yisrael.

    A distinquishing mark of any religious system is their calendar. They all have "holy days" or "holidays," and therefore they must have a system for keeping track of their dates. Throughout history, we can find examples of different calendars that pagan cultures would use to observe their significant religious days. If it is not in line with the Creation Calendar then it is profane. If it is not founded on truth, then it is a lie.

    Since these changes occurred, true Scriptural time has essentially been lost to most people. While Judaism adopted the calculated Hillel II calendar, Christianity currently operates under a solar based calendar called the Gregorian Calendar. Developed by Pope Gregory XIII and decreed on February 24, 1582 by papal bull, it was intended to correct some of the errors found within the Julian Calendar, promoted by its namesake, Julius Caesar in 45 BC. The Julian Calendar was actually an attempt to reform the Roman Calendar which had numerous variations and obvious flaws.[142]

    "The motivation for the Gregorian reform was that the Julian calendar assumes that the time between vernal equinoxes is 365.25 days, when in fact it is presently almost exactly 11 minutes shorter. The error between these values accumulated at the rate of about three days every four centuries, resulting in the equinox occurring on March 11 (an accumulated error of about 10 days) and moving steadily earlier in the Julian calendar at the time of the Gregorian reform. Since the Spring equinox was tied to the celebration of Easter, the Roman Catholic Church considered that this steady movement in the date of the equinox was undesirable."[143]

    There were numerous other calendars used by different cultures throughout the centuries, and there are a variety of different calendars in existence today. This is

important to understand, because they all represent mankind's desire to keep track of time for their own unique purposes. Unless they synchronize perfectly with the Creator's Calendar, they are all flawed. These flaws are recognized as cultures attempt to divide the 365 day solar year by 12 months, which mathematically does not result in a whole number, so there is a leftover fraction of a day.

As a result, some attempt to resolve these discrepancies by inserting or intercalating days and months, but over time, these calendars tend to drift one way or another. This, of course, should be expected if you simply rely upon the sun. As we already discussed, the Scriptures tell us in Beresheet 1:14 that the sun and the moon were created to mark time. The Creator keeps His calendar based upon the sun and the moon. If we fail to use His markers, then we are destined to fail in our attempt to keep His times.

Since both of these celestial bodies were created to help the inhabitants of this planet mark time, it would only make sense to use them both if you want to understand the Creator's Calendar. Many of the problems that we see with the solar based calendars are that they do not synchronize with the markers. Therefore, they are not in synchronicity with the Creator.

While they may appear to calculate a solar year, if they do not properly account for the Appointed Times of YHWH, they are useless in understanding the Covenant path and the Covenant Appointments. In fact, they are often more of a distraction than they are a help. Any attempt to understand Scriptural dating or prophetic events is bound to fail if it is reliant upon a man made calendar system which is out of synch with Creation.

The Covenant people were provided with this

Calendar information so that they can keep their appointments. Since the appointments were with the Creator, we can safely assume that He is keeping the calendar that He asked His Covenant people to keep.

With that having been established, we must remember that all of Creation is based upon physical laws and mathematics that have been determined by YHWH. Scientists rely upon these preexisting mathematical equations, which they are in the process of discovering, to better understand the universe. These mathematics were built into everything at the beginning, and mathematics are at the center of the calendar. The mathematics relating to the calendar were meant to be seen and observed through the signs of the sun and the moon. Again, the Scriptural Calendar is luni-solar.

We currently see the religion of Rabbinic Judaism, which generally follows the mathematical calendar attributed to Hillel II, although there are sects, such as the Karaites, that have their own unique traditions concerning the calendar. The Hillel II calendar was not based upon a perfect mathematical calculation, and only very rarely coincides with the Creator's Calendar. The Rabbinic calendar *arbitrarily* predetermines the month lengths in advance, just as the Julian or Gregorian calendar does. It also operates under certain rules of postponement, contrary to what Mosheh commanded the Covenant community of Yisrael in Debarim 5:32.

All of these man-made determinations have at various times been different than the Creator's true reckoning of time, so those practicing these traditions have essentially "changed" the times and taught others to do so. They are on extremely dangerous ground by doing so. (See Daniel 7:25).

Following a man-made calendar would have had

catastrophic results in the original exodus from Egypt, when keeping Passover on the correct day meant the difference between life and death for some. We shall see that it is also critical as we approach the end of days, when the cost of "not watching" and not observing the Appointed Times as YHWH has instructed, will definitely result in missing an important event. (see Mattityahu 25:1-13).

We have discussed some of the different methods and traditions developed by men, but our discussion has by no means been exhaustive.[144] I find that most people are oblivious to the underlying issue. Most simply want to look at a calendar, and have someone tell them what time it is. It amazes me how people are so willing to follow a tradition. When asked why they observe a certain day, the response is usually: "Because the calendar says so." There is little to no inquiry into who developed the calendar or what it is based upon. They just follow the calendar that somebody has told them to follow.

Now remember, when we are talking about time, we are talking about creation, and walking with the Creator Who created time. This is not something to be taken lightly. In fact, it should be one of the most important issues on any person's mind who wants to be in a Covenant relationship with the Creator.

The Creation Calendar, and the Appointed Times which occur on it, were conceived by the Creator. The Scriptural Calendar is not something that men can change or control. The celestial orbs of the earth around the sun, the moon around the earth and the earth on its's axis, move in the courses established for them from the beginning, and the calendar continues from the beginning. Creation is very mathematical, and the solar system works like a finely tuned clock.

As shown in the beginning, the Creation was made to be in synchronicity with the Calendar. The sun and the moon were set in their places to gauge time. Their movement can be calculated, as the calendar is a mathematical calculation. If we look to ancient records, we can see that the movements of the heavenly orbs have operated in a precise and methodical fashion, perfectly fulfilling the purpose for which they have been created.

The astronomical data from ancient historical records validate the fact that "the moon is a faithful witness." (Tehellim 89:37). And the ancient dates in Scripture clearly indicate that the Yisraelites always oriented their year according to the earth's movement around the sun. Often referred to as the Rule of the Equinox, this ancient calculation used the tequfah to determine the beginning of the year. As a result, it is absolutely in line with the instruction in Beresheet 1:14, as it always uses the sun and the moon to determine time.

Simply stated, the Rule of the Equinox "always places Day 15 of Month 1 *on or after* the Hebrew Day in which the spring equinox occurs. If at the moment of sunset at the end of Month 12, on the evening of the first crescent moon at Jerusalem, there are 15 Hebrew Days or less until the spring equinox, then Month 1 is declared. If there are 16 Hebrew Days or more until the spring equinox, then Month 13 is declared. The spring equinox is defined as the time when the apparent geocentric longitude of the sun (that is, calculated by including the effects of aberration and nutation) is zero degrees."[145]

The Rule of the Equinox is an ancient reckoning understood and used in the past by Yisrael. This has been historically documented.[146] Calculating the year based upon the Rule of the Equinox has been proven to be accurate and valid.[147] It insures that all of the Appointed

Times occur within one complete year. Most importantly, it is also confirmed by Scriptures.[148]

This is an incredible truth that has profound implications. It takes timekeeping out of the hands of men and their subjective determinations which generate corrupted calendars, and places it into the realm of the true science of the movements of the sun and the moon which were created by YHWH.

Another reason why this is so incredible is because once you understand that the Calendar is mathematical, time opens up to you. With the advent of computers we can now easily go forward and backward in time, like a veritable time machine. Both historical and prophetic dates become perfectly positioned on a 7,000 year grid.

Once you realize the method for calculating the beginning of the year through the Rule of the Equinox, there is one more thing to determine – the first day. We have already mentioned that the month begins at the Rosh Chodesh, which literally means "head of the month" or "beginning of the renewal."

The overwhelming evidence is that this was determined at the first sighting of the crescent moon, typically when the moon is at 2 to 3 percent illumination. This is sometimes made difficult in modern times with the existence of atmospheric pollution, and was likely easier in the past. Interestingly though, we now have technological advances that can tell us precisely the illumination of the moon at any given moment.

The point is to see the light. Again, the tradition and spiritual implications of looking up and seeing the visible sign in the sky are overwhelming. Just like evening and morning can be observed, so the renewed moon can be observed. While there are those who hold to the astronomical conjunction dark moon theory, it is

simply not supported by the evidence.[149]

Before we proceed any further, it is important to understand the relevance, and significance of the Appointed Times. It has already been mentioned, but bears repeating. These were not simply legalistic exercises that the Yisraelites were made to follow every year, nor were they arbitrary dates to gather together and worship. They were precisely calculated Appointments with the Creator with incredibly specific purposes.

So then the issue of the Calendar is central to the Covenant, and the Covenant Community assembling together in unity. Failure to observe the same calendar leads to division. This is one of many reasons that continued and perpetuated the division between Rabbinic Judaism and Christianity.

Christianity developed into a religion that claimed to believe the Hebrew Scriptures, but essentially elevated the "New Testament" writings over the "Old Testament." In essence, Christians treat the Torah, the Prophets and the Writings as old historical events describing the ancient Assembly of Yisrael. As a result, they view those texts as having only spiritual application to the Christian Church.

In fact, Christianity has declared the existence of "The Church" over "Yisrael" and has developed new holy days to replace the Appointed Times. Essentially, the things in the "Old Testament" are considered just that - old. Most Christians are taught, and believe, that since the Appointed Times are found in the "Old" Testament, that they are outdated, obsolete, irrelevant and abolished. This is largely due to the Christian notion that the Church has replaced Yisrael, or that the Torah has been done away with. Both of these are untrue and false doctrines.[150]

While some see the significance in the Appointed

Times, they believe that we can no longer "keep" the Feasts, since there is no Temple in Jerusalem. Actually, we are commanded repeatedly to "keep" the commandments of YHWH, not just the Appointed Times. The word "keep" is shamar (𐤔𐤌𐤓) in Hebrew and it means: "to hedge about, to guard, to protect, to attend, to observe, to preserve, to regard, to watch."[151]

The existence or non-existence of a Temple does not affect the Torah, or time for that matter. The planets did not stop their courses simply because YHWH allowed His House in Jerusalem to be destroyed. The Temple was never meant to be there permanently, at least not one built by the hands of man. So the commandments, including those concerning the Appointed Times, are not contingent upon the existence of a structure.

While there are certain rituals and sacrifices that cannot be carried out because there is not an altar or an operating priesthood, it is important to point out that those sacrifices and ceremonies were not originally mentioned with the Appointed Times. The Levitical Priesthood and the sacrificial system in the Temple service was intended to instruct Yisrael during the Age of Instruction. Yisrael was to learn of their need for atonement by the shedding of blood, and of their need for Messiah. This was all realized by many, including the writer of Hebrews, at the beginning of the Age of Messiah.

Thus, the Appointments are still occurring whether you choose to recognize them or not. The point is, the Appointed Times, as well as their significance and meaning – operate not only in the past, but also in the future. If you are observing different times, namely pagan derived times, then you are walking in darkness and following lies. The Appointed Times are mentioned

throughout the "New Testament," and were repeatedly validated by the Messiah.¹⁵²

There are still others who believe that the Appointed Times are exclusively "Jewish Holidays." The Scriptures are clear that the Appointed Times belong to YHWH and no other. They are Times for His Covenant people to observe, as we saw at Sinai. This was later reiterated by Mosheh to Yisrael.

"*¹ And YHWH spoke unto Mosheh, saying, ² Speak unto the children of Yisrael, and say unto them, Concerning the Appointed Times (moadi) of YHWH, which you shall proclaim to be holy convocations, even these are My Appointed Times (moadi). ³ Six days shall work be done: but the seventh day is the Sabbath of rest, a holy convocation; you shall do no work therein: it is the Sabbath of YHWH in all your dwellings. ⁴ These are the Appointed Times (moadi) of YHWH, even holy convocations, which you shall proclaim in their Appointed Times (moadim)."* Vayiqra 23:1-4.

There are a couple of things that should jump right off the page. First, within the first 4 sentences, the Appointed Times are mentioned 4 times, divided into two parts. In each instance where the Appointed Times are mentioned twice, they are also called "holy convocations," and it is clearly stated that these times belong to YHWH. Finally, these two references essentially bracket the Sabbath, which is also called a "holy convocation" and is at the very center of the brackets.

It would appear that at the center of the Appointed Times is the Sabbath. This Sabbath is the seventh day Sabbath. It is being set apart and distinguished from the other Appointed Times, which are mentioned later, but which also include the seventh day Sabbaths. The reason for this separation and distinction is because they are calculated differently. The

seventh day Sabbath is on a seven day cycle which started at Creation. It is a simple count of seven rotations of the earth on its axis. The other Appointed Times occur on specific dates on the lunar cycle, which is calibrated by the solar cycle.

So the first moad that we read about in the comprehensive listing of the moadim is the seventh day Sabbath. The Sabbath is the first moad mentioned in the Scriptures, and it was the first to occur in time – the seventh day. It is connected to the weekly day count and is not tied to both the sun and the moon as are the annual Moadim.

The seventh day Sabbath is clearly special and unique as we have already pointed out on several occasions. It is separate and set apart from the other Appointed Times. Since it is on a different cycle than the other times, it is determined differently. You need to be able to count the passage of days, and you must be able to count to seven.

Just as we saw that the creation week was on a seven day cycle, beginning with the first week of creation, separate from the monthly and yearly cycle, we see the same here. So while the seventh day Sabbath is clearly an Appointed Time, it is weekly and it is not dependent upon the sun and the moon.[153] Because it is so unique and special, the Sabbath is dealt with in a separate text.[154]

The Appointed Times are described as "holy convocations" which is "qadosh miqra" (ᶜ ᵠ ᵠᵐ wᵘᵠ) in Hebrew. A better translation is "set apart gatherings." The word qadosh (wᵘᵠ) is often defined as "holy," but is better described as being "set apart." It describes something not common, or profane. It is usually something meant for YHWH - something acceptable for His presence. The word miqra (ᶜ ᵠ ᵠᵐ) is defined as: "a

summons or assembly, a reading or recitation." It is also defined as a rehearsal.

So on these special days YHWH calls us to essentially read and rehearse something special for Him - something set apart. They can literally be called set apart rehearsals. We read about these times, we learn about them and we act accordingly. These times are likened to rehearsals for a future event. They are set apart because they specifically belong to YHWH.

Sadly, they have been obscured from most of the world because they are mislabeled "Jewish Holidays." While it is true that most in the religion of Judaism recognize the moadim as special days, they have their own traditions and calendar for conducting their celebrations, which do not align with the Scriptures. Just because those in Judaism recognize the significance of these Times, it does not give them exclusive rights to these Times.

The Moadim are for all those who are in Covenant with the Creator. Since Yisrael, not the religion of Judaism or Christianity, represents the Covenant people, the Appointed Times were detailed to them. Therefore, those who belong to Yisrael are expected to meet with YHWH at His times.[155]

So, if you want a relationship with YHWH, you must enter into Covenant with Him, and part of that Covenant relationship involves meeting with Him at His Appointments.[156]

The passage in Vayiqra continues by providing the most comprehensive list of the Appointed Times that can be found in the Scriptures. It also provides more information relative to the timing. There is some debate about how some of the text is translated, but for the purposes of this discussion, we will examine a basic translation. For a more detailed examination of the

subject see the Walk in the Light series book entitled The Appointed Times.

"⁴ These are the Appointed Times (Moadi) of YHWH, set apart rehearsals which you shall proclaim at their Appointed Times (Moadim). ⁵ On the fourteenth day of the first month at twilight is YHWH's Passover. ⁶ And on the fifteenth day of the same month is the Feast of Unleavened Bread to YHWH; seven days you must eat unleavened bread. ⁷ On the first day you shall have a set apart rehearsal; you shall do no customary work on it. ⁸ But you shall offer an offering made by fire to YHWH for seven days. The seventh day shall be a set apart rehearsal; you shall do no customary work on it. ⁹ And YHWH spoke to Mosheh, saying, ¹⁰ Speak to the children of Yisrael, and say to them: When you come into the Land which I give to you, and reap its harvest, then you shall bring ×ᘯ a sheaf of the firsts (resheet) of your harvest to the priest. ¹¹ He shall wave the sheaf before YHWH, to be accepted on your behalf; on the day after the Sabbath the priest shall wave it. ¹² And you shall offer on that day, when you wave ×ᘯ the sheaf, a male lamb of the first (ben) year, without blemish, as a burnt offering to YHWH. ¹³ Its grain offering shall be two-tenths of an ephah of fine flour mixed with oil, an offering made by fire to YHWH, for a sweet aroma; and its drink offering shall be of wine, one-fourth of a hin. ¹⁴ You shall eat neither bread nor parched grain nor fresh grain until the same day that you have brought an offering to your Elohim; it shall be a statute

throughout the age (olam), throughout your generations in all your dwellings. ¹⁵ And you shall count for yourselves from the day after the Sabbath, from the day that you brought את the sheaf of the wave offering: seven complete weeks. ¹⁶ Count fifty days to the day after the seventh week; then you shall offer a new grain offering to YHWH. ¹⁷ You shall bring from your dwellings two wave loaves of two-tenths of an ephah. They shall be of fine flour; they shall be baked with leaven. They are the firstfruits to YHWH. ¹⁸ And you shall offer with the bread seven lambs of the first year, without blemish, one young bull, and two rams. They shall be as a burnt offering to YHWH, with their grain offering and their drink offerings, an offering made by fire for a sweet aroma to YHWH. ¹⁹ Then you shall sacrifice one kid of the goats as a sin offering, and two male lambs of the first year as a sacrifice of a peace offering. ²⁰ The priest shall wave them with the bread of the firstfruits as a wave offering before YHWH, with the two lambs. They shall be set apart to YHWH for the priest. ²¹ And you shall proclaim on the same day that it is a set apart rehearsal to you. You shall do no customary work on it. It shall be a statute throughout the age (olam) in all your dwellings throughout your generations. ²² When you reap the harvest of your land, you shall not wholly reap the corners of your field when you reap, nor shall you gather any gleaning from your harvest. You shall leave them for the poor and for the stranger: I am YHWH your Elohim. ²³ Then YHWH spoke

to Mosheh, saying, **24** Speak to the children of Yisrael, saying: In the seventh month, on the first day of the month, you shall have a Sabbath, a memorial of blowing, a set apart rehearsal. **25** You shall do no customary work on it; and you shall offer an offering made by fire to YHWH **26** And YHWH spoke to Mosheh, saying: **27** Also the tenth day of this seventh month shall be the Day of Atonement. It shall be a set apart rehearsal for you; you shall afflict your souls, and offer an offering made by fire to YHWH. **28** And you shall do no work on that same day, for it is the Day of Atonement, to make atonement for you before YHWH your Elohim. **29** For any person who is not afflicted in soul on that same day shall be cut off from his people. **30** And any person who does any work on that same day, that person I will destroy from among his people. **31** You shall do no manner of work; it shall be a statute throughout the age (olam) throughout your generations in all your dwellings. **32** It shall be to you a Sabbath of solemn rest, and you shall afflict ✘𐤏 your souls; on the ninth day of the month at evening, from evening to evening, you shall observe your Sabbath. **33** Then YHWH spoke to Mosheh, saying, **34** Speak to the children of Yisrael, saying: The fifteenth day of this seventh month shall be the Feast of Succot for seven days to YHWH. **35** On the first day there shall be a set apart rehearsal. You shall do no customary work on it. **36** For seven days you shall offer an offering made by fire to YHWH . On the eighth day you shall have a set apart rehearsal, and you shall offer

an offering made by fire to YHWH. It is a atzeret, and you shall do no customary work on it. ³⁷ These are the Appointed Times (Moadi) of YHWH which you shall proclaim to be set apart rehearsals, to offer an offering made by fire to YHWH, a burnt offering and a grain offering, a sacrifice and drink offerings, everything on His day ³⁸ besides the Sabbaths of YHWH, besides your gifts, besides all your vows, and besides all your freewill offerings which you give to YHWH. ³⁹ Also on the fifteenth day of the seventh month, when you have gathered in the fruit of the Land, you shall "keep the feast of YHWH" (hagag ×𐤉-hag-YHWH) for seven days; on the first day there shall be a Sabbath, and on the eighth day a sabbath. ⁴⁰ And you shall take for yourselves on the first day the fruit of beautiful trees, branches of palm trees, the boughs of leafy trees, and willows of the brook; and you shall rejoice before YHWH your Elohim for seven days. ⁴¹ You shall keep (hagag) it as a feast (hag) to YHWH for seven days in the year. It shall be a statute throughout the ages (olam) in your generations. You shall celebrate it in the seventh month. ⁴² You shall dwell in booths for seven days. All who are native Yisraelites shall dwell in booths, ⁴³ that your generations may know that I made the children of Yisrael dwell in booths when I brought them out of the land of Egypt: I am YHWH your Elohim. ⁴⁴ So Mosheh declared to the children of Yisrael the Feasts of YHWH." Vayiqra 23:4-44.

So there you have it. If you are in Covenant

relationship with YHWH, then these are the Times that you observe as set part days – period. You must keep them at their proper time, according to the Scriptural Calendar. The calendar has been one of many causes of division, and until the Covenant people of YHWH understand and recognize the true Calendar, they will remain divided and miss the important rehearsals that are intended to prepare them for the events that will occur at the end of this age.

This is a clear and unequivocal truth, yet it seems that most of the world is oblivious to this truth. While Judaism appears to recognize the Appointed Times, they celebrate them on the wrong calendar. Christianity, which claims to adhere to the Scriptures, has rejected the Appointed Times and has opted to observe pagan holy days, thus distinguishing itself as a pagan religion.

15

Pagan Christianity

It would not be possible to detail all of the so called "pagan holidays" in existence today within one book. Nor is it even possible to discuss all of the different holy days associated with the numerous denominations of Christianity. For the purposes of this discussion, we will simply highlight some of the significant historical events surrounding the establishment of the Christian religion as well as two of the major Christian Holidays, which both allegedly center on the Messiah.

As was indicated previously, the Messiah did not come to found a new religion called Christianity. He came to restore the Kingdom, and seek and save the Lost Sheep of the House of Yisrael. The Christian religion was actually founded by the Roman Emperor Constantine, and the world headquarters of this new religion has always been in Rome, which was the seat of the Roman Empire.

Christianity is, after all, a religion established by the Roman Empire. This is something often misunderstood by Christians, who believe that the Emperor of Rome became a Christian, and soon thereafter the Roman Empire "converted to Christianity." Sadly, that notion is an idealistic illusion.

What they fail to realize is that the Roman Empire, a pagan empire, actually **created** the religion of

Christianity. It was a politically calculated move to keep the Roman Empire from falling apart. This Emperor that we are referring to was Constantine. Constantine effectively merged the faith in Yahushua with sun worship in the Hellenistic tradition of Alexander the Great.

As far as we can tell, Constantine remained a worshipper of Mithras after his alleged "conversion" to Christianity. Anybody can make a confession, but one must look at their actions to determine what they really believe. Many men have made various claims throughout the ages if they thought it was advantageous to them.

It would seem fairly strange that a newly converted Emperor would establish Christianity as the official state religion of Rome and, at the same time, continue to practice and promote paganism. That is, unless Christianity was actually just another form of pagan religion. Interestingly,  Constantine called the sun-deity: "Unconquered Sun, my companion." He even issued coins proclaiming "Sol Invictus" The Unconquered Sun, which was referring to the sun god he had worshipped most of his life - Mithras.

Besides this, from 330 to 346 C.E. Constantine and his sons issued coins to commemorate the founding of Rome by none other than Romulus and Remus, the mythical twin brothers who were the sons of the pagan god Mars and the Vestal Virgin. On one side, the coins display  the she wolf that allegedly suckled the twins when they were children. The face of the pagan goddess Roma is on the other side. This sounds like something a pagan would

do - not someone who worshipped the Elohim of Yisrael.

Therefore, while Constantine supposedly made a profession with his mouth, his actions betrayed him. That is why James (Yaakob)[157] said "Show me your works."

"[14] *What does it profit, my brethren, if someone says he has faith but does not have works? Can faith save him?* [15] *If a brother or sister is naked and destitute of daily food,* [16] *and one of you says to them, Depart in peace, be warmed and filled, but you do not give them the things which are needed for the body, what does it profit?* [17] <u>*Thus also faith by itself, if it does not have works, is dead.*</u> [18] <u>*But someone will say, You have faith, and I have works. Show me your faith without your works, and I will show you my faith by my works.*</u> [19] *You believe that there is one Elohim. You do well. Even the demons believe - and tremble!* [20] *But do you want to know, O foolish man, that faith without works is dead?* [21] *Was not Abraham our father justified by works when he offered Isaac his son on the altar?* [22] *Do you see that faith was working together with his works, and by works faith was made perfect?* [23] *And the Scripture was fulfilled which says, Abraham believed Elohim, and it was accounted to him for righteousness. And he was called the friend of Elohim.* [24] <u>*You see then that a man is justified by works, and not by faith only.*</u> [25] *Likewise, was not Rahab the harlot also justified by works when she received the messengers and sent them out another way?* [26] *For as the body without the spirit is dead, so faith without works is dead also.*" Yaakob

2:14-26.

This then begs the questions: What did Constantine believe? What exactly was the Christian religion that came out of the Roman Empire? History is clear that the Roman Catholic Church had tremendous pagan influences from its inception. With this type of beginning, is it any wonder that we see the Roman Catholic Church filled with relics, idols and other pagan influences? The Catholic Church is riddled with pagan symbols and beliefs from the concept of The Pope, to the very hat that the Pope wears called a Mitre - which is styled after what the priests of Dagon, the Philistine Fish god used to wear. The exaltation of Mary as The Mother of God and The Queen of Heaven comes straight out of Babylon, and the practice of praying to the dead (saints) is contrary to the instruction in the Scriptures. (Debarim 18:9-14).

The engraved images which fill Catholic Cathedrals and schools are all a violation of the commandments of Elohim.[158] The use of rosary prayer beads is directly linked to other pagan religions including Islam, Hinduism and Buddhism.

"Every one knows how thoroughly Romanist is the use of the rosary; and how the devotees of Rome mechanically tell their prayers upon their beads. The rosary, however, is no invention of the Papacy. It is of the highest antiquity, and almost universally found among Pagan nations. The rosary was used as a sacred instrument among the ancient Mexicans. It is commonly employed among the Brahmins of Hindustan; and in the Hindu sacred books reference is made to it again and again . . . In Tibet it has been used from time immemorial, and among all the millions in the East that adhere to the Buddhist faith . . . In Asiatic Greece the rosary was commonly used, as may be seen from the image of the Ephesian Diana. In Pagan Rome the same appears to have been the case."[159]

The purpose here is not to disparage the Catholic Church, but to show that there is an age old struggle to divert mankind from the truth – a struggle which continues to this day. Just as with Ancient Yisrael, the Catholic Church and Christianity have adopted pagan practices, which they no longer recognize as pagan. Tradition often takes precedence over truth.

The adversary has not just been sitting on the sidelines for the past two thousand years while the Christian church has been building in glory, strength, purity and power. To the contrary, he has been busy, slowly and quietly infiltrating, undermining and "deceiving the elect" whenever possible (see Mattityahu 24:24; Mark 13:22). At the same time he has been building and establishing his kingdom, Babylon, and redirecting the worship of many toward himself rather than the Creator.

Of course this should not be a surprise, because even in the First century there were people who were preaching a false Messiah as we read from Shaul: *"³ But I am afraid that just as Hawah was deceived by the serpent's cunning, your minds may somehow be led astray from your sincere and pure devotion to Messiah. ⁴ For if someone comes to*

you and preaches a Yahushua other than the Yahushua we preached, or if you receive a different spirit from the one you received, or a different gospel from the one you accepted, you put up with it easily enough." 2 Corinthians 11:3-4.

The Christian religion has been preaching a false gospel, and a false messiah for millennia. Christianity is not teaching the Hebrew Yahushua who directed people toward the Commandments and the Covenant path. Rather, Christianity has been advocating a Hellenized christ named Jesus who apparently abolished the Torah. This Christian Jesus directs people away from the Commandments and into lawlessness, the very condition that Yahushua warned against. These changes were so subtle and gradual that those within the system probably did not recognize what was happening. With the advantage of hindsight after nearly 2,000 years of history, it is now easy to see the deception.

Sun god worship has greatly influenced and permeated not only the Catholic Church, but also the entire Christian religion through their various interpretations, doctrines and traditions. There were many different gods in the Roman culture when the Christian religion was established - too many to deal with comprehensively in this text. We already visited the concept of  Hellenism, and determined that the Roman Empire was a polytheistic culture which worshipped many gods.

As already mentioned, one of the pagan gods of particular importance to this discussion is that of Mithras, which was a Persian god said to have been created by Ahura-Mazda and incarnated into the form of a man. According to Persian legend, and in the typical pagan pattern, Mithras was incarnated into the form of a man and was born of Anahita, an immaculate virgin mother on December 25, 272 B.C.E.

Anahita was once worshipped as fertility goddess before her stature was reformed in the sixth and seventh centuries B.C.E. This was undertaken by Zarathustra (also known in Greek as Zoroaster), a prophet from the kingdom of Bactria. Anahita was said to have conceived Mithras, the savior, from the seed of Zarathustra preserved in the waters of Lake Hamun in the Persian province of Sistan. Mithras later ascended into heaven, and this was said to have occurred in 208 B.C.E.

The cult of Mithras was developed and expanded by the Babylonians. Babylonian clergy assimilated Ahura-Mazda to the god Baal, Anahita to the goddess Ishtar (Easter) and Mithras to Shamash, their god of justice, victory and protection and the sun god from whom King Hammurabi received his code of laws in the 16th century B.C.E.*

As a result of the solar and astronomical associations of the Babylonians, Mithras later was referred to by Roman worshippers as "Sol invictus," or the invincible sun. The sun itself was considered to be "the eye of Mithras." The Persian crown, from which all present day crowns derive, was designed to represent the golden sun disc sacred to Mithras.[160]

These sun discs can be seen all throughout Christian art and are often called "halos." These halos are placed above the heads of Christian characters considered to be divine or anointed, in the same fashion that sun worshippers ascribe divinity to their gods. The word

halo derives from the name of a sun god named "Helios," who was another prominent sun god that permeated Judaism as well as Christian theology as has already been mentioned throughout this text.

Helios was a popular sun god and interestingly, the Greek New Testament actually replaces the name of Eliyahu (Elijah) with the name of the pagan sun god Helios. If you look at the Greek manuscripts you will see the Greek name Helios in place of the name Eliyahu. This certainly blows the argument out of the water concerning the inerrancy of the "original Greek" which so many Christians ascribe to. The reason why people did this was the same reason why people wanted to worship Shaul and Barnabas as pagan deities.

You see Helios was often represented as riding a chariot into the sun and since Eliyahu was taken up in a fiery chariot – he resembled what they knew and were familiar with – paganism. Therefore the people who copied and recopied the early manuscripts changed  them to suit their beliefs – this was extremely common – especially considering the fact that there were no professional copyists of the Messianic texts for hundreds of years. Therefore there was no standard or uniformity.[161]

Now most translators recognize this error and have made the appropriate correction in their translations, but one cannot help but wonder what other changes were made by the people who transmitted the earlier Greek texts. It also should make a person wonder about the various traditions which have been inherited from these Hellenized Christians.

For instance, the fact that Mithras was born on December 25 should jump right off the page. Not surprisingly, every sun god throughout history was born on December 25 because they all derive from Babylon. As an example, in the Roman pagan system, Attis was a son of the virgin Nana. His birth was celebrated on December 25. In the Greek pagan religion, Dionysus was a savior-god whose birth was observed on December 25. In the Egyptian pagan religion, Horus was a savior-god born of a virgin Isis on December 25. Of course, Tammuz from Babylon was also born on December 25.

Again, the reason they were born on December 25 was because in ancient times, that was when the winter solstice occurred which was the shortest day of the year in the Northern Hemisphere. After that point the days

grew longer, and this day was a celebration of rebirth. As a result, in pagan traditions it was the time that all sun gods were supposedly born. Therefore we can see how pagan influences infiltrated into Christianity, which now celebrates Christmas – the traditional day for Sun God worship. Those traditions are still practiced to this very day. We even see many ancient traditions being restored, such as the papal camauro worn by Pope Emeritus Benedict XVI.

Etymologically speaking, a mass is traditionally a religious service involving a sacrifice. The Christ Mass was always a pagan celebration involving a ritual sacrifice. It has absolutely nothing to do with Yahushua the Messiah Who was born, as already discussed, on Yom Teruah on Day 1 of Month 7 – an Appointed Time of YHWH. Today, the winter solstice occurs on

December 21, but pagan tradition still clings to the date of December 25 on the Gregorian calendar.

The winter solstice was one of four major celebration times on the pagan calendar which divides the solar cycle into four seasons: the winter solstice, the summer solstice, the spring equinox and the autumnal equinox. This is where the pagan symbol of the sun wheel derives, which is the symbol of Baal. It is also the source of the swastika, which is an ancient sun wheel. It is a well known fact that Adolf 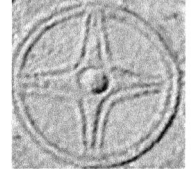 Hitler was an avid pagan, and his selection of the swastika was because of his involvement in sun worship.

The swastika predates Nazi Germany by thousands of years. Notice the Nazi  symbol which depicts Mithra atop of the world. This was the same symbol used by Roman Soldiers, and most will recognize this symbol on many flag poles. As we shall see in the next chapter, sun worship is all around us – we have just not been educated enough to recognize it for what it is – **pagan**.

The modern world is almost exclusively following the pagan solar system. The days of the week are named after pagan gods and goddesses. For instance: Sunday is the Day of the Sun – Sun Day, Monday is the Day of the Moon – Moon Day, Tuesday is Tyr's Day, Wednesday is Wooden's Day, Thursday is Thor's Day, Friday is Friga's Day and Saturday is Saturn's Day. The Scriptural calendar counts the days numerically one through six beginning on Sunday and the seventh day is the Sabbath.[162]

According to the Scriptural calendar, as with the days of the week, the months are numbered and not named. The first month begins at the sighting of the renewed moon in the month of the abib – Month 1. After that, the months continue to progress at the sighting of the first sliver of the renewed moon until 12 or 13 months have elapsed. The Hebrew Month is determined by the moon. The Hebrew Year is determined by the sun and the moon according to the Rule of the Equinox. The Hebrew Day is one revolution of the earth upon its axis. A Hebrew Day begins after sundown, and ends the following evening at sundown.

This was all determined at the beginning of creation, and stands in stark contrast to the pagan system where a day begins and ends at midnight. Also under the  pagan system, the months are named, mostly after pagan gods. The first month January is named after Janus the two headed Roman god. The second month February is named after the pagan goddess Februa.

The third month March is named after the pagan god Mars. The fourth month April is named after the pagan goddess Aprilis. The fifth month May is named after the pagan goddess Maya. The sixth month June is named after the pagan goddess Junio. The seventh month July is named after Julius Ceasar who was believed to have become a god, and the same holds true for the eighth month August, which was named after Augustus Ceasar.

The remaining months are very interesting because they reveal that originally, the months were roughly numbered according to the Scriptural Calendar, because the ninth month September derives from "septum" which means seven. The tenth month October derives from "octo" which means eight. The eleventh month November derives from "novum" which means nine, and the twelfth month December derives from "deca" which means ten. Thus the names of the last four months of the pagan calendar actually reveal the general order which they should fall under the Scriptural calendar.

This is the system within which Christianity was created, currently exists and thrives. The problem is that the current Gregorian calendar is spiritually irrelevant as it is not the Creator's Calendar. However, most people do not even realize that there is another way of reckoning time. <u>Christianty exists within the framework of pagan sun worship</u>. While it contains fragments of truth, that truth has been controlled, manipulated and suppressed by the religion of Christianity, which still operates from Rome, the place of its birth.

There are numerous symbols of sun worship that can be found throughout the Catholic Church – particularly at the Vatican in Rome. The placement of this Holy site of the Catholic Church is quite disturbing, since it is built on top of various pagan temples and tombs. This is in direct contravention to the notions of set apartness,  sanctification, and purity as seen in the Scriptures, and yet this is fairly typical in the Catholic religion. It even contains an intact pagan cemetery.[163]

Actually, many of the alleged Christian holy sites are simply revamped pagan worship sites. Besides the location, the architecture is littered with pagan artifacts which

are an abomination according to the Scriptures. The large obelisk at the entrance of St. Peter's Square is not a copy of an Egyptian obelisk, but rather the very same obelisk that stood in Heliopolis in Egypt, which was the center of worship for none other than Helios – the sun god. Caligula had this obelisk brought from Heliopolis to his circus on Vatican Hill between 37-41 B.C.E.

The obelisk is centered nicely in the middle of a pagan sun wheel, which fills the square. Of course this is a fine compliment to a statute of the sun god Tammuz, which is also located in the Vatican as well as the statute  of the sun god Jupiter, which has been conveniently renamed Peter. These sun god relics should feel right at home in the "Holy City" called the Vatican which sits in Rome on one of the seven hills. (Revelation 17:9). Instead of destroying these pagan sun god images, in accordance with Scriptural directives, the Catholic Church collects them.

Christian holy sites are typically former pagan sites which have been adopted into Christian lore and tradition. Sadly, and shockingly, it is common to see well  meaning Christians scurrying around Jerusalem, and the surrounding area, visiting shrines, which have been set up by the pagan Emperor Constantine's mother Queen Helena. It is understood that she used sorcery and other questionable means to locate these alleged "holy sites." For years, Christian Pilgrims have flocked to the Church of the Nativity in Bethlehem to see the supposed birth site of Yahushua.

The Church is located above a Mithras cave with a Mithra sun god symbol located on the supposed spot of the birth of the Messiah, who they erroneously refer to as Jesus. Like most of the "holy sites" it is dark, depressing and oppressive. It is a Mithras cave located beneath a gloomy sanctuary above, which is separated into numerous sections 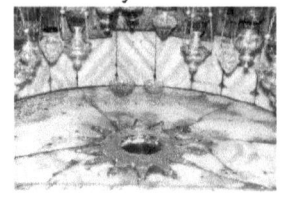 by various divided Christian denominations. Notice the Mithras sunburst, which is placed at the supposed site of the birth of Yahushua.

This cave is just another example of how pagan sun god worship infiltrated Christianity in centuries past. Sadly, these pagan elements are so ingrained into Christian tradition that tour buses now herd bewildered pilgrims to these sights like cattle. The naïve Christians rarely question the  authenticity or origins of these pagan shrines, simply accepting the tradition as truth.

They walk the stations of the cross through the streets of Jerusalem which did not exist at the time  Yahushua was crucified – streets which are 30 to 40 feet above the streets where Yahushua would have walked. All the while, most who walk along this fictitious path believe that they are retracing His steps. As they draw to the completion of their trek, they are led right to the spot where the former Temple of Aphrodite (Easter) was located. The pillars of the former temple are still visible to this day in the outer court of temple complex.

This is where the Church of the Holy Sepulcher is located, where Yahushua was supposedly nailed to the cross, hung, laid out, anointed and then placed into a tomb. Pilgrims come and kiss the stone where Yahushua was crucified, marked by a large mithraic sunburst on the floor. They touch personal effects on the various sites, hoping for some sort of anointing to rub off.

The facility is divided into various sections, as the different denominations of Christianity have marked their territory after having "turf wars" over their individual space. The infighting has gotten so bad that the keys to the church are purportedly held by a Muslim overseer, so that one group of Christians cannot lock the others out. The entire building is filled with icons, idols and symbols of sun worship. It has the look, feel and stench of death, because that is where it is leading people.

An idol is commonly defined as an image used as an object of worship, a false god or a person or thing that is blindly or excessively adored. There are more idols today than ever existed in the entire history of mankind. For some reason, people are deluded about recognizing how wrong it is, unless of course they do not care about the commandments of YHWH. That, after all, is what distinguishes a pagan, from a Yisraelite – the commandments of YHWH Elohim.

Sadly, the Catholic Church makes no excuses about their involvement in idolatry and sun worship. In fact, they flaunt it in the open for all to see. There are other aspects of idolatry which are not so easy to recognize. Idols are not only small wooden and stone carvings that people set up in their homes. Now they are cars in their garages, money in their banks, clothes in their closets, jewelry in their safes as well as their houses, their furniture, their plasma TVs - you name it.

These are the every day objects and temptations which challenge us everyday as we try to live a life according to the instructions of our Creator. We expect these temptations and struggles when we are out in the world, but we do not expect these things in our religious lives and activities. When we assemble together and worship with other Believers, we do so with an expectation that we are no longer in  the world, but have transcended into the spirit – a place where we can fellowship with a Set Apart Elohim.

As a result, it is absolutely shocking, and even unthinkable for some, when they discover that the Church they have been attending their entire life, or the denomination that they belong to, has been involved in harlotry and has perpetuated lies.

Where idolatry is quite obvious in the Catholic Church, it is not so easy to detect in Protestant denominations, although it is still there. One of the first places you will find it is in the Holidays (Holy Days) that they participate in. Again, it comes down to the calendar, and while most Protestant Christians still believe that they have separated from the Roman Catholic Church, they have not.

They still recognize Sun Day, the traditional day of sun worship, as their Sabbath. The change from a seventh day Sabbath to a first day Sabbath is what the Catholic Church deems as her "mark" of authority. Therefore, anyone who considers Sunday to be their

Sabbath is not following the commandments of YHWH, and is under the authority of the Roman Catholic Church. Most Protestants also continue to celebrate the same pagan holidays established by the Catholic Church, namely Christmas and Easter.

Sadly, many people who read the Scriptures get confused on this issue because it appears that the Early Talmidim of the Messiah celebrated Easter, or that Passover was somehow replaced by the Easter celebration. This confusion traces back to an erroneous translation of Acts 12:4 found in the King James Version which reads as follows: "*And when he had apprehended him, he put him in prison, and delivered him to four quaternions of soldiers to keep him; intending after* Easter *to bring him forth to the people.*"

For many people who grew up in the Christian religion, the problem might not be so evident, because Easter is an accepted celebration. But remember that the Easter celebration predates Christianity by thousands of years. When we look at the Greek text the problem becomes evident. You will not find the word Easter in the accepted manuscripts, but rather the Greek word Pascha (πασχα).

The word is Pesach (חספ) in Hebrew. It means Passover, and as we have seen, it is not the same celebration as Easter. So whoever translated this text from Greek to English changed the meaning of the passage by inserting a different word with a very different origin and meaning. This reveals the power of tradition. Since Christianity had replaced the celebration of Passover with Easter, the translator inserted the word Easter into the text. What might seem like a simple and harmless mistake has had a profound impact.

We already saw that Easter derives from Ishtar in Babylon. She was the Great Mother Goddess of the

Saxon people in Northern Europe, and the Teutonic dawn goddess of fertility. Her name was derived from the ancient word for spring: "eastre."

Similar goddesses were known by other names in ancient cultures around the Mediterranean, and were celebrated in the springtime. They are Aphrodite in ancient Cyprus, Ashtoreth in ancient Canaan, Astarte in ancient Greece, Demeter in Mycenae, Hathor in ancient Egypt, Ishtar from Assyria/Babylon, Kali from India and Ostara the Norse Fertility goddess. All of these fertility goddess myths trace back to Babylon and they are all pagan.

The celebration of Easter is a pagan tradition. It was adopted by Christianity in order to separate and distance themselves from the Yahudim. The same holds true with December 25, another ancient pagan celebration of the winter solstice. If Christians want to celebrate the birth of the Messiah, then they should be celebrating the Appointed Time of Yom Teruah. Again, Christianity has rejected the Appointed Times for a pagan celebration, thus establishing itself as a pagan religion.

This religion, which often attempts to view itself as a replacement of Yisrael, calling itself "spiritual Yisrael," has certainly followed the pattern of Yisrael by mixing, compromising and ultimately falling away from the commandments of YHWH in order to chase after other gods. As a result, we see that most nations considered to be "Christian" have actually followed suit with their pagan predecessors.

16

Pagan Society

The United States of America used to enjoy the idea of being a "Christian Nation." There are actually recorded Court cases that have declared the fact that America is a Christian nation.[164] Many Christians find comfort in the "Christian Nation" label, as if that somehow brings continuous divine favor upon this nation. Sadly, whatever that label used to mean, America is clearly not a nation ruled according to the commandments of Elohim.

Interestingly, there was a time when this nation would not celebrate Christmas and Easter. The Puritans, who first came to the shores of this great land, attempted to live pure, undefiled lives – thus the label Puritan. For hundreds of years this land remained a refuge for those seeking to escape the tyranny of oppressive governments and their state controlled religions. In fact, there is  evidence that this land was previously filled with civilizations not formally connected with the religious institutions of the east. Very ancient civilizations once populated the continent long before the Native American Indian, but that is a subject for another discussion.

While America clearly has deep Scriptural roots, we need to be honest about the limitations of that heritage due to the fact that it ultimately became a federal republic. It is not a theocracy, nor was it intended to be one. Indeed, it allows for the freedom of all religions. So if it was a Christian nation, that begs the question: What is a Christian nation? Is it a nation that operates according to the commandments of YHWH? If that is true, then America is disqualified by the fact that it permits the freedom of religion. YHWH does not permit freedom of religion in His Kingdom, nor will He tolerate His people worshipping other deities.

America allows anyone to set up idols and celebrate pagan holidays. In fact, it has essentially adopted numerous pagan holidays such as Halloween, Christmas, Valentine's Day and Easter as national  holidays. America allows people to be satan worshippers, pagans or atheists. It tolerates conduct which the Scriptures forbid and consider abominable. America does not even abide by the Ten Commandments. In fact, it is removing the Ten Commandments from public buildings. Therefore, simply applying the standard set by the Scriptures, America certainly does not willingly serve YHWH.

On the other hand, if you knew nothing about this country and arrived as a traditional immigrant, simply by your observations, you would be forced to conclude that America is a pagan society. It even has a goddess to greet new immigrants into the "promised land." The

Statue of Liberty is the goddess of liberty, and probably the largest pagan statue ever erected. This giant goddess not only greets those who enter into the United States of America, but if they then proceed into New York State they are surrounded by her companions, the goddess of Freedom and the goddess of Justice as well as Mithra himself, who adorn the New York State emblem.

The very fact that this country allows for these pagan statues and images to exist disqualifies it from being a government based upon the Scriptures. If

America were serving the Elohim of Yisrael and obeying His Commandments, then paganism and idolatry would not be tolerated - they would be destroyed. That is what the Scriptures mandate. America would not condone the killing of unborn children, but America follows the pagan practice of killing children. If America followed the Scriptures it would forbid rampant adultery, sexual immorality, rebellious children and other illicit conduct forbidden in the Scriptures.

America still claims to be one nation "under God," but that statement is really meaningless, because it does not say *which* god it is under. If you had to make a judgment based upon outward appearances and the symbols used throughout the country, you would have to admit

Statue of Freedom
Stands atop the dome of the U.S. Capitol building

that it is a pagan god. I say this because statues and idols of pagan gods and goddesses adorn our nation's federal

Entrance to the U.S. Capitol building

The Pagan God, Mars

and state capitals, our courtrooms - even our money. The nation's capital building is adorned

with a statue of the goddess of freedom at its apex, and it is also protected by the Roman god Mars.

Some might argue that our currency states: "In God We Trust." For one thing, those Federal Reserve Notes are printed by a private bank, not by the United States of America. That is a deception and treachery best left for another discussion. The phrase found on those notes is quite meaningless, because it fails to identify *the god* in which we supposedly trust. Many might respond, we trust in the god with the capital "G", you know – that God. No matter how you spell it "god" is just a title and could mean anything or any god. In the case of the Federal Reserve Notes, the god of "mammon" might be most appropriate.

At this point, it may be useful to take a closer look at American currency, in particular the one dollar bill. You see there are numerous well known, as well as  secret, organizations and societies with pagan ideologies that have been influencing and manipulating societies for centuries. Those influences are often hidden in plain sight. For instance, the reverse side of every one dollar bill contains the Great Seal of the United States. I wonder if anyone ever taught you in public school who designed the Great Seal, or how this became the official seal of the country?

You would think that something so common and so important would be taught to every child in every school in America, but it is not. In fact, it is a mystery to most Americans. Did anyone ever explain why there is a pyramid on this American seal? Any reasonable person should quickly ask, "What does a pyramid have to do with the United States of America?" After all, there are no pyramids that exist in the country.

The Great Seal is actually a two sided seal with one side containing the pyramid and the other side containing the bird symbol, which has also been adopted as the Presidential Seal. Both portions of the seal are littered with occult symbolism. It is alleged that the Great Seal was designed by Charles Thompson, William Barton and Pierre Eugene Du Simitiere in 1782.

It is reported by Freemason historian Manly P. Hall that the original design included a Phoenix resting on a nest of flames.

The mythology related to the phoenix was supposed to symbolize a new nation being birthed, but the phoenix has much greater significance in mythology. The phoenix is a Greek name, for a mythical bird which

originated in Ancient Egypt known as the Benu Bird. The Benu Bird, otherwise known as the Sacred Bird of Heliopolis, was one of the primeval forms of the High God and, according to the Pyramid Texts and the Book of the Dead, represented in various forms, the manifestations of Atum, Ra and Osiris. The phoenix is directly associated with sun god worship.

Indeed, the current relevance and significance of the phoenix was clearly demonstrated during the writing of this book. The 2012 Summer Olympic games concluded in London with incredibly sophisticated pageantry filled with pagan and illuminati symbolism. We already discussed the pagan origins of the Olympic games, and there can be no doubt that the same sinister forces that started the tradition remain at the heart of this modern pagan celebration.

During the closing ceremonies, when the fire of Zeus was extinguished, an enormous phoenix rose from the ashes and took flight, consistent with the pagan mythology. How interesting to see this myth consistently and continually woven throughout history. The legend of the phoenix as the "god" who was cast down to earth is directly related to the fall of Thoth, Hermes, Baal, Marduk and Satan – they are all one and the same.

So we see America with this satanic symbol on the very currency that it uses to conduct business. The stars above the head of the phoenix on the One Dollar Bill are all pentagrams, designed in a hexagram pattern, which still remains on the modern seal. The combined pentagram and hexagram reckon back to the Seal of Solomon, perported to have been used in summoning demons. These symbols have a history of use in pagan cult practices, and the fact that they are surrounded by a monstrance, a standard sun god symbol, only adds to the pagan nature of the imagry.

The Benu Bird (Phoenix) was closely associated with a stone called the Benben Stone. The two names are derived from the same word, which means "to rise." The Benben stone was placed on the top of a tall column, an obelisk, to catch the first rays of the rising sun. The obelisk, with the Benben stone on its cap represents the perch rising from the Abyss, which the Benu Bird perched atop, about to call the world into existence. The capstones of pyramids have the same name, and may have had the same function. Obelisks were sometimes erected in pairs, one for the sun and one for the moon. When obelisks occur in pairs, they are called pylons.[165]

Notice that the pyramid on the Great Seal does not have a capstone "[T]he pyramid with its missing capstone is profoundly significant because it alludes to Illuminati control of Freemasonry, but also to the mystery schools of ancient Egypt. In occult terms, the elevated capstone is an allusion to the Great Pyramid with its missing capstone. In ancient Egypt, the  pyramids were used as initiation chambers in the king-making rituals. Each pyramid had a capstone, made either of pure crystal or an alloy of some kind. This capstone was used to attract cosmic rays, which would induce spiritual illumination. The illuminated triangle with the all-seeing eye represents the missing capstone and its accompanying mysteries, both of which only survive now in symbolic form."[166]

The thirteen levels of the pyramid represent the thirteen levels of masonry. The all seeing eye is a Luciferian eye representing Osiris, also known as the Eye of Horus and the Eye of Ra. The Roman numerals MDCCLXXVI translate into Arabic numerals as 1776. The year of the American Revolution, but also the year that the Illuminati was founded, as well as the founding of the House of Rothschild. The Latin inscription surrounding the pyramid proclaims "Announcing the Conception of a Secular New World Order".

It is interesting that we seem to be hearing a similar phrase uttered a lot in the past decade, only now they are speaking it in English. I doubt that many people ever took the time to translate the phrase. It is plain to anyone who looks close enough, that there are things that have been set in motion long ago by powers that go

beyond our elected officials.

There is another Egyptian symbol in this country, which provides more insight into the god that America exalts. Everyone who visits the nation's Capital has likely taken a photo of the giant obelisk, which represents the phallus of Baal, called the Washington Monument. It stands erect in the National Mall, and I would hazard a guess that it is the largest obelisk ever erected in the history of the world.

Interestingly, on the aluminum cap of this immense phallic symbol, one will find inscribed the

words "Laus Deo" which means "Praise be to Deo." Some translate "Deo" to mean "God," but it was originally the name of a pagan fertility goddess, Demeter, who was allegedly the mother of Dionysus, a pagan savior which we already discussed has striking similarities to the Christian Christ called Jesus.

Therefore, the God that America is under appears to be the sun god, Osiris. Knowing that all of these sun gods derive from Babylon, we realize that this is blatant Baal worship. In fact, most of the architecture of the capital city is patterned from the Greco-Roman style, so it even looks like a pagan city filled with pagan temples, and to top it all off – it is designed in the shape of a

pentagram. As mentioned, it includes an enormous sun pillar standing 555 feet and 5 inches tall.

The Supreme Court Building is adorned with sculptures of a variety of pagan gods. A review of the rest of the country reveals much of the same. The goddess of justice is in most state and federal courts, overseeing how justice is meted out throughout the country. You will find her in most lawyers offices, on many business cards  and letterheads. Her name is Themis in the Greek culture and Justicia in the Roman culture.

No matter how you say her name, she is a pagan goddess. True justice comes from Our Heavenly Father, not some pagan goddess. "*³ For I proclaim the name of YHWH: Ascribe greatness to our Elohim. ⁴ He is the Rock, His work is perfect; for all His ways are justice, an Elohim of truth and without injustice; Righteous and upright is He.*" Debarim 32:3-4.

The symbol of Asclepius is seen throughout the medical profession. Known as Asklepios to the Greeks, he is considered a god of healing and was venerated in the ancient world as the patron deity of physicians. "His cult, established in the fourth century B.C., became common throughout the Greco-Roman world, and  even today his symbols – a staff and snake – are used universally as the symbols of medicine."[167]

The study and profession of psychiatry and psychology are named after psyche who was a maiden  loved by Eros, the god of love, and united with him after Aphrodite's jealousy was overcome and who subsequently became the personification of the soul.

Even the dollar sign ($) used to represent currency derives from the snake symbolism, which, in the case of money, most likely symbolizes the wand or caduceus carried by the god Mercury. Mercury is often pictured carrying a caduceus consisting of two snakes

wrapped around each other, rather than a snake wrapped around a pole. The dollar sign was also used by medieval astrologers to denote the planet Mercury. In mythology, Mercury had rule over banking, commerce and financial transactions.

"It is traditional for banks to have sculpted models of either Mercury or the caduceus on their facades or doors. The Bank of England, in London, has a caduceus on either of its main doors. Above the main portal of the Federal Reserve Building, in Washington, D.C., is a sculpture of a female personification of America, holding a caduceus. This was sculpted in 1937, two years after the modern dollar bill was designed and printed."[168]

We already discussed the pagan elements of the solar calendar that we have inherited, and we see from astronomy how all of the planets have been named after pagan gods and goddesses, and the constellations have all been attributed to pagan characters and myths. In March 2004 NASA claimed to have discovered a tenth planet in our solar system, which they promptly named Sedna after the Inuit goddess of the sea. I find it incredible that their natural inclination has been to attach a pagan label to the heavenly bodies, which were specifically designed to be a witness to the Creator of the Universe.

The planets, stars and the constellations were placed in heavens for a reason. The Scriptures tell us that: "*Elohim said, Let there be lights in the firmament of the heavens to divide the day from the night; and **let them be for signs and seasons, and for days and years . . .***" Beresheet 1:14. They are for signs and seasons, they tell the story of the Creator and His plan of restoration yet the pagans have taken hold of them and warped and twisted their true meaning through the occult. The Zodiac is a pagan alteration of what we call mazeroth in Hebrew.[169]

The Scriptures are very clear that His people are not to be using the names of false gods, let alone adorning a nation with their statutes and temple structures. What we see in the United Stated of America is similar to what happened to Yisrael. Instead of tearing down the pagan symbols they ended up falling into idolatry. They were commanded to rid the Land of these symbols and practices. *"² You shall utterly destroy all the places where the nations which you shall dispossess served their gods, on the high mountains and on the hills and under every green tree. ³ And you shall destroy their altars, break their sacred pillars, and burn their wooden images with fire; you shall cut down the carved images of their gods and destroy their names from that place. ⁴ You shall not worship YHWH your Elohim with such things."* Debarim 12:2-4.

The reason for this commandment is to rid the land of these practices so that people would not be led astray and begin participating in abominable acts. We can vividly see the need for this commandment in our present culture. People no longer obey these commandments – even in the modern State of Israel. The landscape is littered with minarets and steeples, domes and pagan imagery. These things continue to  be built. In fact, they are even raising obelisks which were once fallen – in the name of archaeology.[170]

We would do well to heed the following words. *"¹⁴ Therefore, my beloved, flee from idolatry.¹⁵ I speak as to wise men; judge for yourselves what I say.¹⁶ The cup of blessing which we bless, is it not the communion of the blood of*

Messiah? The bread which we break, is it not the communion of the body of Messiah? [17] For we, though many, are one bread and one body; for we all partake of that one bread. [18] Observe Yisrael after the flesh: Are not those who eat of the sacrifices partakers of the altar? [19] What am I saying then? That an idol is anything, or what is offered to idols is anything? [20] Rather, that the things which the Gentiles sacrifice they sacrifice to demons and not to Elohim, and I do not want you to have fellowship with demons. [21] You cannot drink the cup of YHWH and the cup of demons; you cannot partake of YHWH's table and of the table of demons. [22] Or do we provoke the Master to jealousy? Are we stronger than He?" 1 Corinthians 10:14-22.

Our senses are so dulled that most cannot see or recognize the pagan influences that are all around us. As children we hear about "mother nature," and many refer to her when we speak of the weather. By doing so they are attributing power over the elements to a pagan goddess. This is the same Mother Earth that the  pagans worship. We see the symbols for male and female, which stem directly from ancient paganism. We tell our children that the Tooth Fairy is going to come into their room at night, and take their teeth from under their pillow. We sing nice songs asking "Mr. Sandman" to bring us a dream. The list could go on an on.

The movies and toys in modern society promote, glorify and romanticize witches and vampires, sorcery and sex. The holidays that we celebrate generally all have pagan roots. Christmas, Easter, Halloween and Valentine's Day are all pagan celebrations, yet the majority of Christianity, and society at large, is oblivious to the abomination that they are committing in the eyes of Elohim when they participate in these activities.

Every year in the so-called Christian nation of

America, both Christians and pagans are able to join together in the celebration of Easter. Interestingly, it is typically celebrated on Sunday. While Christians claim to celebrate the resurrection of their Messiah on this day, it was not the day that Yahushua was resurrected, and other than the seventh day Sabbath, the Scriptural Appointed Times do not occur on the same week day every year.

So Easter is directly linked with a specific day – Sun day. It is a day named after the sun, and the day which Christianity decided to celebrate as their sabbath, in direct defiance to the commandments of Elohim. Easter Sunday occurs around the vernal equinox, which is a time commonly attributed to pagan fertility celebrations. This makes it very easy for both Christians and sun worshippers to celebrate Easter on the same day, and it is very appropriate, since Easter is, in fact, a pagan fertility rite deriving from Babylon.

This was a day when the pagans would celebrate a sunrise service wherein priests would impregnate women on the altar of Easter. They would sacrifice the infants born from the previous years celebration, and dip eggs in the blood of those sacrificed babies. Incredibly, we not only see pagans celebrating this holiday, but also Christians. The rabbit is a symbol of fertility, as is the egg, and the entire celebration revolves around pagan traditions. Christians now attempt to apply "Christian" meaning to these pagan rites. That is not only absurd, it is expressly forbidden by the Scriptures.

Easter has nothing to do with the death or resurrection of the Messiah. It was simply a pagan tradition that was adopted by Christians after they rejected the Appointed Times of YHWH. Likewise, there is another celebration which both pagans and Christians are able to celebrate – Christmas.

As was already mentioned, the December 25 celebration of Christmas has nothing to do with the Messiah, and is completely grounded in sun god worship. Other related traditions such as Santa Claus, elves, reindeer, flying sleighs and the north pole all have their own pagan derived mythological origins that have been blended together to make the fiction that is now presented to the youth of society. This all knowing santa, who comes into peoples homes through their chimney every year, supposedly rewards or punishes children depending upon their behavior – like a god.

The Christmas tree represents the phallus of Nimrod. It is traditionally decorated with ornamental testicles, and the practice is rooted directly in Babylon. It is an idol which people set up in their homes  once a year to celebrate the rebirth of the sun. The cutting down and raising up at the time of the winter solstice represents a death and resurrection experience.

This type of conduct is clearly an abomination, yet people do not even realize that they are repeating an ancient pagan rite. The Scriptures clearly state that: "*there is nothing new under the sun.*" (Ecclesiastes 1:9). This is particularly true when we are examining sun worship. The abomination committed at Christmas is the same conduct that ancient Yisrael was warned about yet we have not learned from their example.

"*² Do not learn the way of the Gentiles; do not be dismayed at the signs of heaven, for the Gentiles are dismayed at them. ³ For the customs of the peoples are futile; for one cuts a tree from the forest, the work of the hands of the workman, with the ax. ⁴ They decorate it with silver and gold; they fasten it with nails and hammers so that it will not topple.*"

Yirmeyahu 10:2-4 NKJV.

Regardless of this warning, the "Christian Nation" of America has wholeheartedly adopted this Babylonian derived celebration along with many others. This is because the Christian religion, as a whole, has become so polluted with paganism that most simply do not recognize the pagan connection.

Many American Christians who earnestly desire the truth are stunned when their eyes are opened, and they find out how many similarities that they share with pagan religions throughout history and the world. This really should not come as a surprise. After all, if people consider America to be the example of a Christian nation, then all you need to do is look around, watch the news or read a paper to deduce that something must be seriously wrong with Christianity.

America may be a Christian nation, whatever that means, but it surely is a pagan nation. With the rapid moral decline we are witnessing in the country, we need only to examine history to get a glimpse of what is in store for America and the world. Indeed, it has already been described in the Book of Revelation. That is why it is so important to learn the ways of YHWH and separate from the pagan traditions that have consumed this world. Many believe that America is in store for judgment similar to that of Sodom. I believe that this is true, but not for the reasons one might think.

The sin of Sodom was that she had: "[49] . . . *pride, fullness of food, and abundance of idleness; neither did she strengthen the hand of the poor and needy.* [50] *And they were haughty and committed abomination before Me; therefore I took them away as I saw fit.*" Yehezqel 16:49-50. This sounds like an accurate definition of the pagan America that I have described above.

It should be noted that I am simply skimming the

surface in this book. The revelation and truth go so much deeper that it is almost incomprehensible. Most go about their lives completely deluded, chasing after the "American dream," or whatever it is that society presents as the apex of achievement. Most have little understanding of the deception that is being perpetrated upon mankind, but it is time to wake up as we move ever closer to the end of the age.

17

In the End

The Book of Revelation, considered to be a mystery by many, is actually an outline of the end of this age. It details the Day of YHWH – a one year period of time described by the Prophet Yeshayahu (see Yeshayahu 34:8, 61:2 and 63:4).

Most people cannot understand the Book of Revelation, and there is a reason for this. According to Revelation 1:1, the Book of Revelation was written to the servants of Elohim. The servants of Elohim keep the commandments of Elohim, and remain faithful to Yahushua the Messiah according to Revelation 14:12. People who do not keep the commandments of Elohim are not the servants of Elohim, and for this reason they will not understand the Book of Revelation, as the prophecy was not written for them to understand.

People who do not serve Elohim cannot understand the Book of Revelation, because they do not know how to tell time. In order to understand the end, you must go back to the beginning. You must recognize how YHWH reckons time, and you must understand the Appointed Times, which are both keys to our understanding.

As long as Christians continue in their pagan traditions, they will be unable to recognize the times, because they are immersed within "Mystery Babylon."

(see Revelation 17:5). As a result, they will not perceive the events which will take place in the end.

Immediately prior to delivering Yisrael from Egypt, YHWH gave Mosheh and Aharon a lesson on how to tell time. (see Beresheet 12). We are approaching another period in history when YHWH will deliver His people - this time from their enslavement in the world system. In order to be set apart and protected from the coming judgment, our understanding of how to tell time must be restored.

YHWH will again fight for His people as when they were in Egypt. Now they are scattered throughout the world. He will regather and restore His people from the world system represented by Egypt. In the process, He will punish the powers of the world. Just as He punished Egypt and Babylon in the past, He will do so in the future, only this time He will finish the job.

The patterns of the past are for us to learn from. In fact, just as Babylon was the reason why the earth was divided, Babylon will be the reason why the people of Elohim will be regathered. They will actually be gathered out of "Mystery Babylon."

Here is what the Scriptures tell us:

"*¹ After these things I saw another angel coming down from heaven, having great authority, and the earth was illuminated with his esteem. ² And he cried mightily with a loud voice, saying, Babylon the great is fallen, is fallen, and has become a dwelling place of demons, a prison for every foul spirit, and a cage for every unclean and hated bird! ³ For all the nations have drunk of the wine of the wrath of her fornication, the kings of the earth have committed fornication with her, and the merchants of the earth have become rich* through the abundance of her luxury. ⁴ And I heard another voice from heaven saying, <u>Come out of her, My people, lest you share in her sins, and lest you receive of her plagues.</u> ⁵ For her sins have reached to heaven, and Elohim has remembered her iniquities. ⁶ Render to her just as she rendered to you, and repay her double according to her works; in the cup which she has mixed, mix double for her. ⁷ In the measure that she glorified herself and lived luxuriously, in the same measure give her torment and sorrow; for she says in her heart, I sit as queen, and am no widow, and will not see sorrow. ⁸ <u>Therefore her plagues will come in one day - death and mourning and famine. And she will be utterly burned with fire, for strong is YHWH Elohim who judges her.</u> ⁹ The kings of the earth who committed fornication and lived luxuriously with her will weep and lament for her, when they see the smoke of her burning, ¹⁰ standing at a distance for fear of her torment, saying, Alas, alas, that great city Babylon, that mighty city! For in one hour your judgment has come. ¹¹ And the merchants of the earth will weep and mourn over her, for no one buys their merchandise anymore: ¹² merchandise of gold and silver, precious stones and pearls, fine linen and purple, silk and scarlet, every kind of citron wood, every kind of object of ivory, every kind of object of most precious wood, bronze, iron, and marble; ¹³ and cinnamon and incense, fragrant oil and frankincense, wine and oil, fine flour and wheat, cattle and sheep, horses and chariots, and bodies and souls of men. ¹⁴ The fruit that

your soul longed for has gone from you, and all the things which are rich and splendid have gone from you, and you shall find them no more at all. ¹⁵ The merchants of these things, who became rich by her, will stand at a distance for fear of her torment, weeping and wailing, ¹⁶ and saying, Alas, alas, that great city that was clothed in fine linen, purple, and scarlet, and adorned with gold and precious stones and pearls! ¹⁷ For in one hour such great riches came to nothing. Every shipmaster, all who travel by ship, sailors, and as many as trade on the sea, stood at a distance ¹⁸ and cried out when they saw the smoke of her burning, saying, "What is like this great city? ¹⁹ They threw dust on their heads and cried out, weeping and wailing, and saying, Alas, alas, that great city, in which all who had ships on the sea became rich by her wealth! For in one hour she is made desolate. ²⁰ Rejoice over her, O heaven, and you set apart apostles and prophets, for Elohim has avenged you on her! ²¹ Then a mighty angel took up a stone like a great millstone and threw it into the sea, saying, Thus with violence the great city Babylon shall be thrown down, and shall not be found anymore. ²² The sound of harpists, musicians, flutists, and trumpeters shall not be heard in you anymore. No craftsman of any craft shall be found in you anymore, and the sound of a millstone shall not be heard in you anymore. ²³ The light of a lamp shall not shine in you anymore, and the voice of bridegroom and bride shall not be heard in you anymore. For your merchants were the great men of the earth, for by your sorcery all the nations were

deceived. [24] *And in her was found the blood of prophets and saints, and of all who were slain on the earth.*" Revelation 18:1-24.

Notice that Babylon is associated with the woman who claims in her heart to "sit as a queen." This is none other than the so-called Queen of Heaven – Easter. Notice also how Babylon is described as political, religious and economic. We can see how Babylon has influenced all areas of modern society, as people seek their own pleasure through materialism, lust and greed. Babylon ultimately elevates the individual over YHWH.

The command is to "*Come out of her, My people, lest you share in her sins, and lest you receive of her plagues.*" Revelation 18:4. Just as the children of Yisrael were separated in the Land of Egypt, and did not share in the plagues upon Egypt, so those in the Covenant, "am Yisrael," must come out and separate from Babylon. The people of YHWH are supposed to be set apart, "qadosh" in Hebrew, from the world. "*And you shall be set apart (qadosh) unto Me: for I, YHWH, am set apart (qadosh), and have separated you from the peoples, that you should be Mine.*" Vayiqra 20:26.

We must not share in the sins of Babylon, which in large part encompass the false worship that is the source of pagan holidays such as Christmas and Easter. These also lead to other forms of idolatry, such as materialism. One cannot ignore the direct link associated with Christmas and the insane acquisition of material goods. When you read the description of Babylon with discernment, it is easy to see Babylon throughout modern industrial society. The present rulers of darkness have combined our major political, economic and religious systems. Modern society leads people from YHWH and His precepts into Babylonian idolatry.

Yisrael was exiled out of the Land for

participating in such idolatrous practices. The remnant of those who turn to YHWH will someday soon be regathered during a very tumultuous time on this planet

"⁹ For thus says YHWH of hosts, the Elohim of Yisrael: Behold, I will cause to cease from this place, before your eyes and in your days, the voice of mirth and the voice of gladness, the voice of the bridegroom and the voice of the bride. ¹⁰ And it shall be, when you show this people all these words, and they say to you, Why has YHWH pronounced all this great disaster against us? Or what is our iniquity? Or what is our sin that we have committed against YHWH our Elohim? ¹¹ Then you shall say to them, Because your fathers have forsaken Me, says YHWH; they have walked after other gods and have served them and worshiped them, and have forsaken Me and not kept My Torah. ¹² And you have done worse than your fathers, for behold, each one follows the dictates of his own evil heart, so that no one listens to Me. ¹³ Therefore I will cast you out of this land into a land that you do not know, neither you nor your fathers; and there you shall serve other gods day and night, where I will not show you favor. <u>¹⁴ Therefore behold, the days are coming, says YHWH, that it shall no more be said, YHWH lives who brought up the children of Yisrael from the land of Egypt, ¹⁵ but, YHWH lives who brought up the children of Yisrael from the land of the north and from all the lands where He had driven them. For I will bring them back into their land which I gave to their fathers.</u> ¹⁶ Behold, I will send for many fishermen, says YHWH, and they shall fish them; and afterward I will send for many hunters, and they shall hunt them from every mountain and every hill, and out of the holes of the rocks. ¹⁷ For My eyes are on all their ways; they are not hidden from My face, nor is their iniquity hidden from My eyes. ¹⁸ And first I will repay double for their iniquity and their sin, because they have defiled My Land; they have filled My inheritance with the carcasses of their detestable and abominable idols."

Yirmeyahu 16:9-18.

The connection should now be clear. Yisrael was once punished for participating in the abominations derived from Babylon. They were cast out of the Land, but YHWH sent fishermen to fish for them. This was exactly what the Messiah was teaching His talmidim to do - fish for the lost sheep of the House of Yisrael. YHWH will also send hunters. The purpose is to bring Yisrael back. This regathering will be far greater than the deliverance from Egypt. Through this process there will be a doubling of punishment rendered upon Babylon.

From this discussion, the reader should now understand that time is the arena within which the spiritual and the physical come together. It is the framework within which all of creation exists and functions. Time was created in the beginning as a current to gather the Harvest of YHWH - His Covenant people who will fill His House. Within this framework of time there are weekly Appointed Times and annual Appointed Times.

The weekly seven day cycle began at creation, and has continued ever since. This seven day cycle does not require anything except for the passage of seven days. After the passage of six complete days, the weekly Sabbath occurs on the seventh day - from sunset to sunset. So the sun controls this seven day cycle. This weekly Sabbath is a sign (owt) for all who are in the Covenant. (Shemot 31:17).

There are other Appointed Times that operate on an altogether different cycle. They occur annually and they are reliant upon both the sun and the moon. These annual Appointed Times start with a Meal, the Passover, followed by The Feast of Unleavened Bread, the Feast of Shavuot, The Day of Blasting, The Day of Atonements and The Feast of Succot. The cycle ends with "The

Eighth Day." (see Vayiqra 23). There are seven annual Appointed Times which include three Pilgrimmage Feasts, known as hags. The Pilgrimmage Feasts occur at the location where YHWH placed His Name - the dwelling place of YHWH. (Debarim 12).

So what do we do with these Appointed Times? The answer to that question depends upon your relationship with YHWH. If you are in His Covenant, then you must surely keep His commandments, which include His Appointed Times. If you are not in His Covenant, then you are free to participate in the Babylonian holidays. Your actions reflect your heart and determine your destiny.

You see, the Appointed Times are for those in the House. Those who are not keeping those times will not be in the House. They will not be allowed back in the Garden, which is the New Jerusalem.

"*¹ And he showed me a pure river of water of life, clear as crystal, proceeding from the throne of Elohim and of the Lamb. ² In the middle of its street, and on either side of the river, was the tree of life, which bore twelve fruits, each tree yielding its fruit every month. The leaves of the tree were for the healing of the nations. ³ And there shall be no more curse, but the throne of Elohim and of the Lamb shall be in it, and His servants shall serve Him. ⁴ They shall see His face, and His Name shall be on their foreheads. ⁵ There shall be no night there: They need no lamp nor light of the sun, for YHWH Elohim gives them light. And they shall reign throughout the ages and to eternity. ⁶ Then he said to me, These words are faithful and true. And YHWH Elohim of the set apart prophets sent His angel to show His servants the things which must shortly take place. ⁷ Behold, I am coming quickly! Blessed is he who keeps the words of the prophecy of this book. ⁸ Now I, Yahanan, saw and heard these things. And when I heard and saw, I fell down to worship before the feet of the angel who* *showed me these things. ⁹ Then he said to me, See that you do not do that. For I am your fellow servant, and of your brethren the prophets, and of those who keep the words of this book. Worship Elohim. ¹⁰ And he said to me, Do not seal the words of the prophecy of this book, for the time is at hand. ¹¹ He who is unjust, let him be unjust still; he who is filthy, let him be filthy still; he who is righteous, let him be righteous still; he who is set apart, let him be set apart still. ¹² <u>And behold, I am coming quickly, and My reward is with Me, to give to every one according to his work.</u> ¹³ I am the Aleph and the Taw (✕⌁), the Beginning and the End, the First and the Last. ¹⁴ <u>Blessed are those who do His commandments, that they may have the right to the Tree of Life, and may enter through the gates into the city. ¹⁵ But outside are dogs and sorcerers and sexually immoral and murderers and idolaters, and whoever loves and practices a lie.</u>"* Revelation 22:1-15.

This is a description of the New Jerusalem, the restored Garden. Here is the Tree of Life, but only those who obey can gain entry. The pagans are outside, which includes those who love and practice lies. The pagan holidays that derive from Babylon are lies. So you must ask yourself: Do you love pagan traditions such as Christmas and Easter. Do you love to practice these lies? Do you refuse to discontinue observing these times despite the fact that you know they are lies? If so, you will not be permitted into the New Jerusalem. It is really that simple.

It does not matter how many prayers you have said, or if you have "accepted Jesus into your heart." It does not matter whether you have gone to confession or regularly attended mass or other church services. Nor does it matter what Christmas and Easter "mean" to you.

What matters is what you do. You demonstrate your heart and beliefs by your conduct. You demonstrate that you are in the Covenant by keeping the commandments, which include the Appointed Times, and you demonstrate that you are not in the Covenant when you refuse to keep the Appointed Times. For the Scriptures declare, "*One that turns away his ear from hearing the Torah, even his prayer shall be an abomination.*" Proverbs 28:9.

If you are a Christian, then your relationship with YHWH rests upon the shed blood of the Messiah – the Lamb of Elohim. Most Christians understand that the blood provides a covering, and that it was accomplished through the Passover. It is clear that no one can earn their salvation by works. Our salvation rests upon the shed blood of the Lamb of Elohim – Yahushua.

Typically though, Christians ignore or neglect the fact that Passover is a Covenant meal. You must be in Covenant with YHWH in order to participate in the Passover. Essentially most are not in Covenant, because they believe there is a new and different Covenant for the fictitious entity called "the Church."

As a result, Christians do not observe Passover, so admittedly, they are not identifying with the Elohim of Yisrael – the One Who makes Covenant with His people. In fact, many attempt to replace the annual Passover with a tradition called Communion or Eucharist.

The false teaching - that there is a new covenant made with the Church that is different from the Covenant made with Yisrael - has led many astray into the realm of lies. There is no different Covenant, only one renewed through the Messiah. As a result, Christians end up rejecting the Torah of YHWH, which includes the Appointed Times, that lead a person on the narrow way of the Covenant path. They then find themselves operating within Mystery Babylon, participating in pagan holidays and traditions.

They do this to their own destruction and repeat the same error – the same sin as The House of Yisrael – also referred to as Ephraim. Read what the Prophet Hoshea proclaimed: "⁶ <u>My people are destroyed for lack of knowledge. Because you have rejected knowledge, I also will reject you from being priests for Me. Because you have forgotten the Torah of your Elohim, I also will forget your children.</u> ⁷ The more they increased, the more they sinned against Me. I will change their glory into shame. ⁸ They eat up the sin of My people. They set their heart on their iniquity. ⁹ And it shall be: like people, like priest. So I will punish them for their ways, and reward them for their deeds. ¹⁰ For they shall eat, but not have enough. They shall commit harlotry, but not increase, because they have ceased obeying YHWH. ¹¹ Harlotry, wine, and new wine enslave the heart. ¹² My people ask counsel from their wooden idols, and their staff informs them. For the spirit of harlotry has caused them to stray, and they have played the harlot against their Elohim. ¹³ They offer sacrifices on the mountaintops, and burn incense on the hills, under oaks, poplars, and terebinths, because their shade is good. Therefore your daughters commit harlotry, and your brides commit adultery. ¹⁴ I will not punish your daughters when they commit harlotry, nor your brides when they commit adultery; for the men themselves go apart with harlots, and offer sacrifices with a ritual harlot. <u>Therefore people who do not understand will be trampled.</u> ¹⁵ Though you, Yisrael, play the harlot, let not Yahudah offend. Do not come up to Gilgal, nor go up to Beth Aven, nor swear an oath, saying, 'As YHWH lives' - ¹⁶ For Yisrael is stubborn like a stubborn calf; now YHWH will let them forage like a lamb in open country. ¹⁷ <u>Ephraim is joined to idols, let him alone.</u> ¹⁸ <u>Their drink is rebellion, they commit harlotry continually. Her rulers dearly love dishonor.</u> ¹⁹ <u>The wind has wrapped her up in its wings, and they shall be ashamed because of their sacrifices.</u>" Hoshea 4:6-19.

This book contains the knowledge that many need to wake up and repent, before it is too late. You must reject any pagan traditions that you have inherited, and return to the Torah of YHWH - including His Appointed Times contained therein. Christians have rejected knowledge and the Torah. Christianity has willingly relinquished the Appointed Times to the religion of Judaism, because they have no use for them.

Instead, Christianity has developed its own way of worshipping YHWH, and its own times. They have repeated the same sins as Yisrael. By changing the times of YHWH, Christianity observes a different sabbath and different feasts, many of which derive from pagan sun worship. This is specifically prohibited in the Scriptures. (Debarim 12:1-4 and 12:32).

The bottom line is - **the appointments that you keep determine who or what you serve.** If you claim to believe in YHWH and love Him, then you keep His Commandments. (Proverbs 7:2, Yahanan 14:15; 15:10). As we approach the difficult days ahead, only those who obey will be protected from harm.

"*⁷ And to the messenger of the assembly in Philadelphia write, These things says He who is qadosh, He who is true, He who has the key of David, He who opens and no one shuts, and shuts and no one opens: ⁸ I know your works. See, I have set before you an open door, and no one can shut it; for you have a little strength, have kept My word, and have not denied My Name. ⁹ Indeed I will make those of the synagogue of Satan, who say they are Yahudim and are not, but lie - indeed I will make them come and worship before your feet, and to know that I have loved you. ¹⁰ Because you have kept My command to persevere, I also will keep you from the hour of trial which shall come upon the whole world, to test those who dwell on the earth. ¹¹ Behold, I am coming quickly! Hold fast what you have, that no one may take your crown. ¹² He who overcomes, I will* make him a pillar in the Temple of My Elohim, and he shall go out no more. I will write on him the name of My Elohim and the name of the city of My Elohim, the New Jerusalem, which comes down out of heaven from My Elohim. And I will write on him My new name." Revelation 3:7-12.

Notice that only those who keep the commandments will be protected in "the hour of trial."[171] Some put little to no effort into discerning the times, and gladly follow the vain traditions that they have inherited from their fathers. It is time to wake up and come out of Babylon.

It is time to fulfill the words of the Prophet Yirmeyahu who proclaimed: *"[19] O YHWH, my strength and my fortress, my refuge in the day of affliction, the Gentiles shall come to You from the ends of the earth and say, 'Surely our fathers have inherited lies, worthlessness and unprofitable things.' [20] Will a man make gods for himself, which are not gods? [21] Therefore behold, I will this once cause them to know, I will cause them to know My hand and My might; and they shall know that My name is YHWH."* Yirmeyahu 16:19-21.

We must recognize the lies that we have inherited and cast aside the false gods, and the vain traditions. We must acknowledge YHWH and His path. The people of YHWH were cursed because they strayed from the ancient path of YHWII.

"Because My people have forgotten Me, they have burned incense to worthless idols. And they have caused themselves to stumble in their ways, from the ancient paths, to walk in pathways and not on a highway . . ." Yirmeyahu 18:15. It is time to return to those ancient paths - the path of the ages. *"Thus says YHWH, Stand in the ways, and see, and ask for the old (olam) paths, where is the good way, and walk therein, and you shall find rest for your souls. But they said, We will not walk therein."* Yirmeyahu 6:16.

The word olam (ᵐ ⁊ ̊ ⊙) is translated as "old,"

also "ancient." It can mean: "through the ages." The point is that the Ancient Paths have not gone away, they extend to the end – through the ages.

"⁹ Remember the former things of old (olam), for I am Elohim, and there is no other; I am Elohim, and there is none like Me, ¹⁰ Declaring the end from the beginning, and from ancient times things that are not yet done, Saying, My counsel shall stand, and I will do all My pleasure, ¹¹ Calling a bird of prey from the east, the man who executes My counsel, from a far country. Indeed I have spoken it; I will also bring it to pass. I have purposed it; I will also do it. ¹² Listen to Me, you stubborn-hearted, who are far from righteousness: ¹³ I bring My righteousness near, it shall not be far off; My salvation shall not linger. And I will place salvation in Zion, for Yisrael My glory." Yeshayahu 46:9-13.

It is time to be wise and get ready. Yahushua came to set things straight, and guide people away from the traditions of the Pharisees. He revealed the righteous path, and brought it near to the people. While teaching His talmidim on the Mount of Olives, He gave an interesting parable concerning the kingdom of heaven and the end days. That parable concerned 10 virgins - 5 wise and 5 foolish.

"¹ Then shall the Kingdom of Heaven be likened unto ten virgins, which took their lamps, and went forth to meet the Bridegroom. ² And five of them were wise, and five were foolish. ³ They that were foolish took their lamps, and took no oil with them: ⁴ But the wise took oil in their vessels with their lamps. ⁵ While the Bridegroom tarried, they all slumbered and slept. ⁶ And at midnight there was a cry made, Behold, the Bridegroom cometh; go ye out to meet him. ⁷ Then all those virgins arose, and trimmed their lamps. ⁸ And the foolish said unto the wise, Give us of your oil; for our lamps are gone out. ⁹ But the wise answered, saying, Not so; lest there be not enough for us and you, but go ye rather to them that sell, and buy for yourselves. [10] And while they went to buy, the Bridegroom came; and they that were ready went in with him to the marriage: and the door was shut. [11] Afterward came also the other virgins, saying, Lord, Lord, open to us. [12] But He answered and said, Verily I say unto you, I know you not. [13] Watch therefore, for you do not know intuitively (oida) the day or the hour wherein the Son of Man cometh." Mattityahu 25:1-13.

  The virgins represent those waiting for their Groom. They are those who anticipate the return of the Messiah who is coming for His Bride – Yisrael. There is a wedding on the horizon, and they needed to be ready. They were all slumbering and sleeping, and when the cry was given at midnight they all arose and trimmed their lamps. They were all expecting Him, but the foolish virgins were not prepared. When the Groom came, the foolish virgins were off shopping. They missed their opportunity to join the wedding Feast, and they were shut out.

  They were not permitted into the Feast because <u>the Bridegroom does not know, and will not recognize, anyone working lawlessness or unrighteousness</u>. (see Mattityahu 7:23; Luke 13:27). These are people who are not observing the Torah, and violating the Instructions of YHWH.

  We have already discussed the marriage aspect of the Covenant. The entire process is to lead us to the House of YHWH, and back to the Garden. It is there that we can enter into relationship, and dwell with Him. You must be known by the Master, which means your name must be written in His Scroll. Those in His Scroll are those in the Covenant - those who have been covered by the blood, and obey the Commandments. They will be remembered by YHWH.

  You need to have enough oil so that you have

light to see in the darkness. The Scriptures clearly indicate that the Torah is a Lamp. "*Thy Word is a lamp unto my feet, and a light unto my path.*" Tehillim 119:105. "*For the commandment is a lamp; and the Torah is light; and reproofs of instruction are the way of life.*" Proverbs 6:23. "*The light of the righteous rejoiceth: but the lamp of the wicked shall be put out.*" Proverbs 13:9. The Scriptures clearly define the righteous as those who obey, and the wicked as those who do not obey.

The five wise virgins are the firstfruits of the harvest. "*These are they which were not defiled with women; for they are virgins. These are they which follow the Lamb whithersoever He goeth. These were redeemed from among men, being the firstfruits unto Elohim and to the Lamb.*" Revelation 14:4. If you want to be ready for the Master's return, then you had better not delay. You need to prepare and make sure that your lamps are lit and full of oil. That involves the Word of YHWH, the Instructions found in the Torah. If you are participating in the sins of Babylon then you are in darkness. In fact, the Scriptures clearly state: "*the light of the lamp shall not shine in [Babylon] anymore.*" Revelation 18:23.

Those who have oil are those who are walking in righteousness and obeying the Torah, which includes the Appointed Times. The Appointed Times will soon be a guide through darkness and judgment just as they were for Yisrael when they were enslaved in Egypt. Those who keep the Appointed Times will be ready for the Master's arrival. Those living and participating within Mystery Babylon will not.

The Appointed Times clearly reveal the Covenant path, and as we saw with Yisrael in Egypt, the Passover is the beginning of that path. Those who desire to journey on that Covenant path must first be in the Covenant. They must bear the sign of the Covenant –

circumcision.

 Once in that Covenant, they must enter the house through the door, which is covered by the blood of the Lamb. As they partake of the Covenant meal, and eat of the lamb whose blood was shed, they are acknowledging that the firstborn require the protection of the lamb. This of course is symbolic of the Lamb of Elohim, the Messiah. The First of YHWH died so that the firstborn of Yisrael might live.

 That Appointment revealed that the Son of YHWH, the Lamb of Elohim, was the fulfillment of the pattern of the Passover Lamb. Once we partake of the Covenant meal we are delivered from death, and provided a Sabbath rest - which is the First Day of the Feast of Unleavened Bread. This Feast is an annual event, a Pilgrimage Feast, when we are supposed to meet with YHWH at His House. We are to refrain from leaven, which represents sin. When we properly observe this Appointed Time we reflect upon any sin, including pagan influences, that may have crept into our lives. We purge them from our beings, understanding that we must be pure to be in the presence of YHWH.

 During this Feast, a sheaf (omer) of the first (resheet) of the barley would be cut by the Priest. The resheet offering was the first cutting of the harvest, and it was waved before YHWH by the Priest on behalf of Yisrael. This event began a count of seven sevens, or rather seven weeks, which is what the Scriptures call the Feast of Weeks. During this period of time the people were harvesting their grain. First the barley, and then the wheat. Toward the end of the wheat harvest, on the 50th day, the people gathered at the House and presented their bikkurim - the firstfruits of their crops. Through this act, they were really presenting themselves as firstfruits.

 This 50th day called Shavuot (weeks) is

connected to the Feast of Unleavened Bread through the counting of weeks and days. Due to this connection, it is often considered the "atzeret" of Passover, although the Scriptures never describe it as such. The combined barley and wheat harvets involved grain crops that needed to be separated from weeds (tares), which grew among them. After the separation, the grain was brought to the threshing floor where it was threshed, winnowed and placed safely in the storehouse (barn). The tares and the chaff were destroyed by fire.

How appropriate that the people would come with their harvest offerings to the House of YHWH, which was built on a threshing floor. (see 2 Shemuel 24:18-21). The symbolism cannot be ignored. Of course, Yahushua often taught in parables, which would expound upon the meaning of the Appointed Times.

"[24] *Another parable put He forth unto them, saying, The Kingdom of Heaven is likened unto a man which sowed good seed in his field:* [25] *But while men slept, his enemy came and sowed tares among the wheat, and went his way.* [26] *But when the blade was sprung up, and brought forth fruit, then appeared the tares also.* [27] *So the servants of the householder came and said unto him, Sir, didst not thou sow good seed in thy field? From whence then hath it tares?* [28] *He said unto them, An enemy hath done this. The servants said unto him, Wilt thou then that we go and gather them up?* [29] *But he said, Nay; lest while ye gather up the tares, ye root up also the wheat with them.* [30] *Let both grow together until the harvest: and in the time of harvest I will say to the reapers, Gather ye together first the tares, and bind them in bundles to burn them, but gather the wheat into my storehouse (barn)."* Mattityahu 13:24-30.

This is one of many parables that Yahushua used relative to the agriculture and harvest season, which was at the heart of the Appointed Times. The patterns of the

Covenant Land are meant to symbolize the spiritual teaching, and plan of YHWH for His Covenant people. All of the patterns are applicable to our spiritual walk. Indeed, Yisrael is referred to as *"trees of righteousness, the planting of YHWH."* Yeshayahu 61:3. Therefore, those in the Covenant, the people of Yisrael, should be bearing good fruit, which they can present to YHWH at His House.

We can see this in the progression of the crops as they begin as seeds. Some seeds are good while others are bad. The seeds planted fall upon various types of ground. Yahushua showed this in a parable. Some seed fell on good ground producing a great yield, while others fell on bad soil producing less. There are also weeds, known as tares, which grow up with the good seed. In the end they will all be separated. (See Mattityahu 13). Therefore, the Covenant progression as "rehearsed" through the Appointed Times actually reveals how YHWH will gather His people, His Harvest, in the end.

So the first offering made during Unleavened Bread began the grain harvest, and it was presented without yeast. It was pure and represented the Messiah as the first offering of the harvest of YHWH. Messiah, of course, is the First, and as the Lamb of Elohim, His blood covers the house, saves the firstborn from death and makes way for the adoption of the firstborn of Yisrael, represented by the Levites. The firstborn are then able to enter into the House, partake of the meal and join into the wedding celebration.

The seven weeks are then counted when the people are harvesting their crops. The harvest season culminates with the 50th day, when the people gather together at the House of YHWH to celebrate the Feast of Weeks. This is the harvest of YHWH. This process is revealing one aspect of the Covenant plan, when

YHWH would gather His people to thresh and sift them.

Of course, the fact that it occurs on the 50th day then connects us to the 50th year - the Jubilee, which begins in the Sabbath month. By now the cycles of seven are extremely prevalent, but no more so than in the seventh month - the Sabbath month. The firstborn of the month - the renewed moon is a special day. It is marked by the blasting of a trumpet, and calls us to repentance. We then count ten days until Yom Kippurim, the Day of Atonements. Those who are covered by the blood are atoned, and those who are not covered receive no atonement.

Those who receive atonement proceed to the Feast of Ingathering. Instead of grain, now the harvest is fruit. This occurs at the end of the harvest - the end of days. This is aptly described in the Book of Revelation.

"*^{14} I looked, and there before me was a white cloud, and seated on the cloud was one 'like a Son of Man' with a crown of gold on his head and a sharp sickle in his hand. ^{15} Then another messenger came out of the Hekal and called in a loud voice to him who was sitting on the cloud, 'Take your sickle and reap, because the time to reap has come, for the harvest of the earth is ripe.' ^{16} So he who was seated on the cloud swung his sickle over the earth, and the earth was harvested. ^{17} Another messenger came out of the Hekal in heaven, and he too had a sharp sickle. ^{18} Still another messenger, who had charge of the fire, came from the Altar and called in a loud voice to him who had the sharp sickle, 'Take your sharp sickle and gather the clusters of grapes from the earth's vine, because its grapes are ripe.' ^{19} The messenger swung his sickle on the earth, gathered its grapes and threw them into the great winepress of Elohim's wrath. ^{20} They were trampled in the winepress outside the city, and blood flowed out of the press, rising as high as the horses' bridles for a distance of 1,600 stadia." Revelation 14:14-20.*

According to this passage it becomes quite apparent that the earth will be harvested around the Appointed Time of Succot - The Feast of Ingathering. So during the final Sabbath month in the 120th Jubilee, the earth will be harvested, and the firstfruits of the Covenant will be gathered to dwell with YHWH.[172] The grapes will be thrown into the winepress of Elohim's wrath.

So this process of harvesting over the course of seven months, within the framework of seven Appointed Times, involving seven Sabbaths and culminating with the eighth day is the context for the entire Covenant process involving the people of YHWH.

If you are in a Covenant relationship with YHWH, then you should keep the commandments. Those commandments include the Appointed Times. We keep them by watching over, protecting and guarding these Times, because they are our guide back to Eden. As we keep and proclaim the Appointed Times we are participating in rehearsals that will affect our future. The prophets foretold an exciting future for the Covenant people, known as am Yisrael.

This divided people will soon be reunited, and there will be a deliverance involving the Appointed Times. The patterns of the past are there for future generations to learn from. If you are participating in the rehearsals prescribed by YHWH, then your fate is secure. If you are participating in any other rehearsals, then you have good reason to be concerned.

With that in mind, the importance of discerning the times cannot be emphasized enough. Yahushua repeatedly warned His followers to watch.[173] When He approached Jerusalem before His crucifixion, He wept because the people failed to discern the times. (Luke 19:41-44). They failed to recognize Him, and they were

blinded concerning their impending doom. Many were killed when Jerusalem and the Temple were destroyed in 70 CE.

YHWH has stated many times that He does not desire the blood of sacrifices. *"For I desire mercy and not sacrifice, and the knowledge of Elohim more than burnt offerings."* Hoshea 6:6. The offerings and sacrifices presented during the Appointed Times were meant to instruct us during the Age of Instruction.

As we approach the end of days, the "m'qetz yomim," it is vitally important to understand the times in which we are living. Through the Appointed Times YHWH has provided the outline for His plan. Those Times were established from the beginning, and are there to guide the Covenant people in the end.

"³ Hearken unto me, O House of Yaakob, and all the remnant of the House of Yisrael, which are borne by Me from the belly, which are carried from the womb . . . ⁹ Remember the former things of old: for I am Elohim, and there is none else; I am Elohim, and there is none like Me, ¹⁰ Declaring the end from the beginning, and from ancient times the things that are not yet done, saying, My counsel shall stand, and I will do all My pleasure." Yeshayahu 46:3, 9-10.

The Appointed Times are not simply historical events from days gone by. They are special rehearsals in the plan of YHWH, which lead up to a crescendo in the end of the age – the Age of Messiah. In fact, it can be safely stated that the Appointed Times may be more important today than ever before as we approach the end of days.

It could mean the difference between life and death in the future. The Yisraelites in Egypt needed to precisely follow the commandments concerning the Passover in order to be spared from death. Those same commandments will prove critical in the end, but we

need to watch. If the Children of Yisrael had not diligently obeyed the commandments concerning the Passover in Egypt, their firstborn would have perished. The same will be true in the end. Those who are not watching, those who are not wise, those who do not have sufficient oil in their lamps, will find themselves in darkness, shut out of the House and the Feast occurring therein

Yahushua Himself warned: *"Remember therefore how thou hast received and heard; and hold fast and repent. If therefore you shall not watch, I will come as a thief, and you shall not know what hour I will come upon you."* Revelation 3:3. In other words, if we do not watch we will be surprised, but if we watch we will not be surprised. A person's readiness hinges upon their diligence in discerning time.

The river of time that flowed from the beginning is soon approaching the end of its journey. The river that sprang from the Garden flows back to the Garden, the New Jerusalem. The New Jerusalem, better known as the Renewed Jerusalem includes a river. The Scriptures begin with a river and end with a river - the River of Life.

The Appointed Times chart our course back to the Garden where only one river flows. To properly navigate our passage on this river, YHWH provided us with the Torah, which acts as a lighthouse, a channel marker and a warning beacon. It keeps us on couse, on the way to life.

Contained within the Torah are the instructions concerning Appointed Times, which act as currents in the cycles of time. These cycles of righteousness continue from the beginning to the end and are there for our benefit. (Psalm 23:3). They are ports of harbor along our journey where we are able to rest, refresh, resupply

and do business with YHWH. They help to correct our course and keep us from the shallows, the rocks, the winds and the waves that would send us into harms way.

When we stay on the straight and narrow, we are assured that things will be well with us. "*³² You shall observe to do therefore as YHWH your Elohim hath commanded you: you shall not turn aside to the right hand or to the left. ³³ You shall walk in all the ways which YHWH your Elohim hath commanded you, that you may live, and that it may be well with you, and that you may prolong your days in the land which you shall possess.*" Debarim 5:32-33.

If we stray to the right or the left, those paths lead to death and destruction. If you have strayed from the straight path by participating in pagan traditions, you have a choice to make. You can repent and discontinue those activities, choosing to walk the straight path by keeping the true Appointed Times as set forth in the Scriptures. This conduct is pleasing to YHWH as you obey Him and follow His Covenant path.

The other choice is to continue participating in the pagan derived traditions. You can try to convince yourself that your actions are harmless, and YHWH is not displeased with your actions. You can think that it is all simply a matter of the heart, and it does not matter what you actually do. Regardless of what you think, or how you might try to justify your actions, the Scriptures are quite clear, that you are operating in self delusion.

The sad truth is that many would rather maintain their traditions than actually obey YHWH. A person's conduct reveals what is in their heart. If you put YHWH first, then you will obey Him. If you put yourself first, then you will do what you want, regardless of what YHWH commands. This, of course, is nothing new. It is exactly what the Messiah was dealing with when He confronted the Pharisees.

The Pharisees were very religious, but through their desire to be zealous, they lost something. They replaced YHWH and His Torah with their traditions. As a result, they went their own way instead of His Way. By doing so they lost their relationship with YHWH, and they did not know Him when He appeared – in the flesh. This is the problem with religion. It can delude you into thinking and believing that you have a relationship with the Creator, when in fact you do not.

Religion can convince you that by following prescribed traditions you draw closer to the Creator, when, in fact, they separate you from Him. Religion will try to convince you that its doctrines and traditions provide the true path, the way to "heaven" or "paradise." This is in spite of the fact that Messiah proclaimed: "*I am the way, the truth, and the life. No one comes to the Father except through Me.*" Yahanan 14:6.

When people have to make a choice between the truth and tradition, many choose their traditions over the Messiah. They choose the way of religion over the way of the Torah, as walked by the Messiah. They decide to walk in the path that they find most comfortable or enjoyable.

We saw this with the Pharisees, and we see it in Judaism and Christianity today. Traditions reign supreme over the simplicity and purity of the Torah. Yahushua said: "*[29] Take My yoke upon you and learn from Me, for I am gentle and lowly in heart, and you will find rest for your souls. [30] For My yoke is easy and My burden is light.*" Mattityahu 11:29-30.

We all have a choice to make. Will we take the yoke of the Messiah, or the yoke of men. Rest assured, YHWH is very concerned with our actions, as well as our thoughts. It is what we do that demonstrates what we believe. Messiah could not have made it any clearer when He proclaimed: *"If you love Me, keep My commandments."* Yahanan 14:15. In fact, He shows mercy to those who "keep" His Commandments. If your religion acknowledges the Ten Commandments, then you should take note of the Second Commandment spoken by the voice of YHWH.

"⁴ You shall not make for yourself a carved image - any likeness of anything that is in heaven above, or that is in the earth beneath, or that is in the water under the earth; ⁵ you shall not bow down to them nor serve them. For I, YHWH your Elohim, am a jealous Elohim, visiting the iniquity of the fathers upon the children to the third and fourth generations of those who hate Me, ⁶ but showing mercy to thousands, to those who love Me and keep My commandments." Shemot 20:4-6.

His commandments include specific Appointed Times to be kept and observed. It is these times that are to be kept, not times created by man or derived from Babylon. It is through the keeping of the Appointed Times that we demonstrate our love, and our belief in YHWH. The Appointed Times had significance in the past, and they continue to be relevant in the present and future. They are not just interesting historical events, they are a treasure map that guides us back to paradise.

The Messiah could not have made it any clearer when He said, *"He that believes the Son has the Age of Life, but he that does not obey the Son shall not see life, for the wrath of Elohim abides on Him."* Yahanan 3:36. Belief and obedience are interlocking concepts which religious men attempt to separate, but which a servant of Elohim would never separate.

Hopefully, the reader will understand the need to "come out of Babylon," and step into synchronicity with the plan of YHWH as it plays out through His Appointed Times. It may seem foreign at first, especially when you start discerning between tradition and the

Scriptural commandments. This is to be expected, and it is part of the process where we learn to meet with YHWH and learn His Ways. Just as a newborn learns to crawl before he can walk, the same holds true as we are "born again" into the Covenant, and begin to traverse the Covenant journey back to the Garden.

The point at first is simply obedience. We may not always know why we are required to do things, but that is exactly why we must simply obey. Through our continuous obedience, we begin to learn and understand the purpose of these rehearsals. There will be a time when they will no longer be rehearsals. Just as Yisrael once journeyed from slavery to freedom, protected from the judgments of YHWH, there will be a time in the future when Yisrael, the Covenant people, will be gathered and delivered through their diligent obedience to these rehearsals.

The pagan traditions adopted by many religions are rehearsals for the worship of the sun, and ultimately hashatan – the adversary. If we are in a Covenant relationship with YHWH, then we must reject those traditions, remain set apart from Babylon and rehearse the events associated with His Covenant.

Your conduct and observance of time must be examined within the context of the Covenant. The Appointed Times are prescribed by YHWH to perfect and establish His Covenant, and His Covenant people. If you are a part of His Covenant then you must understand the Moadim – the Appointed Times. You must also avoid all false and profane traditions that derive from Babylon, and refrain from observing and participating in Babylonian holy days – Pagan Holidays.

Endnotes

[1] The term "god" is a generic term which can be attached to any number of powerful beings described in mythology and worshipped in pagan religions. Some use a capital "G" to refer to "the God of the Bible" but I find it a disservice to apply this label to the Creator of the Universe when the Hebrew Scriptures clearly refer to Him as Elohim. The pagan origins of the word "god" are discussed in the Walk in the Light series book entitled "Names." Elohim (𐤌𐤉𐤄𐤋𐤀) is technically plural, but that does not designate more than one Creator. The singular form is El (𐤋𐤀) and could refer to any "mighty one," but because the plural is used to describe the Creator, it means that Elohim is qualitatively stronger or more powerful than any singular El (𐤋𐤀). In Hebrew, the plural form can mean that something or someone is qualitatively greater not just quantitatively greater. We see in the first sentence of the Scriptures that "In the Beginning Elohim created" the Hebrew for "created" is bara (𐤀𐤓𐤁) which literally is "He created." It is masculine singular showing that while Elohim is plural He is masculine singular. For an excellent discussion of the Hebrew Etymology of the Name of Elohim I recommend *His Name is One* written by Jeff A. Benner, Virtualbookworm.com Publishing 2002. The Hebrew language currently in use, often called modern hebrew, is not the language used when the Scriptures were first spoken and written. The original Hebrew language is often called "ancient" or "paleo" Hebrew.

[2] While the notion that the Hebrew Language is the "mother tongue" of the planet is not a popular notion with secular scholars, there is evidence pointing to that fact. See *The Origin of Speeches Intelligent Design in Language*, Isaac E. Mozeson, Lightcatcher Books, 2006.

[3] The current modern Hebrew character set is sometimes referred to as Chaldean flame letters. This language was brought with the Yahudim after their Babylonian exile. It is

important to understand a bit of history involving the Kingdom of Israel (Yisrael). After the death of King Solomon (Shlomo), the Kingdom was divided in two. The Northern Tribes were referred to as the House of Yisrael and the Southern Tribes were referred to as the House of Yahudah. The House of Yisrael was conquered and exiled by the Assyrians in the North. The House of Yahudah was conquered and exiled by the Babylonians in the South. There is a great deal of mystery associated with this language which is really a modern language. One thing is certain, it is not the original language of Yisrael. In fact, it is really a language that exclusively belongs to the Yahudim. Those from the House of Yisrael who desire to truly learn about their Hebrew Roots should be looking at the original Hebrew Language often referred to as Ancient Hebrew or Paleo Hebrew. This would have been the language used by Abraham, Yitshaq, Yaakob, Mosheh and the Assembly of Yisrael.

4. There are many different Ancient Hebrew scripts discovered through archaeology. Since they were all written by different individuals, there are stylistic variances between them. The modern Hebrew used today is not the same language as the Ancient or Paleo Hebrew used by Ancient Yisrael. Therefore, throughout this text we will attempt to provide examples of words and phrases in their Ancient Script in order to glean the depth of their meaning.

5. The Paleo Hebrew font primarily used in this book is an adaptation and interpretation of the various examples of Paleo Hebrew found throughout archaeology. Since there are a variety of scripts found in academia, this one script font developed by the author is being used for consistency and clarity in an attempt to represent the Creator's meaning in the "original" language. The author has developed a Font intended to represent the ancient language as might have been written by an individual person thousands of years ago.

6. It is important to recognize that there was a spiritual universe before "the beginning" of the physical universe. The *time* between the *foundation of the world* in the *spiritual universe*, and Day One of the *physical universe* is referred to as Olam She'avar or The World that Was in Hebraic thought . . . Everything in the *spiritual universe*, including

the angels and the *souls* of all people, were created *before the time of the ages* according to 2 Timothy 1:8-11, Titus 1:1-3 and Jude 1:6. This time in history is referred to as Olam She'avar or The World that Was in Hebraic thought. This was when the *foundation* of the earth was laid according to Job 38:4, Psalms 102:25, Isaiah 48:13, Zechariah 12:1 and Hebrews 1:10. Olam She'avar is referred to as the time *before the disruption of the world* in John 17:24 and 1 Peter 1:17-21. The children of Elohim were chosen during Olam She'avar *before the disruption of the world* according to Ephesians 1:3-6. See *The 7000 Year Plan*, www.torahcalendar.com.

7 The Hebrew Scriptures contain numerous instances of what are commonly called jots and tittles. These typically include enlarged, diminished or reversed characters intended to draw the readers attention to something. No one knows exactly how they came into existence, although the popular opinion is that Mosheh included them in the original Torah. One thing is certain, they are not considered to be scribal errors and they have been maintained in all copies of the Hebrew texts, although you will not see them in a translation.

8 The word shi (⟂ש) is used only three times in the Scriptures - Isaiah 18:7 and Psalms 68:29 and 76:11. In each case it has profound prophetic significance.

9 It is important to recognize that there is no such thing as a Hebrew numeral set, separate and apart from the Hebrew letters. As a result, each Hebrew character has a corresponding numeric value. This adds an interesting dimension to the study of Scriptures. Commonly called gematria, the study of the numeric values of characters and words can be quite revealing.

10 The numerical value of "beresheet" (Xיwﬠפב) is 913, calculated as follows: ב = 2, ר = 200, א = 1, ש = 300, י = 10, ת = 400. The numerical value of "beit" (Xיב) is 412, calculated as follows: ב = 2, י = 10, ת = 400. The numerical value of "rosh" (wאר) is 501, calculated as follows: ר = 200, א = 1, ש = 300.

11 The word et (Xא), otherwise known as the Aleph Taw, consists of two Hebrew characters - the aleph (א) which is the first character in the Hebrew alphabet, and the taw (ת) which is the last letter in the Hebrew alphabet. "This word Xא is used over 11,000 times (and never translated into

English as there is no equivalent) to point to the direct object of the verb." (from Benner, Jeff A., *Learn to Read Biblical Hebrew*, Virtualbookworm.com 2004 Page 41.). It is embedded throughout the Hebrew Scriptures and while it has a known grammatical function, the Sages have long understood that it has a much deeper and mysterious function – many believe that it is a direct reference to the Messiah. As such, it plays an important part in understanding the Scriptural Covenants so we will, at times, examine its existence and relevance throughout this text.

[12] For further information concerning the language in and through the process of creation see the Walk in the Light series book entitled *Scriptures*.

[13] Time is often described as a physical dimension. Just as height, length and width constitute the dimensions of our three dimensional physical world, so time is another dimension in the world as we know it.

[14] The Torah (𐤀𐤅𐤓𐤄) is generally found within and consists of the first five books of the Hebrew and Christian Scriptures. Traditionally, it is contained in a Scroll and the first scroll was written by Moses (Mosheh), and placed within the Ark of the Covenant. The Torah is often referred to as "The Law" in many modern English Bibles. Law is not an accurate word to describe the Torah which often results in the Torah being confused with the laws, customs, and traditions of the religious leaders as well as the laws of particular countries. The Torah is more accurately defined as the "instruction" of YHWH for His set apart people. The Torah contains instruction for those who desire to live righteous, set apart lives in accordance with the will of YHWH. Contrary to popular belief, people can obey the Torah. (Deuteronomy 30:11-14). It is the myriads of regulations, customs and traditions which men attach to the Torah that make it impossible and burdensome for people to obey. The names of the five different "books" are transliterated from their proper Hebrew names as follows: Genesis - Beresheet, Exodus - Shemot, Leviticus - Vayiqra, Numbers - Bemidbar, Deuteronomy - Debarim.

[15] YHWH (יהוה) in Modern Hebrew and (𐤉𐤄𐤅𐤄) in Paleo Hebrew, is the four letter Name of the Elohim described in the Scriptures. This four letter Name has commonly been

called the "Tetragrammaton" and traditionally has been considered to be ineffable or unpronounceable. As a result, despite the fact that it is found nearly 7,000 times in the Hebrew Scriptures, it has been replaced with such titles as "The Lord," "Adonai" and "HaShem." I believe that this practice is in direct violation of the First and Third Commandments. Some commonly accepted pronunciations are: Yahweh, Yahuwah and Yahowah. Since there is debate over which pronunciation is correct, I simply use the Name as it is found in the Scriptures, although I spell it in English from left to right, rather than in Hebrew from right to left. For the person who truly desires to know the nature of the Elohim described in the Scriptures, a good place to start is the Name by which He revealed Himself to all mankind.

16 The word "Bible" has traditionally been the word used to describe the collection of documents considered by Christianity to be inspired by Elohim - I prefer the use of the word Scriptures. The word Bible derives from Byblos which has more pagan connotations than I prefer, especially when referring to the written Word of Elohim. This subject is discussed in greater detail in the Walk in the Light Series book entitled *Scriptures*.

17 It is important to recognize that some things get "lost in translation." This is particularly true when translating from an eastern language to a western language. This does not mean that the Word of Elohim is not perfect. We are talking about imperfect men translating words from one language to another while attempting to maintain their complete power and meaning. For a detailed discussion of this matter read the Walk in the Light series book entitled *Scriptures*.

18 One cannot ignore the parallels within the book of Revelation between the 144 thousand and the 24 elders before the throne to YHWH Echad. It appears that time was fashioned to reveal the Kingdom of YHWH. This will be discussed further in the Walk in the Light series book entitled *The Final Shofar*.

19 Mazzaroth is a term which refers to the constellations. It is important to recognize that they were set in their place in the heavens on Day 4 of creation. They are there for "signs" and they are very important for the story that they tell. There is much that we can learn from the celestial bodies

which were given for "signs" among other things. (Beresheet 1:14). For more information concerning these matters a good starting point would be: *Mazzaroth* by Frances Rolleston Weiser Books 2001; *The Witness of the Stars* by E.W. Bullinger Kregel Publications; *The Gospel in the Stars*, Joseph A. Seiss, Kregel Publications 1972.

20 December 25 used to be the summer solstice and thus the day when sun worshippers would celebrate the "rebirth" of the sun. It is a day traditionally associated with the birth of sun gods throughout the planet. Now, the winter solstice occurs on December 21. For a further discussion of this matter see the Walk in the Light series books entitled *Restoration*.

21 The date of the birth of Isaac (Yitshaq) is quite significant as his life has many Messianic patterns built in. This will be discussed later in the text and is discussed in the Walk in the Light series books entitled *Covenants* and *The Messiah*.

22 Yisrael (1ɣ ۴w˞) is often translated to mean "he will rule as El." This is because the name actually contains the root of the name of Sarah – sar (۴w). Sar means: "ruler or prince." Interestingly, we can break the name Yisrael (1ɣ ۴w˞) down further in the Ancient Script, which provides even more detail. We could define the word as "the possession (w˞) of El (1ɣ) with El in the center, as the head (۴)." The root yisr (۴w˞) means "straight" so Yisrael could mean "those who belong to El, who follow El and walk straight in His path."

23 The first time that we read about Yisrael is when the son of Yitshaq, named Yaakob, was returning to the Promised Land with his family. He wrestled with a mysterious man and would not let go. The man then told him: "*Your name will no longer be Yaakob, but am (ᴍ ɣ) Yisrael, because you have struggled with Elohim and with men and have overcome.*" Beresheet 32:28. He then blessed Yaakob, but He would not tell him His name. There is another very interesting item in the passage describing the name change. If you were simply reading a translation you would miss it completely. In the Hebrew text the word am (ᴍ ɣ) appears right next to the name Yisrael. This was the am (ᴍ ɣ) that we discussed earlier, and it was signifying that the Covenant points to Yisrael. The people of Yisrael are the Covenant people promised from the beginning. They are the noble family

24 that would be in the Kingdom.

25 Gematria is the study of the numerical values of Hebrew words and letters. For more information see Appendix B or visit the website at www.shemayisrael.net.

25 It is well established that YHWH has a 7,000 year plan for creation patterned upon the first seven words of the Hebrew Scriptures and the seven day weekly cycle. There are six days for man, or flesh, and the seventh is the Sabbath of YHWH. This time is divided into 50 year Jubilee cycles so the time allotted to man is 120 Jubilee Cycles, which is 6,000 years. (see Beresheet 6:3).

26 For further discussion on the end of days see the Walk in the Light series book entitled *The Final Shofar*.

27 For further discussion on the seventh day see the Walk in the Light series book entitled *The Sabbath*.

28 This subject is discussed in the book *Why Not Women?* by Loren Cunningham and David Joel Hamilton, YWAM Publishing 2000.

29 Wikipedia citing Cyrus H. Gordon and Gary A. Rendsburg, *The Bible and the Ancient Near East* fourth edition, 1997, Norton & Co. The modern Hebrew script was replaced with Paleo Hebrew script by the author for consistency.

30 It is a popular tradition that the fruit of the Tree of Knowledge of Good and Evil was an apple, but this could simply be tradition associated with pagan traditions involving Athena, the goddess of wisdom, with an apple. There is no mention of an apple in the Scriptures, nor is any particular fruit mentioned. According to some tradition, the forbidden fruit was the fig, and this would make sense since the man and the woman sewed fig leaves to cover themselves. It could be that they reached for the closest thing that they could find. (see Rabbi Nehemia Berachos 40a; Sanhedrin 70a. See also *The Rod of An Almond Tree in God's Master Plan*, Peter A. Michas Wine Press WP Publishing 1997).

31 Qayin (ן־יק) means: "acquired" and is an accurate transliteration of the name commonly referred to as Cain. Hebel (לבה) means: "breath" and is an accurate transliteration of the name commonly referred to as Abel. This name also can mean "vanity," and the Book of Yasher actually states that this was the intended meaning of the name as Hawah declared: "In vanity we came into the

³² earth, and in vanity we shall be taken from it." Book of Yasher 1:13.

³³ According to the Book of Yasher 1:12 Adam knew his wife Hawah on the day he was expelled from the Garden of Eden.

³⁴ Adapted from *A Mechanical Translation of the Book of Genesis* Jeff A. Benner, Virtualbookworm.com Publishing Inc. 2007.

³⁵ There are some interesting omissions in the account of the birth of Qayin and Hebel which leaves room for speculation. The Targums are famous for attempting to fill in those gaps and Targum Pseudo-Jonathan provides the following account: "¹ Adam knew his wife Hawah who had conceived from Sammael, the angel of YHWH. ² Then from Adam her husband she bore his twin sister and Abel. Abel was a keeper of sheep, and Qayin was a man tilling the earth." Beresheet 4:1-2. According to the notes for verse 1: "This verse could also be translated as follows: "Adam knew that his wife [Hawah] . . ." Ed. Pr. Has a different version of this verse: "Adam knew [Hawah] his wife, who desired the angel, and she conceived and bore [Qayin]. And she said, 'I have acquired a man, the angel of [YHWH].'" The belief that [Qayn] was the child of Sammael . . . was derived from the fact that Gen 5:3 says that Seth was in the likeness and image of Adam. Since this is not said of [Qayin] in 4:1, the conclusion was drawn that he was not Adam's son. Ps.-J states explicitly in 5:3 that [Hawah] bore [Qayin], who was not from Adam and who did not resemble him. B. Shabb. 146a (738), Yebam. 103b(711), Abod. Zar. 22b(114) say that the serpent copulated with Eve and/or infused her with lust, but they do not say that he fathered [Qayin]. PRE 21 (150) says that he (ie. Sammael) came to her riding on the serpent, and she conceived. We conclude that the "he" in question was Sammael, since PRE 13 (92) tells us that Sammael mounted the serpent and rode on it. In effect, then, Ps.-J. is the earliest text that explicitly identifies Sammael as the father of Cain (cf. Cashdan, 1967, 33)." *The Aramaic Bible Volume 1B*, Targum Pseudo-Jonathan Genesis, Translated, with Introduction and Notes by Michael Maher, M.S.C., The Liturgical Press 1992.

³⁵ Tanchuma Bereishis 9 says Qayin and Hebel were both 40 years old when they brought their offerings, and therefore Hebel was 40 when he died.

³⁶ See Yeshayahu 41:26, 46:10, 48.

³⁷ Mosheh (𐤌𐤔𐤄) is the proper transliteration for the name of the Patriarch commonly called Moses. The name Mosheh is actually an Egyptian name which refers to his miraculous appearance from water.

³⁸ See Jenni-Westermann Theological Lexicon.

³⁹ See Strong's Hebrew Concordance # 8141.

⁴⁰ It is a well established Hebraic concept that 1,000 years are like a day to YHWH. This idea was first taught by Mosheh in Psalm 90:4. Peter said in II Peter 3:8 that the brethren should not be ignorant of this one thing. The 1,000 years for a day concept is also to be found in the Talmud in Sanhedrin 97A-97B, the Epistle of Barnabas 15:1-9 and the Secrets of Enoch 33:1. It was also spoken of by Irenaeus in *Against Heresies* Book 5/28/3, by Cyprian in chapter 11 of *The Treatises of Cyprian* by Lactanius in *The Divine Institutes* Book 7 Chapters 25-26, by Methodius in *The Banquet of the Ten Virgins* Discourse 9, Chapter 1, by Latimer and by Hippolytus of Rome. Sir Isaac Newton, who was very interested in the subject apparently said, "About the times of the end, a body of men will be raised up who will turn their attention to the prophecies and insist upon their literal interpretation in the midst of much clamor and opposition."

⁴¹ Michael Wise, Martin Abegg Jr., and Edward Cook, *The Dead Sea Scrolls - A New Translation*, Harper Collins, 2005, p. 94.

⁴² For further discussions concerning this issue, reference is made the Walk in the Light series books entitled *The Messiah* and *The Final Shofar*.

⁴³ The instructions of YHWH are known as the Torah. In a very general sense, the word Torah is used to refer to the first five books of the Scriptures which some call the Pentateuch, or the five books of Mosheh. Torah may sound like a strange word to anyone who reads an English translation of the Scriptures, but it is found throughout the Hebrew text. The reason is because it is a Hebrew word which translators have chosen to replace with "the Law." Whenever the word "Torah" is found in the Hebrew, it has been translated as "the Law" in English Bibles. Therefore, if you grew up reading an English Bible then you would never have come across this word. On the other hand, if you read the Hebrew Scriptures the word Torah is found throughout

the text. The word Torah (𐤀𐤅𐤓𐤄) in Hebrew means: *"utterance, teaching, instruction or revelation from Elohim."* It comes from horah (𐤄𐤅𐤓𐤄) which means **to direct**, **to teach** and derives from the stem yara (𐤉𐤓𐤄) which means to **shoot** or **throw**. Therefore there are two aspects to the word Torah: 1) aiming or pointing in the right direction, and 2) movement in that direction. The Torah (𐤀𐤅𐤓𐤄) is the first five books of the Hebrew and Christian Scriptures. The Torah is more accurately defined as the "instruction" of YHWH for His set apart people. The Torah contains instruction for those who desire to live righteous, set apart lives in accordance with the will of YHWH. Contrary to popular belief, people can obey the Torah. (Debarim 30:11-14). It is the myriads of regulations, customs and traditions which men attach to the Torah that make it impossible and burdensome for people to obey. The Torah has been in existence as long as Creation and arguably forever, because the instructions of YHWH are the ways of YHWH. The names of the five different "books" are transliterated from their proper Hebrew names as follows: Genesis - Beresheet, Exodus - Shemot, Leviticus - Vayiqra, Numbers - Bemidbar, Deuteronomy - Debarim. While it is generally considered that the Torah is contained exclusively within the 5 Books of Mosheh, in a broader sense one might argue that they are included in the entire Tanak - The Torah, The Nebiim (The Prophets) and the Ketubim (The Writings).

44 Interestingly, "sakar" is the root of "Issachar" which is the Tribe of Yisrael responsible for the calendar according to I Chronicles 12:32. No doubt there are great rewards associated with knowing the times of YHWH, as we shall see.

45 Yeshayahu (𐤉𐤔𐤏𐤉𐤄𐤅) is the proper transliteration for the Prophet commonly called Isaiah. His name in Hebrew means "YHWH saves."

46 The description of the rainbow in the Throne Room in Heaven is actually found in the Book of Revelation at 4:3.

47 *Nechama Leibowitz*, New Studies in Bereshit, p. 86.

48 As we continue to examine the Covenant process between YHWH and man, including the Appointed Times, it becomes increasingly clear that the Messiah, represented by the Aleph Taw, is at the center of it all. The Aleph Taw and

the Messiah are discussed in greater detail in the Walk in the Light series book entitled *The Messiah*.

49 Throughout this text you may find that the words "*Jewish*," "*Jews*" and "*Jew*" are in italics because they are ambiguous and sometimes derogatory terms. At times these expressions are used to describe all of the genetic descendents of the man named Yaakob (Jacob), later named Yisrael (Israel). At other times the words are used to describe those who adhere to the religion of Judaism. The terms are commonly applied to ancient Israelites as well as modern day descendents of those tribes, whether they are atheists or Believers in YHWH. The word "*Jew*" originally referred to a member of the tribe of Judah (Yahudah) or a person who lived in the region of Judea. After the different exiles of the House of Yisrael and the House of Yahudah, it was the Yahudim who returned to the Land while the Northern Tribes, known as the House of Yisrael, were scattered to the ends of the earth (Yirmeyahu 9:16). The Yahudim retained their identity to their culture and the Land and thus came to represent all of Yisrael, despite the fact that the majority of Yisrael, the 10 tribes of the Northern Kingdom, remained "lost". As a result, the word "*Jew*" is erroneously used to describe a Yisraelite. While this label became common and customary, it is not accurate and is the cause of tremendous confusion. This subject is described in greater detail in The Walk in the Light Series book entitled *The Redeemed*.

50 See Vayiqra 19:15, Debarim 1:17 and 16:9, 2 Samuel 14:14, 2 Chronicles 19:7, Proverbs 24:23 and 28:21, Ezekiel 18:20-32, Matthew 22:16, Acts 10:34, Romans 2:11, Ephesians 6:9, Colossians 3:25, James 2:1 and 2:9, 1 Peter 1:16-17.

51 Yahuhanan (ᕁᕁXᛁᛙᕁ) is a Hebrew name which means "YHWH has given." Many pronounce his Hebrew name as Yochanan (ᕁᕁᛘᛁᕁ) but that pronunciation loses the Name of YHWH. According to McClintock and Strong it is "a contracted form of the name Jehohanan." Therefore, in an effort to keep the original flavor of the name I use the Yahonatan, Yahuhanan or Yahanan when referring to Yahanan the Immerser or the New Testament individual commonly called John.

52 There are numerous legends concerning who killed Nimrod and the sources are often obscure. There are some who

suggest that it was Esau who actually killed Nimrod. See *Targum Jonathan* on Beresheet 25:27.

53   Pirke R. El. xxiv.; "Sefer ha-Yashar" l.c.; comp. Gen. R. lxv. 12. http://www.jewishencyclopedia.com/view.jsp?artid=295&letter=N&search=nimrod. (Elohim replaced God and Hawah replaced Eve for accuracy and consistency.)

54   *Nimrod and Babylon: The Birth of Idolatry*, Steve and Terri White http://koinonia-all.org/bible/nimrod.htm. The Name of YHWH and the title Elohim replaced by author for consistency. The word God replaced with Elohim for consistency and accuracy.

55   *The Pagan Origin of Easter*, David J. Meyer, Last Trumpet Ministries International, PO Box 806, Beaver Dam, WI 53916, www.lasttrumpetministries.org/tracts/tract1.html.

56   Some believe a great planetary event may have occurred resulting in the breakup of the continents. This would have created diversity among the population on the planet. Seder Olam I says that Abram was 48 at the time of the dispersion. Midrash Yalkut Divrie HaYamim I says that construction on the Tower of Babel ended when Abram was 48.

57   See *Worlds in Collision*, Immanuel Velikovsky, Paradigma Ltd. 2009.

58   For further discussion on the end of days see the Walk in the Light series book entitled *The Final Shofar*.

59   Encarta.msn.com/dictionary_/pagan.html

60   en.wikipedia.org

61   The word "shaw" (שׁוא) often translated as "vain" is better translated as "naught, nothingness or emptiness." So rather than commanding us not to take the Name of YHWH "in vain," it is really telling us not to bring the Name "to nothing." The Name of YHWH is to be exalted before all the earth.

62   *The Nephilim and the Pyramid of the Apocalypse*, Patrick Heron, Xulon Press 2005.

63   *Some Significant Antecedents of Christianity* by Julian Morgenstern, E.J. Brill, Leiden, Netherlands 1966, pp 91-92.

64   Eustace Mullins, *The Curse of Canaan*, p. 8 (1987).

65   en.wikipedia.org/wiki/Moloch

66   Edwin O. James, *Sacrifice and Sacrament*, p. 94 (1962).

67   The Book of Yasher is not a "canonized" text, but it is referenced in "canonized" Scriptures, which would appear

68   to validate its existence and validity. See Joshua 10:13 and II Samuel 1:18. The issue of canonization is discussed in the Walk in the Light series book entitled *Scriptures*.

Obviously, after the cataclysm of the flood, and the dispersion after the Tower of Babel, we do not necessarily have archaeological evidence of specific locations that existed previously. We do have patterns that are revealed through the Scriptures, and if we look at the mysterious "Red Heifer" sacrifice that occurred "outside the camp" of Yisrael, essentially "east of Eden," we can see a pattern established from the very beginning at the door, a threshold covenant if you will. The sacrifice of the "Red Heifer" occurred outside the camp, and that sacrifice was required to purify people from their uncleanness so that they could enter the House of YHWH. So this sacrifice of the Only Son of YHWH was needed "outside the door" so that the Redeemed can get clean and reenter the Garden. See also Endnote 70.

69   Shaul of Tarsus, commonly referred to as the Apostle Paul in Christianity, recognized that the Seed of Abraham was the Messiah. In his Torah teaching to the Galatians he writes: *"Now to Abraham and his Seed were the promises made. He does not say, 'And to seeds,' as of many, but as of one, 'And to your Seed,' who is Messiah."* Galatians 3:16. Shaul was a well educated man, allegedly taught by the renowned Sage Gamaliel. Through his various writings he was apparently attempting to instruct Gentiles in the Hebrew Scriptures. Sadly, many of his writings have been twisted and misconstrued, and some actually believe that he was the founder or a co-founder of the Christian religion.

70   The Miphkad Altar is the place where the Red Heifer sacrifice was made, east of the House of YHWH. It is located outside the camp. The ashes of the Red Heifer mixed with water were necessary to cleanse a person who was defiled from a dead body, in order that the person might enter the Tabernacle or the temple – the House. Every person is tarnished from sin, which is the transgression of the Torah perpetuated from the Garden. All must be made clean before they can be reconciled to YHWH. This process of becoming clean, so that you can enter into the House of YHWH is provided through the picture of the Red Heifer, which is slaughtered "outside the

⁷¹ camp," not on the Altar which is within the courts of the House of YHWH. The Red Heifer sacrifice provides cleansing so that one can approach YHWH to do business with Him. Only when you have entered the House do you receive atonement, and offer up sacrifices on the Altar before the House. The description of the Red Heifer slaughtering can be found in Numbers (Bemidbar) 19.

⁷¹ *Jewish and Early Christian Methods of Bible Interpretation*, Judah Gross, Hashtaumd, Quoting [ix] Levenson 181 [x] Manns 60.

⁷² *Ancient Egypt*, Lorna Oaks and Lucia Gahlin, Barnes & Noble Books, 2003.

⁷³ The Scriptures detail many matters that relate to time and the number seventy. For instance, there are 70 years for the life of a man (Psalm 90:10). The House of Yahudah was exiled for 70 years for failing to observe the laws regarding the Sabbath Year that necessitated letting the Land rest and releasing slaves from servitude. (Yirmeyahu 35:11). The Book of Daniel also speaks of 70 weeks. (see Daniel 9). Therefore, the number 70 is quite significant when examining time. We can see this with the multiples of seven involving the seven day week, the seven week count in Shabuot as well as the 7,000 year plan of YHWH for creation.

⁷⁴ The mixing and deliverance from Egypt was a precursor for another greater fulfillment of this Covenant that will occur through another cycle in the end. The Covenant people are currently mixed within the nations, and will some day be delivered from the Nations as Yisrael was once delivered from Egypt. This issue is discussed further in the Walk in the Light series books entitled *Covenants*, *The Redeemed* and *The Final Shofar*.

⁷⁵ en.wikipedia.org/wiki/Midian

⁷⁶ There is much speculation concerning whether or not Jethro was a pagan idolater. Since the text describes him as a priest of Midian (Shemot 3:1), and since Midian was a pagan culture, it would seem that Jethro, at least initially, was a pagan priest. It appears that he gave YHWH esteem after the deliverance of Yisrael and may have been responsible for introducing the Midianites to YHWH. For a detailed discussion of Jethro see www.jewishvirtuallibrary.org.

⁷⁷ The man Aaron, whose Hebrew name is better

transliterated as Aharon, was the brother of Mosheh. They both were born into the Tribe of a Levi, although Mosheh had been adopted into the household of Pharaoh.

78 Durant, Will. *The Story Of Civilization (Vol. 1): Our Oriental Heritage.* MJF Books. 1935 p. 201.

79 For an interesting article on the application of each plague to the specific Egyptian gods see Against All the Gods of Egypt by David Padfield, www.padfield.com 2002.

80 Beresheet 33:17.

81 The mikvah is where the Christian doctrine of baptism derives, although it did not begin with Christianity. The mikvah is an ancient practice commanded by YHWH long before the existence of Christianity. It is a very Hebrew notion, since the word "Hebrew" carries the connotation of "crossing over." Thus passing "through the waters" is something every Hebrew must do. As a result, it was a natural thing for Yisraelites to do. In fact, there were numerous mikvaote (plural form of mikvah) at the Temple in Jerusalem, and it was required that a person be immersed in a mikvah prior to presenting their sacrifice. The Hebrew word for baptize is tevila (ה⁻ל⊕), which is a full body immersion that takes place in a mikvah (ΨΡΡᴹ). This comes from the passage in Beresheet 1:10 when YHWH "gathered together" the waters. The mikvah is the gathering together of flowing waters. The "tevila" immersion is symbolic for a person going from a state of uncleanliness to cleanliness. The priests in the temple needed to tevila regularly to insure that they were in a state of cleanliness when they served in the Temple. Anyone going to the Temple to worship or offer sacrifices would tevila at the numerous pools outside the Temple. There are a variety of instances found in the Torah when a person was required to tevila. It is very important because it reminds us of the filth of sin, and the need to be washed clean from our sin in order to stand in the presence of a set apart Elohim. Therefore, it makes perfect sense that we be immersed in a mikvah prior to presenting the sacrifice of the perfect lamb as atonement for our sins. It also cleanses our temple which the Spirit of Elohim will enter in to tabernacle with us. The tevila is symbolic of becoming born again and is an act of going from one life to another. Being born again is not something that became popular in the 1970's within the Christian

religion. It is a remarkably Yisraelite concept that was understood to occur when one arose from the mikvah. In fact, people witnessing an immersion would often cry out "Born Again!" when a person came up from an immersion. It was also an integral part of the Rabbinic conversion process, which, in many ways is not Scriptural, but in this sense is correct. For a Gentile to complete their conversion, they were required to be immersed, or baptized, which meant that they were born again - born into a new life. Many people believe that immersion is a newly instituted Christian concept. Because of the exchange between Messiah and Nicodemus, many people believe that immersion is a newly instituted Christian concept. Let us take a look at that conversation in the Gospel according to Yahanan: "¹ Now there was a man of the Pharisees named Nicodemus, a ruler of the Yahudim. ² He came to Yahushua at night and said, 'Rabbi, we know you are a teacher who has come from Elohim. For no one could perform the miraculous signs You are doing if Elohim were not with him.' ³ In reply Yahushua declared, 'I tell you the truth, no one can see the kingdom of Elohim unless he is born again.' ⁴ 'How can a man be born when he is old?' Nicodemus asked. 'Surely he cannot enter a second time into his mother's womb to be born!' ⁵ Yahushua answered, 'I tell you the truth, no one can enter the kingdom of Elohim unless he is born of water and the Spirit. ⁶ Flesh gives birth to flesh, but the Spirit gives birth to spirit. ⁷ You should not be surprised at My saying, You must be born again. ⁸ The wind blows wherever it pleases. You hear its sound, but you cannot tell where it comes from or where it is going. So it is with everyone born of the Spirit.' ⁹ 'How can this be?' Nicodemus asked. ¹⁰ 'You are Yisrael's teacher,' said Yahushua, 'and do you not understand these things? ¹¹ I tell you the truth, We speak of what We know, and We testify to what We have seen, but still you people do not accept Our testimony. ¹² I have spoken to you of earthly things and you do not believe; how then will you believe if I speak of heavenly things? ¹³ No one has ever gone into heaven except the One who came from heaven - the Son of Man. ¹⁴ Just as Mosheh lifted up the snake in the desert, so the Son of Man must be lifted up, ¹⁵ that everyone who believes in Him may have eternal life.'" Yahanan 3:1-15. From this exchange it seems that Nicodemus is unfamiliar with immersion, and was surprised by the fact that a person needed to be "born again." His first question:

"*How can a man be born when he is old?*" demonstrated he did not see how it applied to him, because he was already a Yahudim. His second question "*How can this be,*" only affirmed that fact. And this is why Yahushua asked: "*You are Yisrael's teacher and do you not understand these things?*" In other words, "you're supposed to be the one teaching Yisrael about these spiritual matters and you're not. You think only the Gentiles need to be immersed and born again, but you all need it because you are all sinners and this needs to be taught to everyone, not just the Gentiles." So you see, being born again through immersion was not new to Yisrael. This is why many readily were immersed by Yahanan the Immerser - they understood their need. But often, the leaders, like Nicodemus, failed to see their need for cleansing because they were blinded by the notion that their Torah observance justified them, when in fact, it is the blood of the Lamb that justifies a person. It is important to note that the tevila must occur in "living waters" - in other words, water which is moving and ideally which contains life. These living waters refer to the Messiah. In a Scriptural marriage, a bride would enter the waters of purification prior to her wedding. These are the same waters that we are to enter when we make a confession of faith and become part of the Body of Messiah - His Bride.

The Shema is arguably one of the most important, commandments, statements and prayers found within the Scriptures. The Shema begins at Debarim 6:4. In fact, it was declared to be the first (resheet) of all the commandments by Yahushua. (see Mark 12:29). The Shema proclaims: "*⁴ Hear, O Yisrael: YHWH our Elohim, YHWH is one. (echad) ⁵ Love YHWH your Elohim with all your heart and with all your soul and with all your strength. ⁶ These commandments that I give you today are to be upon your hearts. ⁷ Impress them on your children. Talk about them when you sit at home and when you walk along the road, when you lie down and when you get up. ⁸ Tie them as symbols on your hands and bind them on your foreheads. ⁹ Write them on the doorframes of your houses and on your gates.*" Debarim 6:4-9. The command to write the commands on our doorposts and our gates means that YHWH is in control of that space. His Commandments are the rule of that property, which represents His Kingdom on the Earth. So we are instructed to essentially establish the

Kingdom of YHWH in every area of our lives. The text of the Shema in Hebrew is quite profound and contains an enlarged ayin (ע) at the end of the word "shema" and an enlarged dalet (ד) at the end of the word "echad". The ayin dalet (דע) is essentially announcing that we should "see" (ע) the "door" (ד). The Shema text is provided in Appendix D.

[83] See the Creation Calendar at www.torahcalendar.com.

[84] There are new theories concerning the new moon which attempt to persuade people to believe that the new moon occurs at the conjunction, rather than at the sighting of the first sliver. This notion is not warranted by any historical information, and borrows on the astronomical determination of a conjunction which actually only lasts for a matter of minutes. The moon is in darkness before and after the actual conjunction and can be in darkness for days at a time. Therefore, the determination of the moment of conjunction requires great mathematical precision. It was not possible to determine the conjunction of the moon in ancient times, and because it is so brief, the determination of when to recognize the new moon day would have involved great debate and discussion, none of which is found in the historical records. The first sliver is a visible sign, or "owt" that can be seen by all, versus a dark moon which remains unseen for days. There is ample historical proof that the new moon was considered to be the crescent moon when the first sliver was observed. See Philo, *Treatise on the Special Laws*, Book II, XI (41) which states: "[It] is that which comes after the conjunction, which... [is] the day of the new moon in each month . . . at the time of the new moon, the sun begins to illuminate the moon with a light which is visible to the outward senses, and then she displays her own beauty to the beholders." Etymologically, it has been asserted that the word chodesh (חדש) derives from chadash (חדש) which can mean "to polish with a sword." So the chodesh would appear as a chadash, a scimitar or curved sword common in the Middle East. See Gesenius' Hebrew-Chaldee Lexicon.

[85] It has been well documented that the most probable exodus route went through Wadi Watir on the Sinai Penninsula; and the Red Sea crossing occurred at Nuweiba, Egypt, where an underwater land bridge has been located

86   containing remnants of Egyptian chariot wheels. The Scriptures specifically provide that YHWH made the Egyptian's chariot wheels fall off. (Shemot 14:25). The location of Mt Sinai is located in Saudi Arabia according to Galatians 4:25 where altars and other relics have been found confirming the presence of the Yisraelites along with the mixed multitude that departed Egypt. For a detailed discussion of this issue see the book entitled *The Exodus Case New Discoveries Confirm the Historical Exodus* by Dr. Lennart Möller, Scandinavia Publishing House, 2002.

87   A Ketubah (ה ב ו ת כ) is simply a marriage contract. It was quite common in ancient cultures and continues to be common primarily in eastern cultures. It establishes the rights and responsibilities of the parties and often includes the damages for a parties' breach of the contract. In western culture similar contracts are used and called pre-nuptial agreements.

88   The name rendered Joshua in English is actually rendered several ways in Hebrew. It could be Yahushua, Yehoshua or Yeshua. They are all essentially the same Hebrew name. Since it is also the Name of the Messiah, when referring to the assistant of Mosheh, I will continue to use Joshua, in order to avoid confusion.

89   *Ancient Egypt*, Lorna Oakes and Lucia Gahlin, Barnes & Nobles Books, 2003, Page 283.

90   The word "Bible" has traditionally been the word used to describe the collection of documents considered by Christianity to be inspired by Elohim - I prefer the use of the word "Scriptures." The word Bible derives from Byblos which has more pagan connotations than I prefer, especially when referring to the written Word of Elohim. This subject is discussed in greater detail in the Walk in the Light Series book entitled *Scriptures*.

91   Pictures from www.biblelarkeologi.no/exodusklippenhoreb.htm. It is my understanding that Jim and Penny Caldwell as well as the late Ron Wyatt located and photographed this site. I would encourage the reader to visit their websites and read about their exciting adventures. You can visit these sites at wyattmuseum.com and jimandpenny.com.

92   *The Exodus Case*, Dr. Lennart Möller, Scandinavia Publishing House, 2002.

   The maps that you have in the back of your Bible are wrong

in some cases because tradition has taken precedence over the truth. The process by which Queen Helena discerned the supposed locations of Scriptural cites was conducted using divination and sorcery. She was, after all, a pagan sun worshipper as was her son and apparent lover - Emperor Constantine.

[93] It is interesting to read that YHWH has a Scroll with names written in it. While this verse does not have any added detail, the point is clear - YHWH has a register of those who are included in His Covenant. If you join in and obey the terms, your name gets written in the Scroll. If you refuse to obey, your name can be blotted out. This flies directly in the face of a popular Christian doctrine "once saved always saved." Sadly, many in Christianity believe that their destiny relies upon whether they said a simple prayer at some point in their lives. The fact is that actions speak louder than words, and while we all need the atonement freely provided by the Messiah, once we join the family of YHWH, we are expected to obey His rules.

[94] This entire renewal process turns out to be a Messianic allusion. The Messiah is the one who meets with YHWH and transmits His Words, He came with the esteem of YHWH hidden behind a veil of flesh. They fasted 40 days and 40 nights, which would turn out to be a Messianic trademark.

[95] "According to Rashi, Moses ascended Mount Sinai no less than three times for forty days and forty nights. The first ascent began on the 6th if Sivan [month 3], 50 days after the Exodus, when Moses first received the Ten Commandments . . . When he descended and saw the people worshipping the Golden Calf, however, he smashed the tablets (Exod. 32:19). According to tradition, this occurred on the 17th of Tamuz [month 4] . . . On the following day Moses burned the Golden Calf and judged the transgressors. He then reascended on the 19th of Tamuz [month 4] and interceded on behalf of Israel for 40 more days (until the 29th of Av [month 5]) . . .God then called Moses the following day, on Elul [month 6] 1, to ascend a third time to receive a new set of tablets. Forty more days and nights were spent receiving the revelation of Torah at Sinai. Moses finally descended on Tishri [month 7] 10 - Yom Kippur - with the second set of tablets in hand and the

reassurance of God's forgiveness." Quoted from www.hebrew4christians.com (correct month numbers inserted). With recent technological advances we can now discern with precision when these events took place. According to the work of Eliyahu David ben Yissachar, the First ascent occurred on Day 8 of Month 3 and the descent occurred on Day 18 of Month 4. The Second ascent occurred on Day 19 of Month 4 and the descent occurred on Day 29 of Month 5. The Third ascent occurred on Day 30 of Month 5 and the descent occurred on Day 10 of Month 7. The Golden Calf was worshipped on Day 17 of Month 4 and the Tablets were broken on Day 18 of Month 4. Interestingly, there can only be 143 days between Day 8 of Month 3 and Day 10 of Month 7 in a year where Month 3, 4, 5 and 6 each contain 30 days, which is indeed the case in the year of the Exodus. According to 1 Kings 6:1, the year of the Exodus occurred 480 years before year 4 of King Solomon's (Shlomo's) reign.

[96] See Shemot 16:23

[97] For a detailed discussion of the Covenants found within the Scriptures see the Walk in the Light series book entitled *Covenants*.

[98] Bemidbar (𐤁𐤌𐤃𐤁𐤓) is the Hebrew word for the text often referred to as "Numbers." The word Bemidbar actually means: "in the desert."

[99] Yahudah (𐤉𐤄𐤅𐤃𐤄) is the proper English transliteration for the Hebrew name often pronounced as Judah.

[100] Since there is no "J" in the Hebrew language, the name Joseph is more accurately rendered as Yoseph.

[101] This is pointed out because it is very significant and prophetic. The fact that these two sons were born in a pagan context and later adopted by Yisrael speaks to their future redemption.

[102] Yisrael has often been likened to the moon, as Yisrael is supposed to reflect the light of YHWH.

[103] Judges, known as shoftim, were those appointed to mete out justice and right rulings among the Yisraelites. They always existed from Mosheh onward, but became increasingly important after the death of Joshua (Yahushua) to the time of King David, when there were individual "judges" who were raised up to lead Yisrael. Since Yisrael was divided into twelve tribes, the judges added some cohesiveness to an

often divided nation.

¹⁰⁴ The name of the man often called Samuel in English translations of the Scriptures, is more accurately pronounced Shemuel (שׁמואל). In modern Hebrew it is often written and pronounced as Sh'muel.

¹⁰⁵ The Tabernacle, also known as the Mishkan, was constructed by Mosheh and the skilled craftsmen of Yisrael while they travelled through the Wilderness. It was made to be portable - as a tent, and it was the House of YHWH. Although shortly after Joshua (Yahushua) died, the Tabernacle moved to Shiloh and became a permanent structure with stone walls with a fabric roof, according to the Talmud in Zebahim 112B. The physical appearance and layout of the Tabernacle is a pattern of the Garden of Eden. It also provides an image of a person's body, and is intended to show us how YHWH desires to dwell or "tabernacle" within us. These two concepts of the Tabernacle combined, show us how YHWH desires to dwell with us and in us. The description of the building of the Tabernacle is provided in Shemot 25 - Shemot 28.

¹⁰⁶ We repeatedly see the word shamar (שׁמר) throughout the Scriptures, although we do not always recognize the consistency because it can be translated as "watch," "guard," "keep" etc. The word is meant to stress to us that we are to act as watchmen over the commandments so that we are diligent to obey. Adam did not watch over the Garden as he was commanded, and the serpent entered and deceived Hawah and him - the consequences were devastating. As the Son of Adam, we see that Messiah did what Adam failed to do. Where Adam failed in the Garden of Eden, Yahushua stepped in and broke the cycle in another Garden. Right before the death of Yahushua, we see Him keeping vigil in the Garden of Gethsemane as He is about to complete His mission. While He stays awake and prays - His disciples kept falling asleep. In the Hebrew Mattityahu we get a vivid picture of His instructions, as He tells His disciples the same thing that the Creator instructed Adam - He tells them to watch and He gives them something to do. In Mattityahu 26:38 He says: "Support *Me and watch with Me.*" The word for watch is shamar. In Mattityahu 26:40 He asks: "So *you are unable to watch with Me one hour?*" Again the word is shamar. In Mattityahu 26:41 He states: "Watch *and*

pray – lest you fall into temptation." Again we see the word shamar. In each case this presents the picture of a watchman keeping guard. And notice the connection - Watch and pray lest you fall into temptation. Adam failed in his duty to watch, just as the disciples did, and as a result both he and the woman fell into temptation. Yahushua the Messiah stayed awake and watched - like a watchman over Yisrael just as was written: "*He who watches (shamar) over Yisrael will neither sleep nor slumber.*" Psalms (Tehillim) 121:4. The purpose of His watching is to preserve and protect and guard our souls - our very lives - we read this in Psalms (Tehillim) 121:7-8. Again to watch over (shamar) our souls is to keep and to protect us. He also instructs us to watch and an important part of our watching involves the Torah. Over and over again we are instructed to keep the commandments, and to watch the commandments and to guard the commandments. This is the same word shamar, and we are given this instruction so that we stay within the hedge of protection provided by the Torah - so that we don't fall into temptation - so that we are kept from evil. The purpose of a hedge is to make a separation between those things on one side and those things on the other side. The Torah provides us with distinctions and draws a line for us to understand right from wrong, clean from unclean, righteous conduct from abominable conduct. On this foundation of Truth the Kingdom is established, and it will only be populated with those who will also <u>obey</u> the Truth.

[107] Tehillim (אױלהת) is a proper transliteration for the word Psalms. The Book of Psalms would thus be rendered Sefer Tehillim.

[108] We know from the text that Abraham went to the "region" or "land" of Moriah, better translated as Moriyah (הױרמ), which means "shown by YHWH." Tradition holds that this was the same site that the altar was built on before the Temple was built by Solomon, although the Scriptures do not specifically state that fact.

[109] There are two similar, but also differing accounts of David's purchase of the threshing floor of Araunah. According to 2 Shemuel 24:18-25: "[18] *On that day Gad went to David and said to him, 'Go up and build an altar to YHWH on the threshing floor of Araunah the Jebusite.'* [19] *So David went up, as YHWH had commanded through Gad.* [20] *When Araunah looked and saw*

the king and his men coming toward him, he went out and bowed down before the king with his face to the ground. ²¹ Araunah said, 'Why has my lord the king come to his servant?' 'To buy your threshing floor,' David answered, 'so I can build an altar to YHWH, that the plague on the people may be stopped.' ²² Araunah said to David, 'Let my lord the king take whatever pleases him and offer it up. Here are oxen for the burnt offering, and here are threshing sledges and ox yokes for the wood ²³ O king, Araunah gives all this to the king.' Araunah also said to him, 'May YHWH your Elohim accept you.' ²⁴ But the king replied to Araunah, 'No, I insist on paying you for it. I will not sacrifice to YHWH my Elohim burnt offerings that cost me nothing.' So David bought the threshing floor and the oxen and paid fifty shekels of silver for them. ²⁵ David built an altar to YHWH there and sacrificed burnt offerings and fellowship offerings. Then YHWH answered prayer in behalf of the land, and the plague on Yisrael was stopped." The weight of the silver was around 1 pound or .6 kilograms. According to 1 Chronicles 21:25-26: "²⁵ David paid Araunah six hundred shekels of gold for the site. ²⁶ David built an altar to YHWH there and sacrificed burnt offerings and fellowship offerings. He called on YHWH, and YHWH answered him with fire from heaven on the altar of burnt offering." The gold amounts to a weight equivalent to about 15 pounds or seven kilograms. Notice the difference in prices which appear, on the surface, to be a discrepancy, but at second glance is not. The writer in Shemuel simply stated that David purchased the threshing floor and the oxen to sacrifice, and paid 50 shekels of silver for the oxen. The writer in I Chronicles was concerned about the site and indicated the price for the threshing floor was six hundred shekels of gold. Notice also that fire came down from heaven, as with Eliyahu.

[110] http://en.wikipedia.org/wiki/Threshing_floor

[111] It is important to note that the House of YHWH was built upon a threshing floor. This is significant because all of the adult males of Yisrael were commanded to appear before YHWH three times a year at the place where He chose to put His Name - in other words - where He lived. That place has been Jerusalem ever since David set up the Tabernacle there. The Appointed Times were centered around the harvests and no one was to come empty handed. In other words, they were supposed to bring the best - their

firstfruits – just as Hebel had done long ago. It is there, at the threshing floor of YHWH, that the hearts of men would be sifted as they did business with their Elohim

[112] There are significant parallels between the Tabernacle in the Wilderness, and the House which David planned to build for YHWH. The House of YHWH took a journey with Yisrael and was portable while Yisrael was moving. It was semi-permanent while it was at Shiloh for 3 ½ centuries. It was only when David became king and established his throne in Jerusalem that we see the transition of the House of YHWH to a permanent building. This is significant and is a Messianic reference to a future time when Messiah will rebuild the House as foretold to David: "[11] *YHWH declares to you that YHWH Himself will establish a house for you:* [12] *When your days are over and you rest with your fathers, I will raise up your offspring to succeed you, who will come from your own body, and I will establish His kingdom.* [13] *He is the One who will build a House for My Name, and I will establish the throne of His kingdom throughout the ages.*" 2 Shemuel 7:11-13. This House, built by Messiah, will be the New Jerusalem, only He will be the Chief Cornerstone (Capstone) (Yeshayahu 28:16; Zekaryah 10:4; Ephesians 2:20; 1 Peter 2:6) and He will build this House with Living Stones (1 Peter 2:5).

[113] Shlomo (שׁלמה) is the proper English transliteration for the Hebrew name which is traditionally pronounced as Solomon.

[114] This is all that YHWH asks of His people and they continually refuse to do what He says. There are rich blessings for those who obey – like David. There are also curses for those who disobey – like Shlomo.

[115] Interestingly, what Jeroboam did is exactly what Christianity has done to the true worship of YHWH. Jeroboam established places of worship other than Jerusalem, he got rid of the Levite priests, and set up his own priesthood. He worshipped false gods and he established new holidays. The Roman Catholic Church, from which most of modern Christianity derives, has established Rome as their headquarters, rather than Jerusalem. They have established a priesthood separate from the Levitical priesthood. They celebrate Christmas, Easter and numerous holidays with pagan origins, all while

essentially ignoring the Appointed Times of YHWH. They have replaced the Sabbath with Sunday and set up images which are adored and worshipped – all contrary to the Torah. As of June 29, 2008, the Congregation for Divine Worship and the Sacraments by explicit directive of Pope Benedict XVI has prohibited the use of YHWH in Catholic worship. Instead, it has been directed that the Name should be replaced by the Latin "Dominus," Greek "Kyrios," Hebrew "Adonai" or a word of "equivalent meaning" in the local language. See www.catholicnewsagency.com. I could go on, but trust that the point is abundantly clear, the Christian faith, including the Catholic Church and its progeny in the Protestant factions have fallen into the same error as Jeroboam and the House of Yisrael.

[116] While the House of Yisrael went into exile, that did not mean that YHWH gave up on His Firstborn. In fact, Mosheh and the Prophets were very clear that they would be regathered and restored with the House of Yahudah. First, the Messiah had to make atonement for the sins that caused the exile, and the time of the punishment needed to expire. That time was revealed through the very unusual prophecy "acted out" by Ezekiel (Yehezqel) (see Yehezqel 4). This matter is discussed in greater detail in the Walk in the Light series book entitled *The Redeemed*.

[117] The name of the prophet commonly known as Ezekiel is more properly transliterated into the English language as Yehezqel (לאקזחי).

[118] Sheol is a Hebrew word which is used to mean "the grave," while Gehenna is a Greek word which is used to describe a place of punishment known as "hell" or "the lake of fire."

[119] The current modern Hebrew character set is sometimes referred to as Chaldean flame letters. This language came with the Yahudim after their Babylonian exile. There is a great deal of mystery associated with this language, which is really not so modern at all. One thing is certain, it is not the original language of Yisrael. In fact, it is really a language that exclusively belongs to the Yahudim. Those from the House of Yisrael who desire to truly learn about their Hebrew Roots should be looking at the original Hebrew Language often referred to as Ancient Hebrew or Paleo Hebrew. This would have been the language used by Abraham, Yitshaq, Yaakob, Mosheh and the Assembly of

Yisrael.

120 Both the religions of Judaism and Christianity are guilty of mixing pagan traditions and practices. This issue is also discussed in the Walk in the Light series books entitled *Restoration*.

121 Pritchard, James, *Ancient Near Eastern Texts Relating to the Old Testament*, Princeton University Press, 1969, p. 309-310.

122 Eliyahu David ben Yissachar of www.torahcalendar.com. Belshazzar was apparently aware of the seventy (70) year prophecy of Yirmeyahu 29:10-14, but miscalculated the date. Why else would he be throwing a party using the implements from YHWH's Temple in absolute defiance of YHWH? The great banquet was almost certainly given to celebrate the non-fulfillment of Yirmeyahu 29:10-14, as evidenced by the fact that YHWH had NOT caused the Yahudim to return to Jerusalem at this time. Belshazzar started the party a little early for Yirmeyahu 29:10-14, but he was right on time for Yirmeyahu 25:11-12. For Belshazzar did not understand that Yirmeyahu had given two individual seventy (70) year prophecies. The seventy (70) years of Yirmeyahu 25:11-12 began to be counted from Jehoiachin's Captivity, and ended with the destruction of Babylon. The seventy (70) years of Yirmeyahu 29:10-14 began to be counted from the Seventh Captivity mentioned in Yirmeyahu 52:30, and ended with the return of the exiled Yahudim to Jerusalem. Belshazzar was apparently celebrating the non-fulfillment of Yirmeyahu 29:10-14 on the very night that Yirmeyahu 25:11-12 was fulfilled! Belshazzar was obviously interested in history, prophecy and chronology, but as he did not fear Elohim, and as he was not in covenant with YHWH, YHWH did not allow him to perceive what was about to happen to him. The same thing is getting ready to happen to many people who are not in covenant with YHWH, as prophesied by Yahushua in Mattityahu 24:48-51. This group will also include the five foolish virgins of Mattityahu 25:1-13.

123 In a very vivid method of illustrating a prophetic word, Yehezqel was told to lay on his left side to illustrate the punishment upon the House of Yisrael and then to lie on his right side to illustrate the punishment upon the House of Yahudah. "⁴ *Then lie on your left side and put the sin of the House of Yisrael upon yourself. You are to bear their sin for the*

number of days you lie on your side. ⁵ I have assigned you the same number of days as the years of their sin. So for 390 days you will bear the sin of the House of Yisrael. ⁶ After you have finished this, lie down again, this time on your right side, and bear the sin of the House of Yahudah. I have assigned you 40 days, a day for each year." Yehezqel 4:4-6. So there would be 390 years for the House of Yisrael and 40 years for the House of Yahudah. There is a mystery in the Torah about multiplying the term of punishment which needs to be applied. Yisrael was told that they would be punished if they disobeyed and these punishments were clearly explained. They were then warned of the time of their punishment being multiplied if they continued to disobey. "²⁷ If in spite of this you still do not listen to Me but continue to be hostile toward Me, ²⁸ then in My anger I will be hostile toward you, and I Myself will punish you for your sins seven times over." Vayiqra 26:27-28. As a result, the punishment for the House of Yisrael would turn out to be 390 years times 7 for a total of 2,730 years. This seven-fold punishment of 2,730 years began in 723 – 714 BCE and will end in 2007 – 2016 CE.

[124] The Elephantine Letters are a collection of more that twenty ancient documents written primarily in Aramaic between priests and family members who were exiles of Yahudah. They were found on an Island in the Nile in Egypt where a community of Yahudim resided. The documents provide corresponding dates between the Persian calendar and the Egyptian calendar that can be helpful in accurately placing historical events which occurred during the period of time that they were written.

[125] Jubilee years and Shemitah years can be viewed using the data contained in www.torahcalendar.com. The final week of the word given by Gabriel to Daniel will be discussed further in the Walk in the Light Series book entitled "The Final Shofar."

[126] The Book of Maccabees is not a "canonized" text and is considered to be apocryphal and pseudepigraphical depending upon the different religions that recognize that text. The subject of "canonization" is a man-made concept and relies upon a number of factors that determine whether a particular text is "accepted" and deemed reliable. Sometimes these factors are political, sometimes they are doctrinal. Whether men and their methods of "canonizing"

127   texts is reliable is a subject discussed in the Walk in the Light series book entitled "The Scriptures."

128   Beresheet 41 describes the interpretation of Pharaoh's dream by Yoseph involving the seven cows and the seven years. Daniel was also given prophetic words concerning sevens. The Torah has some very specific times associated with sevens, and these all culminate in the end of days as described in the Book of Revelation, which is based upon the number seven. Interestingly, the seventh letter in the Hebrew Aleph Bet is zayin (ז) which represents a weapon or a "sword."

128   www.bdancer.com/history/BDhist2a.html

129   *The Origins of Christianity and the Bible* - The cultural background of early Christianity, www.religious-studies.info.

130   *Backgrounds of Early Christianity*, Everett Ferguson, Second Edition, William B. Eerdmans Publishing Company, 1993, p. 11.

131   Ibid, *The Origins of Christianity and the Bible.*

132   Ibid.

133   Ibid. (Items in brackets added by this author for clarity and consistency in the text).

134   Josephus, *Antiquities*, 14/10/5/200-201.

135   Some information adapted and obtained from www.unrv.com. Dates provided by www.torahcalendar.com.

136   From the article entitled *"Until Shiloh Comes"* by Chuck Missler from his Book *"The Creator Beyond Time and Space."* (Replacement of Yahudim instead of Jews and Judah by the author for consistency sake.)

137   Those that continue to attempt to argue that the regathering has already occurred are typically motivated by a particular prejudice, doctrine or position. Some are from the Yahudim who are attempting to position themselves as "first class" citizens and relegate the rest of the Redeemed to "economy class" as "Gentile Believers" - this label being a contradiction in terms. Some are Christians who do not want to have anything to do with the "Old Testament" and would rather consider themselves "Spiritual Israel" or "The Church," thus elevating themselves above Yisrael, or at least putting themselves into a different category. Whatever their motivation, their teachings are divisive and clearly in

138 contradiction to the prophecies which indicate that this regathering will occur at the end of the Age of Messiah when the Messiah will rule over the united kingdom from that point on. For numerous examples of prophecies regarding the regathering, see Chapter 16 of the Walk in the Light series book entitled *The Redeemed*.

138 For a further discussion, see the Walk in the Light series book entitled *The Messiah*. For more detailed information you can also read *The Star that Astonished the World* by Ernest L. Martin, and the article *The Birth of the Messiah* at www.torahcalendar.com.

139 For greater detail on the significance of the works of the Messiah, see the Walk in the Light series book entitled *The Messiah*. For calendar calculations regarding dating see the work of Eliyahu David Ben Yissachar, Jerusalem, Israel.

140 See en.wikipedia.org/wiki/Council_of_Jamnia. Also see the book entitled *Rabbi Akiba's Messiah* by Daniel Gruber.

141 "In the fourth century, Hillel II established a fixed calendar based on mathematical and astronomical calculations. This calendar, still in use, standardized the length of months and the addition of months over the course of a 19 year cycle, so that the lunar calendar realigns with the solar years. Adar I is added in the 3rd, 6th, 8th, 11th, 14th, 17th and 19th years of the cycle." www.jewfaq.org/calendar.htm

142 Wikipedia, Roman Calendar.

143 Wikipedia, Gregorian Calendar.

144 As YHWH is not an Elohim of confusion, all of the dates contained in the Scriptures can be mathematically retrocalculated and forecalculated on His Calendar. This means that every date, past, present and future in the Scriptures, from Beresheet to Revelation, is destined to occur on the Creator's Calendar. Although there have been counterfeit calendars throughout Yisrael's history, including the Enoch calendar, the Qumran calendar, the Karaite calendar and the Rabbinic calendar, YHWH keeps time on His Calendar. For further discussion on the development of the calendar up until the Rabbinic calendar in 359 CE, see the book entitled *Calendar and the Community A History of the Jewish Calendar Second Century BCE - Tenth Century CE* by Sacha Stern, Oxford University Press, 2001.

145 www.torahcalendar.com see article entitled *Determining the*

Hebrew Year.

146 *Calendar and the Community* A History of the Jewish Calendar Second Century BCE - Tenth Century CE by Sacha Stern, Oxford University Press, 2001, Section 4.2.2 Calendrical rules. The Creation Calendar found at www.torahcalendar.com follows the rule as described in the first rescension. The rule of the equinox is attested in a single passage of the Babylonian Talmud (B. RH 21A), which exists in two different rescensions.

147 As one might expect, the Land bears witness to the accuracy of the true Scriptural Calendar. The Rule of the Equinox, which relies on no opinion from any man or religious ruling body, has repeatedly and faithfully been confirmed by the harvests in the land of Israel. I have travelled to Israel on many occasions to confirm this fact and document the evidence, especially in years which have been controversial such as 2008 and 2011. The Creation Calendar has been perfectly in synch with the harvests of the Land, while other manmade calendars have been in error. If the ancients would have tried to follow the modern man-made calendars that are currently being promoted, it could have been devastating to them, as it might have restricted them from harvesting at the appropriate time and resulted in the loss of crops. Proofs can be found at www.shemayisrael.net and www.torahcalendar.com.

148 By using the powerful algorithms underlying the Creator's Calendar found on www.torahcalendar.com we are able to go backward in time. We are able to confirm certain days, months and years that have been provided in the Scriptures which confirm that the Rule of the Equinox was used by Ancient Yisrael and more importantly, YHWH Himself. Supporting research and evidence remain unpublished at the time of this printing, but are hoped to be available in the near future. The Creator's Calendar and related research can be found at www.torahcalendar.com.

149 Those who follow the conjunctionist position essentially equate a Scriptural new moon (rosh chodesh) with an astronomical new moon or dark moon. The astronomical new moon cannot be visually observed because it is a dark moon. The modern astronomical definition is not the method historically used by Yisrael. While modern science may define a dark moon as a new moon, it is not a good idea

to let modern scientific astronomical definitions interpret the ancient practices of the Yisraelites recorded in the Scriptures. We have seen the problems in this regard with Creation and evolution. False science is often at odds with the Scriptures. The Sun and Moon were specifically called the greater light and the lesser light. The operative word being light. They were meant to be a visible witness of the calendar. The first sliver of the renewed moon is a visible sign of renewal when we actually see the light. We know that the moon was made for Signs and Appointed Times and Days and Years. (Beresheet 1:14; Tehillim 104:19). A sign is something that is meant to be seen and observed. The moon is in a dark phase for more than a day, so there is no precision and nothing to observe. Therefore, the conjunctionists rely upon darkness for their sign, which is inconsistent with the Scriptures. Their primary argument is premised upon the interpretation of one word in Psalm 81:3 which states: "Blow the chodesh shofar fullness (kesah) in the day of our solemn feast." Some translations provide for blowing the shofar at "the full (kesah) moon." The conjunctions position then points out that the word kesah (ץף𝑤) means: "clothed or covered." They then indicate that this must mean it is covered in darkness, but that is an incorrect assumption. When something is in darkness it is not covered with anything. While the word can certainly mean covered or clothed, the intention is that it is clothed in light, not in darkness. Indeed, this is aptly demonstrated in one of the Psalms (Tehillim) which speaks of the majesty of creation. "¹ Bless YHWH, O my soul. O YHWH my Elohim, You are very great; You are clothed with honor and majesty. ² Who coverest Thyself with light as with a garment: who stretchest out the heavens like a curtain." Tehillim 104:1-2. So the covering is light, and light is the sign we should be looking for. As we shall see later in the discussion, there are two Feasts that occur in the middle of the month when the shofar is to be blown. So there are Appointed Times that occur around the Full Moon, in the middle of the month. According to Psalm 81:3 the shofar is to be blown on the New Moon, and on the full moon during the Feast of Passover/Unleavened bread in the spring, and at Succot in the fall.

[150] There is a false doctrine that has infiltrated the Christian

Religion that is causing tremendous harm and confusion, as people attempt to identify with YHWH and His Covenant. The doctrine is referred to as Replacement Theology, and it essentially teaches that the Christian Church has replaced Yisrael - the Covenant people of YHWH. It teaches that the Church is now "Spiritual Israel" and makes a separation between that which is considered to be "Old" and that which is considered to be "New." As a result, the "New Testament" is often considered to be newer, better and more relevant than the "Old Testament." As a result, many are not taught the Covenant Path found within the Torah, and they end up rejecting the path established by YHWH, believing that it is old, outdated and irrelevant to the new Israel - the Church. This, of course, is not consistent with the Torah or the Prophets, but it is the framework within which many in the Christian religion find themselves, and it ends up controlling their reading and interpretation of the Scriptures, which leads them away from the Covenant into a life of confusion and lawlessness. Proverbs 28:9 says, "One that turns away his ear from hearing the Torah, even his prayer is an abomination." The Messiah does not have good things in store for those who reject the Torah and live lawless lives contrary to His commandments. (See Mattityahu 7:23; Luke 13:27).

[151] Strong's Hebrew Concordance Number 8104

[152] For a discussion of the Messiah and events involving the Appointed Times see the Walk in the Light series entitled *The Messiah*.

[153] The Lunar Sabbath is a fairly new idea that seems to be circulating in the Messianic/Hebrew Roots movement, and has caused a tremendous amount of confusion. It has no basis in history, and essentially promotes the notion that the weekly Sabbath cycle is controlled by the lunar cycle, which is exactly the opposite of what is demonstrated by Vayiqra 23, which clearly separates and sets apart the weekly Sabbath from the other Appointed Times. The weekly Sabbath is a memorial of Creation week, and exists on a completely independent seven day count separate from the lunar-solar reckoning of the annual Appointed Times. The matter is discussed in an Appendix in the Walk in the Light series book entitled *The Sabbath* as well as the book *Appointed Times*.

154 For an in depth discussion regarding the Sabbath day, the reader is referred to the Walk in the Light series book entitled *The Sabbath*.

155 It is important to understand the distinction between "am Yisrael" and Judaism. The Assembly, or people, of Yisrael consists of all who enter into Covenant with YHWH. This includes anyone from the nations regardless of genetics, lineage or culture. Judaism is a religion that originated from ancient Yisrael, namely the Pharisaic sect. It has adapted and evolved since the destruction of Jerusalem in 70 CE. While it may contain many physical descendents of the House of Yahudah, called Yahudim or Jews, it is by no means the narrow way of keeping the Covenant. For in many ways, Judaism has added to and taken away from the Torah which is specifically prohibited according to Debarim 5:32.

156 For a detailed discussion of the Scriptural Covenants, see the Walk in the Light series book entitled *Covenants*.

157 Yaakob is a proper transliteration for the Hebrew Patriarch commonly called Jacob. The author of the New Testament text entitled James was actually named Yaakob.

158 See Shemot 20:4, Vayiqra 26:1, Debarim 4:8-10, Debarim 4:15-25, Debarim 27:15.

159 *The Two Babylons*, Alexander Hislop, Chick Publications, pp. 187-188.

160 Information gleaned from Mithraism: an essay by David Fingerhut, www.ukans.edu. Dating provided by Eliyahu David ben Yissachar.

161 Textual criticism is a necessary aspect of restoration when the motivation of the "critic" is to discern the original meaning of a document. This is particularly important concerning the "New Testament" manuscripts because there are no original "autographs" of any "New Testament" manuscripts. Today, there are somewhere around 25,000 to 30,000 texts, some of which are merely fragments, all of them being copies of copies of copies. There are numerous textual variants within these texts which require diligent efforts to discern which variant best represents the original text. Most of the time these variations are inconsequential syntax matters, but there are some very important variations that can affect doctrinal issues. Now some textual critics set out on their quest with the exclusive

purpose of disproving the validity of the Scriptures, while I understand the realities of the fact that we are dealing with writings almost 2,000 years old. It is incredible that we have so many documents that involve our faith. I find it to be an exciting endeavor, and it in no way diminishes my faith to admit that the New Testament copies are not perfect.

162 For a more detailed discussion on the Sabbath, I would recommend the Walk in the Light Series book entitled *The Sabbath*. The Catholic Church has made no excuses concerning the fact that they "changed" their Sabbath from the seventh day to the first day – Sun Day. They consider this to be their "mark" of authority, and they openly admit that this is not taught anywhere in the Scriptures – because you will not find it in the Scriptures. The seventh day is still the Sabbath day. For more information concerning this important subject see the Walk in the Light series book entitled *The Sabbath*.

163 *The Vatican's Pagan Cemetery* By Barbie Nadeau Oct. 13, 2006 - Just inside the Vatican's fortified walls, directly below the street connecting its private pharmacy and its members-only supermarket, lies a 2,000-year-old graveyard littered with bizarre, often disturbing displays of pagan worship. Under one metallic walkway, the headless skeleton of a young boy rests in an open grave. At his side, a marble replica of a hen's egg, which to pagans represented the rebirth of the body through reincarnation. Nearby, countless skeletons lie scattered among the remnants of terra cotta vases used in pagan ceremonies. The underground air is damp with the smell of wet dirt, and the clay tubes used by the pagans to feed their dead with honey and syrup still protrude, fingerlike, from the ground. Walking among the exposed bones of any ancient graveyard would be chilling enough. But when it's a pagan necropolis directly beneath Vatican City, arguably Christianity's holiest shrine, then the situation redlines right into completely unnerving. Or it would be if it weren't so enthralling, especially for anyone who has ever pondered Roman Catholicism's pagan roots. The Necropoli dell'Autoparco (literally Necropolis of the Parking Garage), a 2,000-year-old burial ground, which opens to the public Oct. 20, offers a rarely seen glimpse of the close ties between pagans and Christians during the Augustan era (23

B.C.- 14 A.D.). "You see a mix of social class and even religious beliefs here," says Francesco Buranelli, director of the Vatican Museums, who believes that including the pagan graveyard as part of the Vatican's museums will foster awareness of the roots of Catholicism and the importance of its Roman history. www.informationliberation.com/?id=16977.

164 *Church of the Holy Trinity v. United States*, 143 U.S. 226 (1892). While the subject of this case was not to decide whether or not America is a Christian Nation – Justice Brewer in his decision writes: "beyond all these matters no purpose of action against religion can be imputed to any legislation, state or national, because this is a religious people." He then proceeds to present a dissertation on American religious history and several pages later makes the following comment: "These, and many other matters which might be noticed, add a volume of unofficial declarations to the mass of organic utterances that this is a Christian nation." I will let you be the judge as to what this actually means – if anything at all.

165 *The Cosmic Conspiracy*, Stan Deyo, Deyo Enterprises, 2010. See also www.phoenixfestivals.com.

166 Michael Howard, *The Occult Conspiracy* (Rochester, Vermont: Destiny Books 1989), pp. 84-86.

167 *Healing Waters*, Estee Dvorjetski, Biblical Archaeology Review, July/August 2004, Vol. 30, No. 4, Page 21.

168 *The Secret Symbols of the Dollar Bill*, David Ovason, Harper Collins Publishers, 2003 p. 10.

169 Some interesting information concerning the Mazzaroth can be found in the following books: *Mazzaroth* by Frances Rolleston Weiser Books 2001; *The Witness of the Stars* by E.W. Bullinger Kregel Publications; *The Gospel in the Stars*, Joseph A. Seiss, Kregel Publications 1972.

170 There is an incredible archaeological site in Israel between Haifa and Tel Aviv known as Cesarea, which was the place where the Apostle Shaul was imprisoned on his way to Rome. At this location there are ancient ruins of a circus where they would conduct chariot races – among other things. Traditionally, the Romans who were sun worshippers would place obelisks at the center of the arena. At this particular site the archaeologists discovered a fallen obelisk, which they raised in direct contravention to the

Torah. This reflects the attitude that secular modern day Israel has concerning the non-application of the Torah to life in the Land. It is for this reason that Yahanan equates Jerusalem to Sodom and Egypt at this time in history (Revelation 11:8).

[171] This essentially puts to rest the notion of the "Pre-Tribulation" Rapture. The patterns provided in the Scriptures are clear. YHWH did not remove His people during the plagues, He separated and protected them. While He will certainly remove His people while His wrath is being poured out upon the earth, it is important to note when that event occurs. This issue is discussed in greater detail in the Walk in the Light series book entitled *The Final Shofar*.

[172] For a further discussion see the Walk in the Light series book entitled *The Final Shofar*.

[173] See Matthew 24:42; Matthew 24:43 Matthew 25:13 Mark 13:35; Mark 13:37; Luke 12:38; Luke 21:36.

A Note on Dates

Historical dating has long been a subject of controversy and debate in the academic community. While certain dates involving particular aspects of a civilization may be agreed upon, others remain in dispute. This sometimes leads to problems creating a complete timeline of history. Very recently some intensive and compelling work has been completed by using astronomical data, particularly eclipse data, which can then be used to lock together histories of various cultures, thereby providing an accurate view of history in totality. The dates used in this book may not always be the same as academia purports, but they are believed to be the most accurate available. Dates provided by Eliyahu David ben Yissachar, Jerusalem, Israel, through the work displayed on www.torahcalendar.com have been denoted by placing an asterisk (*) next to them.

Appendix A

Tanak Hebrew Names

Torah - Teaching

English Name	Modern Hebrew	English Transliteration
Genesis	בראשית	Beresheet
Exodus	שמות	Shemot
Leviticus	ויקרא	Vayiqra
Numbers	במדבר	Bemidbar
Deuteronomy	דברים	Devarim

Nebi'im - Prophets

Joshua	יהושע	Yahushua
Judges	שופטים	Shoftim
Samuel	שמואל	Shemu'el
Kings	מלכים	Melakhim
Isaiah	ישעיהו	Yeshayahu
Jeremiah	ירמיהו	Yirmeyahu
Ezekiel	יחזקאל	Yehezqel
Daniel	דניאל	Daniel
Hosea	השוע	Hoshea
Joel	יואל	Yoel
Amos	עמום	Amos
Obadiah	עבדיה	Ovadyah

Jonah	יונה	Yonah
Micah	מיכה	Mikhah
Nahum	נחום	Nachum
Habakkuk	חבקוק	Habaquq
Zephaniah	צפניה	Zepheniyah
Haggai	חגי	Chaggai
Zechariah	זכריה	Zekaryah
Malachi	מלאכי	Malachi

Kethubim – Writings

Psalms	תהלים	Tehillim
Proverbs	משלי	Mishle
Job	איוב	Iyov
Song of Songs	שיר השירים	Shir ha-Shirim
Ruth	רות	Ruth
Lamentations	איכה	Eikhah
Ecclesiastes	קהלת	Qohelet
Esther	אסתר	Ester
Ezra	עזרא	Ezra
Nehemiah	נחמיה	Nehemyah
Chronicles	דברי הימים	Divri ha-Yamim

Appendix B

Hebrew Language Study Chart

Gematria	Letter	Paleo	Modern	English	Picture/Meaning
1	Aleph	ש	א	A	ox head
2	Bet	⌂	ב	B, Bh	tent floor plan
3	Gimel	∧	ג	G	foot, camel
4	Dalet	▽	ד	D	door
5	Hey	ᛉ	ה	H	man raised arms
6	Waw	⸠	ו	W, O, U	tent peg, hook
7	Zayin	⤳	ז	Z	weapon
8	Het	目	ח	Hh	fence, wall
9	Tet	⊕	ט	T, Th	basket, container
10	Yud	⌐	י	Y	closed hand
20	Kaph	॥	כ	K, Kh	palm, open hand
30	Lamed	⌐	ל	L	shepherd staff
40	Mem	ᚳ	מ	M	water
50	Nun	↘	נ	N	sprout, seed
60	Samech	⟊	ס	S	prop, support
70	Ayin	⊘	ע	A	eye
80	Pey	⌐	פ	P, Ph	open mouth
90	Tsade	✝	צ	Ts	hook
100	Quph	ᛡ	ק	Q	back of the head
200	Resh	ᚱ	ר	R	head of a man
300	Shin	ᚹ	ש	Sh, S	teeth
400	Taw	×	ת	T	mark, covenant

Note: Gematria in a very simple sense is the study of the various numerical values of the Hebrew letters and words. Since there is no separate numerical system in the Hebrew language, all Hebrew letters have a numerical value so it is a very legitimate and valuable form of study. There are many different forms of Gematria. The Gematria system used in this chart is mispar hechrachi, also known as Normative value. The Paleo font used is an attempt to blend the ancient variants into a uniform and recognizable font set that accurately depicts the original meaning of each character.

Appendix C

The Walk in the Light Series

Book 1	Restoration - A discussion of the pagan influences that have mixed with the true faith through the ages which has resulted in the need for restoration. This book also examines true Scriptural restoration.
Book 2	Names - Discusses the True Name of the Creator and the Messiah as well as the significance of names in the Scriptures.
Book 3	The Scriptures - Discusses the origin of the written Scriptures as well as many translation errors which have led to false doctrines in some mainline religions.
Book 4	Covenants - Discusses the progressive covenants between the Creator and His Creation as described in the Scriptures which reveals His plan for mankind.
Book 5	The Messiah - Discusses the prophetic promises and fulfillments of the Messiah and the True identity of the Redeemer of Yisrael.
Book 6	The Redeemed - Discusses the relationship between Christianity and Judaism and reveals how the Scriptures identify True Believers. It reveals how the Christian doctrine of Replacement Theology has caused confusion as to how the Creator views the Children of Yisrael.
Book 7	The Law and Grace - Discusses in depth the false doctrine that Grace has done away with the Law and demonstrates the vital importance of obeying the commandments.
Book 8	The Sabbath - Discusses the importance of the Seventh Day Sabbath as well as the origins of the tradition concerning Sunday worship.
Book 9	Kosher - Discusses the importance of eating food prescribed by the Scriptures as a aspect of righteous living.

Book 10	Appointed Times – Discusses the appointed times established by the Creator, often erroneously considered to be "Jewish" holidays, and critical to the understanding of prophetic fulfillment of the Scriptural promises.
Book 11	Pagan Holidays – Discusses the pagan origins of some popular Christian holidays which have replaced the Appointed Times.
Book 12	The Final Shofar – Discusses the walk required by the Scriptures and prepares the Believer for the deceptions coming in the End of Days.

The series began as a simple Power point presentation which was intended to develop into a book with twelve different chapters but ended up being twelve different books. Each book is intended to stand alone although the series was originally intended to build from one section to another. Due to the urgency of certain topics, the books have not been published in sequential order.

For anticipated release dates, announcements and additional teachings go to:
www.shemayisrael.net

Appendix D

The Shema
Deuteronomy (Devarim) 6:4-5

Traditional English Translation

Hear, O Israel: The LORD our God, the LORD is one!
You shall love the LORD your God with all your heart, with all
your soul, and with all your strength.

Corrected English Translation

Hear, O Yisrael: YHWH our Elohim, YHWH is one (unified)!
You shall love YHWH your Elohim with all your heart, with
all your soul, and with all your strength.

Modern Hebrew Text

שְׁמַע ישראל יהוה אלהינו יהוה אחד
ואהבת את יהוה אלהיך בכל־ לבבך ובכל־ נפשך ובכל־ מאדך

Ancient Hebrew Text

⏃⌇⊏⌇ ⌇⌇ ⌇⌇⌇ ⌇⌇⌇ ⌇⌇⌇ ⌇⌇⌇ ⌇⌇⌇
⌇⌇⌇ ⌇⌇ ⌇⌇⌇ ⌇⌇⌇ ⌇⌇⌇ ⌇⌇⌇ ⌇⌇⌇
⌇⌇⌇ ⌇⌇⌇

Hebrew Text Transliterated

Shema, Yisra'el: YHWH Elohenu, YHWH echad!
V-ahavta et YHWH Elohecha b-chol l'vavcha u-v-chol
naf'sh'cha u-v-chol m'odecha.

The Shema has traditionally been one of the most important prayers in
Judaism and has been declared the first (resheet) of all the Commandments.
(Mark 12:29-30).

Appendix E

Shema Yisrael

Shema Yisrael was originally established with two primary goals: 1) The production and distribution of sound, Scripturally based educational materials which would assist individuals to see the light of Truth and "Walk in the Light" of that Truth. This first objective was, and is, accomplished through Shema Yisrael Publications; and 2) The free distribution of those materials to the spiritually hungry throughout the world, along with Scriptures, food, clothing and money to the poor, the needy, the sick, the dying and those in prison. This second objective was accomplished through the Shema Yisrael Foundation and through the Foundation people were able to receive a tax deduction for their contributions.

Sadly, through the passage of the Pension Reform Act of 2006, the US Congress severely restricted the operation of donor advised funds which, in essence, crippled the Shema Yisrael Foundation by requiring that funds either be channeled through another Foundation or to a 501(c)(3) organization approved by the Internal Revenue Service. Since the Shema Yisrael Foundation was a relatively small and operated very "hands on" by placing the funds and materials directly into the hands of the needy in Third World Countries, it was unable to effectively continue operating as a Foundation with the tax advantages associated therewith.

As a result, Shema Yisrael Publications has effectively functioned in a dual capacity to insure that both objectives continue to be promoted, although contributions are no longer tax deductible. To review some of the work being accomplished you can visit www.shemayisrael.net and go to the "Missions" section.

We gladly accept donations, although they may not be tax deductible. To donate, please make checks payable to: Shema Yisrael Publications and mail to:

Shema Yisrael
123 Court Street • Herkimer, New York 13350

You may also call (315) 939-7940 to make a donation
or receive more information.

www.ingramcontent.com/pod-product-compliance
Lightning Source LLC
Chambersburg PA
CBHW060338170426
43202CB00014B/2808